Richard Wainwright, the Liberals and Liberal Democrats

Manchester University Press

Richard Wainwright, the Liberals and Liberal Democrats

Unfinished business

MATT COLE

Manchester University Press

Manchester and New York

distributed exclusively in the USA by Palgrave Macmillan

Published by Manchester University Press

Published by Manchester University Press
Oxford Road, Manchester M13 9NR, UK
and Room 400, 175 Fifth Avenue, New York, NY 10010, USA
www.manchesteruniversitypress.co.uk

Distributed exclusively in the USA by
Palgrave, 175 Fifth Avenue, New York,
NY 10010, USA

Distributed exclusively in Canada by
UBC Press, University of British Columbia, 2029 West Mall,
Vancouver, BC, Canada V6T 1Z2

British Library Cataloguing-in-Publication Data
A catalogue record for this book is available from the British Library

Library of Congress Cataloging-in-Publication Data applied for

ISBN   978-0-7190-8253-5 *hardback*

First published 2011

The publisher has no responsibility for the persistence or accuracy of URLs for any external or third-party internet websites referred to in this book, and does not guarantee that any content on such websites is, or will remain, accurate or appropriate.

Typeset in Minion by
Koinonia, Manchester
Printed in Great Britain by
TJ International Ltd, Padstow, Cornwall

To Sue and Jess

Contents

List of figures

Foreword

Vince Cable, MP

Richard Wainwright was one of the major figures of post-war Liberalism. Matt Cole performs a valuable service in bringing alive his life and times to a generation of Lib Dems for whom his name is unlikely to have the recognition he deserves.

I am fortunate to have seen him in action. As a student at Cambridge I followed in his footsteps as President of the Liberal Club before embarking on my long excursion into the Labour wilderness. He was one of the guest speakers at the Club and I joined a group which motored up to Colne Valley for the 1963 by-election campaign which laid the foundations for his General Election victory in 1966.

To be frank, the Presidency of the Liberal Club was not a post of great importance in his time or mine. He said that he was one of two active members – at a time (in the late 1930s) when the Liberal Party was split into three and seemed to be heading for extinction. The Club had only expanded a little three decades later. The parliamentary Liberal Party was also of very modest proportions – in my day, six. Apart from the party's superstars – Grimond and Thorpe – there was a small but respected group of MPs and candidates whom we endeavoured to attract to – usually tiny – meetings. I recall Richard for his Yorkshire accent, and rather dry, uncharismatic manner (Grimond was, by contrast, inspirational and Thorpe was wickedly funny). The content I have long since forgotten but I seem to recall a strong strain of Methodism and an approach to economic matters which relied heavily on an appeal to simple common sense and basic accounting which jarred somewhat with what we were being taught in the lecture halls by the disciples of Keynes and the very clever Nobel Prize winners who graced the economics faculty.

There is little doubt that he would today be regarded as an 'economically liberal' Liberal. He was a strong believer in traditional liberal values like free trade. He had an accounting and business background and had little taste for Socialism (not only because he fought Labour in Colne Valley). At that time, the main intellectual influences on Liberal economic policy came from innovative, free market, thinkers like Professor Alan Peacock. This ideological current later became associated with the Thatcherite revolution in the Conservative Party but (as I am reminded when I go to speak at some of the – so-called 'right wing' – think-tanks like the Institute of Economic Affairs) the Liberal Party was then its natural home. The books of Jo Grimond from this period reflect that thinking, espousing, long before it became fashionable, ideas like education vouchers. *The Orange Book*, by contrast, is almost pink. One of the reasons I, and others, migrated to Harold Wilson's Labour Party was that we felt more comfortable with the social democratic, more egalitarian values of some of its leading people like Anthony Crosland than we did with the views of Richard Wainwright and his contemporaries.

Eventually however I finished up in the same place. In the 1983 election when I stood in York for the SDP/Liberal Alliance, he was one of my main speakers. And I was indebted to him since a bitter schism had opened up in York between the SDP which had been allocated the seat and the local Liberals who had been advancing in local government. York was – somewhat implausibly – seen as a target seat and attracted the Gang of Four, Roy Jenkins for a spectacularly successful rally. But Cyril Smith ostentatiously boycotted the campaign, David Steel kept a discreet distance and only Richard Wainwright of the top Liberals would come. His lay preacher style of speaking and homespun common sense went down much better with a Yorkshire public than they had with the undergraduates. Predictably, but sadly, we doubled the third party vote but still came third. He retained his seat in Colne Valley.

Apart from those fleeting experiences two decades apart I never met him and this book adds greatly to my knowledge and understanding of him. I was surprised to read of his key role in the dumping of Jeremy Thorpe as party leader and of some of the rather poisonous relationships which rendered a small parliamentary party much more difficult to manage than today's. But Wainwright was quintessentially a party man who became involved when the Liberal Party was in the depth of despair and stuck with it through over half a century of ups and downs – mostly downs – helping to steer it into the new merged party. He was a Liberal, a community campaigner and internationalist through and through, a role model for any aspiring Lib Dem politician.

Acknowledgements

Several individuals and institutions have been vital in supporting the completion of this biography, and I offer them my most sincere thanks. First of all the Wainwright family and the Scurrah Wainwright Trust for their personal co-operation and financial support; Sue Donnelly and all the staff at the London School of Economics Archives for their generous assistance in using the Wainwright papers, and Becky Webster for their classification; and King Edward VI College in Stourbridge for flexibility in allowing me time to undertake research. Thanks are similarly due to the staff of all other archives on whose collections the book draws, and especially to the many dozens of interviewees who came forward so readily to talk at length about their memories of Richard Wainwright. I am grateful to Tony Mason and the staff at MUP for their support in preparing and presenting the work, and for academic support and advice I am particularly indebted to Prof. David Dutton, Prof. David Denver, Dr Richard Grayson, Dr Peter Catterall, Dr Ruth Fox, Dr Roy Douglas, Dr Chris Cook, Dr Andrew Russell and Dr Nick Crowson. The opinions offered here, however, are entirely the author's.

Chronology

1976   Resignation of Jeremy Thorpe
1977   Lib-Lab Pact begins
1978   Lib-Lab Pact ends
1979   Retains Colne Valley at General Election
1981   Formation of SDP-Liberal Alliance
1983   Retains Colne Valley at General Election
1985   Announces retirement
1987   Colne Valley lost at General Election; retires from Parliament
1988   Formation of Liberal Democrats
1989   Becomes Yorkshire Liberal Democrats' President
1992   General Election
1995   Saddleworth by-election
1997   Retires from Presidency of Yorkshire Liberal Democrats and other political offices
2003   Death at Leeds, 16 January

Introduction

Winston Churchill told his grandson that political parties are like horses: the politician, like the rider, should simply 'go to the stable and pick the best hack'.[1] This is a book about a man, his times and particularly his Party. Richard Wainwright was an enigma in that he was both an idiosyncratic personality and a fierce Party loyalist; a millionaire who promoted a minimum wage; a reputed teetotaller who could enjoy 'good dinners with healthy red wine' and even 'go slightly pink';[2] a public school Cambridge graduate who preferred Yorkshire fish and chips to London society; who was raised by Victorian Liberals and fought against Labour but supported New Liberalism to fight the Conservatives. Like Churchill, many of the 'greats' of twentieth-century politics left their Party, and Liberals had reason during Wainwright's time to find it easy. It is staying in parties through difficult times, or reviving parties thought dead, which is hard.

Richard Wainwright joined the Liberal Party at its lowest ebb; he helped lead its return from the wilderness when others drifted elsewhere; he showed it could win in northern, urban areas which some Liberals had forsaken; and he rescued it from the weaknesses of its members and leaders in the years after its recovery. Finally he saw it transformed into another Party which he came to embrace. These acts alone make his life worthy of study, but he was in addition a pacifist in a time of war and a man of faith in a secular age.

This is a political biography and only touches on Wainwright's personal life and his charitable work where these have relevance for his impact as a politician. There is within that limitation an interest in Wainwright's life for a range of readers: his former followers; those loyal to the north of England (like the Liverpudlian Professor of Politics who immediately remembered him as 'a great Northerner');[3] historians of the Liberal Party and of Britain in the twentieth century; Liberal Democrats and aspirant politicians of any sort who want to do the job well; and anyone who has convictions. The dilemmas faced by Party loyalists with strong individual beliefs in an era of change are not simply resolved, but Wainwright's life is the story of one struggle to resolve them – with remarkable success.

Notes

1 This remark was reported by Churchill's grandson and namesake in the first edition of Martin Gilbert's television biography *Churchill: Renegade and Turncoat* (BBC TV 1992).

2 RSW never claimed to be a teetotaller, but was quite often reported as being, for example in Roth, A., *The MPs' Chart* (London: Parliamentary Profiles 1966), p. 79, where it is also wrongly stated that RSW was a non-smoker. His ability to enjoy a social drink was testified to by Joe Egerton, Economics Director of the British Chambers of Commerce (correspondence with the present author, 9 June 2009), RSW's secretary Caroline Cawston (interview, 2 June 2008) and Menzies Campbell, not quoted here, but with whom RSW and Joyce enjoyed two evenings' drinking when they met on holiday in Belaggio.

3 Prof. Denis Kavanagh in conversation, 10 July 2008.

1 'A privileged education, isolated from most 1930s schoolchildren': Wainwright (front row, third from the right) as a leaver from Streete Court preparatory school, where he studied from 1928–31 (courtesy of Mr Nigel Giles, Streete Court Club).

2 Wainwright (far left) on an outing with fellow boarders at Shrewsbury School in 1934 (with the permission of the London School of Economics Archives).

3 Wainwright as a fresher at Clare College, Cambridge in autumn 1936, when he joined the Liberal Party for the first time (courtesy of the Cambridge University Liberal Club).

4 Wainwright (to the right of the door in a light coat) on active service with the Friends Ambulance Unit in Einbeck, Germany, November 1945 (with the permission of I. B. Tauris & Co.).

5 'She's the one that gets me in, every election. She's the one people like to see': Wainwright's tribute to his wife Joyce, seen here at their wedding in January 1948 (courtesy of Mrs Joyce Wainwright).

A letter to you

from

Richard
WAINWRIGHT

Dear Elector,

If things were properly managed, you and I *ought* to be feeling right bang on top of the world. Why? Because our district has been pretty well at the peak of a huge trade boom, in which most of the world is also taking part. And breathtaking new inventions are here, which could speed production, bring down prices, and open wonderful chances for the children. What an opportunity! But what is being done with it?

Well, some folk are doing very well—good luck to them. They are mostly working for really go-ahead firms, and sharing in the harvest. Their problem is: "Will the boom burst?" **And if they're saving money, will it keep its value until they want to draw it?**

PRICES UP & UP

But many others find their increased money does not keep far enough ahead of rising prices. And those who are elderly (after a lifetime's work), those with large families, those with no big Union to help them—they find the cost of living running in front all the time.

IS SPECIAL EFFORT REWARDED?

Those who have worked at special training are not always rewarded for it. Those with big responsibilities find life getting more complex and anxious. Those with routine jobs often find little or no outlet for their talents.

THE LIGHTS ARE ALWAYS "RED"

We are officially told that the nation's finances are dangerously balanced on a knife edge. Partly on this excuse, more and more power and "say" is taken out of our district, to "experts" outside who reckon to know just what's good for us.

Who is it, then, who gets the really fat share of this trade boom? It is the Government.

Despite a few small reductions, we are still the most heavily taxed people in the world—including the ordinary family with an ordinary wage. You suffer high taxes through so many day-to-day items, from vegetables and entertainments to textiles, tea, and National Insurance, that it is very difficult to realise what the total weekly tax bill amounts to in your home.

NINETEEN BOB A WEEK EACH

For the *average* manual worker and family, the *average* tax bill *per person* is only just under £1 each week. For many others, the figure is of course even higher. **I do not think you get value for money.**

GIVE JOHN BULL & HIS WIFE A CHANCE

The answer—not an easy one—to these problems is for the Government to give real and full scope to the gumption and skill of the common-sense man and woman. More radicals and liberals in Parliament would lead the way in doing this.

Two enormous party machines, grinding away at the dreary game of "In and Out," cannot do this job. They do not push their punches home—it would make life too uncomfortable when their turn comes to sit in the seats of power. For instance, the Socialist M.P.s have very rarely bothered to muster their full strength in this Parliament.

From the six years I have worked in your Constituency, I believe you would prefer to have a Member free to speak your mind, and his mind, to Parliament; and pledged to work for peace, freedom and reform.

If elected, I shall continue to live in the district, and be ready to help whenever and wherever I can do so.

Yours sincerely,

Richard Wainwright

6 Wainwright at the Liberal Party's nadir: this was Wainwright's 1955 address to the electors of Pudsey as one of just 110 Liberal candidates at that year's general election (with the permission of the University of Bristol Special Collections).

7 Wainwright in conversation with Liberal Party Leader Clement Davies at the 1956 Liberal Assembly in Folkestone (with the permission of Halksworth Wheeler Ltd).

8 'He was thrilled, because it was what he had always wanted': the description Joyce Wainwright (right) gave of the reaction of Henry Scurrah Wainwright (left) to his son's election to Parliament in March 1966 when this photo was taken.

9 Wainwright (seated, left of Leader Jo Grimond at the centre) and his colleagues in the Liberal Parliamentary Party of 1966. Future Liberal Leaders David Steel and Jeremy Thorpe are on the far left and right respectively (with the permission of the University of Bristol Special Collections).

10 Wainwright in contemplation in his beloved garden at The Heath in 1973, not long after his tour of Guinea-Bissau (with the permission of the London School of Economics Archives).

11 Wainwright bathing in a stream at Eastergate in August 1973 in one of many publicity campaigns which helped him win back his seat (with the permission of the *Huddersfield Daily Examiner*).

12 Wainwright celebrating with supporters at Slaithwaite in Colne Valley after winning back his seat in 1974 – the only Liberal MP to do so since the Second World War (with the permission of the London School of Economics Archives).

13 Wainwright visiting a colliery in the eastern districts of the Colne Valley in 1975 (with the permission of the *Huddersfield Daily Examiner*).

14 and **15** 'Looks more and more like a Toby jug' was the description given by *The Guardian*'s Derek Brown of Wainwright's disarmingly modest, cheerful demeanour. Its development is represented by the work of cartoonists for *The Yorkshire Observer* in 1950 (Plate 14) and *Parliamentary Profiles* in 1984 (Plate 15) (courtesy of Terry Roth).

16 Wainwright on the day the Liberal Assembly voted for the alliance with the SDP. In the foreground are David Steel (left) and Bill Rodgers (right). Jo Grimond is on the left reading *The Guardian* (courtesy of Lord Rodgers of Quarry Bank).

Amiable face of politics

Weekend
PEOPLE

ALEC RAMSDEN
reports on a special
day for the Liberal
MP, Richard
Wainwright. Pictures
by LAURIE MERCER

WHEN the Liberal MP, Richard Wainwright lunched with a few friends at the weekend there was an extra course to complement the minestrone soup, roast turkey and raspberry vacherin.

It was a tasty slice of nostalgia which Mr. Wainwright, MP for Colne Valley for 14 years, but the constituency's official candidate for a quarter of a century, and his 200 guests at a Huddersfield hotel devoured with relish.

Officially the event was the handing over of a portrait in oils of the amiable Mr. Wainwright, a portrait in oils of him by the Yorkshire artist, Trevor Stubley. But it was also an occasion for reunion; for talk of the past and particularly of the early days of his campaign, including a 1959 election when he polled a mere quarter of the votes — and was in third place.

Then there were accounts of how he came closer in 1963 and 1964 and of how victory was achieved in 1966 when the sitting MP, Pat Duffy, now a Parliamentarian for Sheffield, was vanquished. There was talk, too, of a temporary setback in 1970 when a young Labour candidate by the name of David Clark snatched Colne Valley back until 1974 — the start of Mr. Wainwright's unbroken run.

He recalled: "The Yorkshire Liberal Federation approached me in 1956 after I had fought Pudsey twice — and it was obvious I was not going to win it. I took to Colne Valley straight away. As a student of history I had always been fascinated by the accounts of a former MP, Philip Snowden, and I was convinced the Liberals could win there."

Ironically, said Mr. Wainwright, his efforts to put Colne Valley back on the Liberal map received a publicity setback when a rather more newsworthy Colne Valley worthy — ex-Prime Minister Harold Wilson — was elected Leader of the Opposition.

Admiring the portrait, picturing a studious-looking Mr. Wainwright in a somewhat out-of-character light jacket, were a host of friends he and his wife Joyce have made over their years in politics.

There was former Liberal leader Lord Grimond, who was making his tenth incursion to the Huddersfield area.

Another member of "the best club in the land," Lord Wade knows the district much better, for he was formerly MP for Huddersfield West — part of which constituency, through boundary changes now has Mr. Wainwright as MP.

There was Ernest Gilpin, a former Liberal Association chairman, Coun. James Crossley, who led a team of Oxford University students spearheading the first Colne Valley drive. Free Democrat representatives from the German "twin" town of Unna, three generations of the Wainwright clan, and a man who probably knows Richard Wainwright better than any of his political friends.

Edward Dunford has been his agent since before the Colne Valley campaign began, and there was recognition of this in the form of a carriage clock presented by the party's secretary general, John Spiller.

Richard Wainwright, right, with Lord Grimond, left, and the artist Trevor Stubley, who painted the MP's portrait.

For Mrs. Wainwright there was a decorative bell-pull embroidered Danish-style by Mrs. Lise Newsome, a hand-stitched tablecloth, and, of course, flowers.

It was an event that the veteran Liberal thoroughly enjoyed, and nostalgia ruled in his speech, although he could not avoid a hint of politics in saying that the Liberal approach was more urgently needed today than it was when the Colne Valley campaign began.

He was firmly non-committal about whether he will be the candidate at the next election. With a Mona Lisa-like smile, he said: "On that my lips are sealed."

Mrs. Joyce Wainwright, left, and Edward Dunford, Liberal agent, admire the embroidered bell-pull made by Lise Newsome, centre.

17 A report of the celebration of Wainwright's quarter-centenary as Liberal candidate for Colne Valley from the *Yorkshire Post* of 5 November 1984 (with the permission of *The Yorkshire Post*).

18 Wainwright (right) on polling day of the 1987 general election with the Liberal candidate for the Colne Valley, Nigel Priestley (left) and Priestley's wife Sue (with the permission of the *Yorkshire Post*).

19 Wainwright as Yorkshire Liberal Democrat President, chatting with former MP Gwynoro Jones at their 1991 conference (with the permission of the *Yorkshire Post*).

20 Wainwright at work in the Commons (with the permission of *The Reformer*).

PART ONE: BEFORE PARLIAMENT

1 Early life

There is a strong case for describing 1918 as the worst year in the Liberal Party's history. The Liberals approached the General Election of that year as two separate organisations: one led by Lloyd George and allied to the Conservatives, who gave a free run to any Liberal candidates in possession of the 'coupon' – a joint message of support from Lloyd George and Tory Leader Andrew Bonar-Law; the other led by the previous Prime Minister, H.H. Asquith, whose candidates fought independently against candidates from the Conservatives and the newly strengthened Labour Party. These were reduced to thirty-six seats, Asquith himself losing his place in Parliament; Lloyd George's National Liberals survived only with Tory support. After eventually being forced to stand against Asquithian Liberals at by-elections and then being ejected from the Party conference, Lloyd George was abandoned by the Conservatives in 1922. The Party which a decade earlier had enjoyed a majority of 273 over the Conservatives in the Commons was in 1918 shattered – apparently permanently.

This was also the year of the birth of Richard Scurrah Wainwright on 11 April in Leeds. There is more than poetic coincidence to the fact that in the year that the Liberal Party suffered such apparently fatal wounds, another Liberal was born, only fifteen miles from Asquith's birthplace, who was to build a political base in West Yorkshire from which he would be one of the pioneers of the Liberal Party's recovery. Richard Wainwright was born into an environment which thrived on confident and active Liberalism and became one of its most vital leaders by building upon what remained of that foundation when the feud between Asquith and Lloyd George was over. But he still had to meet the challenges of further internal struggles, of threats from the Party's foes and some of its friends and of personal dilemmas and tragedies. He was a major reason why the Liberal Party and ultimately the Liberal Democrats survived as well as they did in the form that they did. His political life is a significant part of the recent history of the Liberal Party.

Leeds

Wainwright was born into a prosperous, respectable household enjoying the benefits of the development of Leeds as a centre of industry and politics. His father, Henry Scurrah Wainwright was born in 1877 and at the start of the twentieth century was an accountant living in Potternewton with his mother and grandmother. In 1902 Henry Scurrah established Thackray Medical Supplies, manufacturing and repairing surgical supplies and training nurses to offer home care. Richard Wainwright remained a shareholder and Director of the company until the time of his political career.[1] This was only one of a portfolio of investments made by Henry Scurrah, most notably a substantial interest in the Leeds Metropole Hotel, in which Richard Wainwright acquired shareholdings during the Second World War.[2] The sale of this helped to fund the increasingly prestigious and comfortable lifestyle the Wainwrights enjoyed as Richard grew up, one measure of which is that in his mid-twenties Richard kept a current account of at least £600 – at the time an MP's annual salary, or to put it another way about the same purchasing value as £15,000 in 2010 – which he himself thought too high.[3]

Henry Scurrah married within his class – indeed almost within his street – when he took Emily White, the daughter of a manufacturing chemist,[4] as his bride before the First World War, and as Leeds grew the Wainwrights moved out at its advancing suburban frontier. Henry Scurrah, whose mother had been born in Holbeck near the centre of Leeds in the 1840s, had moved from Potternewton on the north-eastern fringes of Leeds Parish to Roundhay, only incorporated into the City in 1912, by the time Richard Wainwright was a small boy. In 1937, the family moved again to a large property called The Heath at Adel, an area in the north of Leeds which was only subsumed into the City in 1925. This was to be the Wainwrights' family home for the next fifty years.

Richard Wainwright's upbringing lacked neither resources nor emotional support. As well as an expensive education, he was used to domestic staff, his family were patrons of Leeds charities, subscribers to the founding of public monuments in the City and his father was eventually awarded the OBE. He learned to drive at seventeen and before that holidayed in Torquay, visited Newnham College, Cambridge, and the Chelsea Flower Show. Gardening was a keen interest of the Wainwright family and one which Richard continued. The acres of gardens at The Heath were tended by professional gardeners, noted for their delphiniums and featured on the cover of a gardening text-book.[5] At the age of nine, Richard Wainwright kept a detailed Royal Horticultural Society diary of the management and care of the gardens and at thirteen he was first Secretary of the Roundhay Amateurs' Horticultural Society. This illustrates Wainwright's background and developing character: firstly, he was able to persuade local Labour MP James Milner to be the Society's President because of his family's contacts: 'Milner is a friend of ours and is Member of Parliament for South-East Leeds', Wainwright explained to the Society's Treasurer, adding confidently: 'he will probably be Lord Mayor in the near future.' In fact Milner went on to be Deputy Speaker of the Commons before being made Baron Milner of Leeds. Secondly, Wainwright showed his organisational dynamism, recruiting officers of the Society and ordering its stationery from a firm in Sussex whose services he had seen advertised in a national newspaper and which he told the Treasurer proudly were 'very cheap'.[6]

Wainwright also had the advantage of being a cherished only son. Henry Scurrah and Emily had been married a decade before Richard Wainwright was born, and he was the subject of devotion in childhood which produced assurance and even precociousness. At boarding school he received parental visits more often than the average boy, and was kept off at Leeds for whole terms with illness. His mother objected tearfully to his being sent away to school, and kept infant photographs of him around her until her own death.[7] Richard Wainwright did not, it should be stressed, emerge from this as a feeble or vain person – his father showed in his relations with Richard's children high expectations, especially in education, good manners and clear speech, and a sense of duty to others.[8] Like other boys, he enjoyed seeing motorcycle stunt-riding shows, followed the fortunes of Leeds United and went on camping trips with the Boys' Brigade. However, in significant ways his upbringing was different from that of his contemporaries.

Richard Wainwright's social background was similar in its significance to that of a leading Liberal of the previous generation, David Lloyd George. Like Wainwright, in national politics Lloyd George was an outsider, proud to come from a part of the United Kingdom unfamiliar to most of its rulers, and even in Wainwright's case, not quite from a social class able to command automatic acceptance amongst metropolitan dilettantes. Lloyd George's first language made him literally incomprehensible to most of his colleagues in government; but Wainwright too was by turns amused and angered by the limited understanding of the world of his origins which he encountered at Westminster. At the same time, both men were doted upon as children, and within the world of their origins, they were part of what Lloyd George's biographer John Grigg calls 'the Welsh patriotic elite', or what in Wainwright's case was a network of professional, religious and political leaders who were recognised as the advocates to the outside world of Yorkshire interests. Grigg describes these circumstances in Lloyd George as 'not-so-humble origins'.[9] Both men had Janus-faced political identities: at Westminster they were provincial outsiders; in their constituencies, acknowledged notables.

Lloyd George is said to have announced at thirteen that he would be Prime Minister; Liberal ambitions were tailored after the First World War but expectation was still strong. Asked what Henry Scurrah's reaction was when Richard

Wainwright was elected to Parliament in the former's eighty-ninth year, Richard's wife says 'he was thrilled, because it was what he had always wanted'.[10]

Shrewsbury

Richard Wainwright had a privileged education, isolated from most 1930s schoolchildren. It nurtured talents and ideas which were to be essential to his political career and immunised him from the difficulties of the Liberal Party at national level. It began at a private school in Leeds but at the age of nine Richard was sent to a boarding school called Streete Court at Westgate-on-Sea in Kent. His mother was extremely reluctant, and deeply upset, to see him go; but he was to study away from home for the next eleven years.

Streete Court was established by J.V. Milne, father of A.A. Milne, the creator of Winnie the Pooh, in 1894 as a nursery for major public schools. It offered a traditional robust and highly structured experience, and drew other pupils from beyond the South-East: several of Wainwright's Streete Court contemporaries caught the train from Leeds, sometimes to be mocked by locals on arrival at the station in Kent. Wainwright showed his interest in writing by compiling the 1929 edition of Streete Court's magazine – although, as so often in later life, he did not make any acknowledged contribution of his own. Most of the boys at Streete Court went to leading public schools, including Charterhouse, Rugby, Uppingham, Marlborough, Wellington, Malvern, Eton and Harrow. Wainwright went with the largest contingent, to Shrewsbury School.[11]

Joyce Wainwright believes her husband's liberalism was strengthened by even this early stage of education:[12] it is true that some Liberal names were on the register at Streete Court around Wainwright's time, including Peter Calvocoressi, who was on the prosecution team at Nuremberg, a Liberal candidate in 1945 and later a renowned historian; members of the Benn family – then still within Liberal ranks – also went to Streete Court. Wainwright certainly seems to have been happy there. However, there is little about the school or its intake which was distinctively Liberal. That claim could be made somewhat more convincingly for Shrewsbury.

Wainwright took up his place at Shrewsbury School in September 1931. Shrewsbury was a senior public school, but one with relatively modest origins as a King Edward VI Grammar School, and its clientele embraced a large contingent of the ambitious northern professional, commercial and industrial bourgeoisie.[13]

The result was a mixture of the social exclusivity and physical hardships of public school life, tempered by less certainty of destiny to rule than characterised Eton, Westminster or Harrow; and a greater sense of provincial civic purpose than was inculcated in those places. Shrewsbury, for example, still maintains the mission house it established for the poor of Liverpool and which was extended during Wainwright's time, whilst most senior public schools have abandoned such activity as a Victorian fad. Noted Salopians emerging from this idiosyncratic environment a generation later included broadcasters Michael Palin and John Peel, *Private Eye* founders Richard Ingrams and Willie Rushton, and radical journalist Paul Foot.[14] The maverick quality of the School extended to some of the staff who taught Wainwright, challenging his already active political mind. The blend of academic pride and personal aspiration on one hand, and intellectual dynamism with a sense of social justice on the other, suited him down to the ground.

Much of the day-to-day life at Shrewsbury reflected that of other English boarding schools: daily chapel, sports, traditional scholarship, and a densely layered hierarchy determining what collar boys wore, whether or not they had a cushion in chapel and a good deal more. Upon arrival at Shrewsbury, new pupils assimilated a vocabulary of fifty new words and nicknames, many reinforcing the rigid social order: newcomers were 'scums', or 'douls' when required to do menial work; day boys were 'skites'; teachers 'brushers'; 'sap' was hard study; and 'wazz' described the anxiety inspired by the prospect of discipline.

House Masters and Monitors habitually used beatings to establish their authority, and Wainwright's House Master, C.W. 'Cuddy' Mitford, had a reputation for harsh sarcasm and an overbearing use of his disciplinary powers. One of Wainwright's contemporaries in Mitford's House at Severn Hill, the painter Kyffin Williams, described it as 'a hard, philistine place': boys were beaten for not reciting their sports colours accurately; beaten for speaking in regional accents; even beaten for not correcting others' accents.[15] Another Salopian of the early 1930s, later *Spectator* Editor Brian Inglis, recalled 'licensed bullying', heavy drinking amongst staff and sexual relations between boys. 'Shrewsbury for the first couple of years,' wrote Inglis, 'was a hell for anybody who was not an exceptionally gifted footballer or cricketer.'[16] Even affectionate accounts of the era acknowledge 'a general consensus of correct and incorrect behaviour – what was "done" and "not done"; a withering reproof for a remark or action which lay outside the code was that it was "not much done". It doesn't sound much but it stung.'[17]

None of this seems to have troubled Wainwright, who within four months of arrival was writing diaries in fluent Shrewsburyese, and though not a natural athlete – at thirteen he had reached neither five feet tall nor six-and-a-half stone – he found a niche in the boat house, gaining House colours for coxing. He recorded witnessing Mitford beat seven small boys, but disapproved only because the House Master had insisted on carrying out the punishment himself. 'Why can't the man leave it to his monitors?' asked Wainwright. It is in fact disapproval of individuals' incompetence which emerges as the strongest negative theme of Wainwright's time at Shrewsbury. From his earliest days at the School, Wainwright felt confident to pass judgement on those he found wanting at all levels of the hierarchy: the Archdeacon's remarks on war debts in chapel were 'quite good', but the Bishop of Liverpool's sermon was 'very bad'; Rev. R.H.J. Brooke, a 'new brusher ... took us quite well', but when new Headmaster H.H. Hardy had been in place less than a month in September, Wainwright condemned him as 'so far too "machine-like". Where's his personality?' Mitford was commended for a concert in his study, where Wainwright also listened to the Prince of Wales on the radio, which was 'not bad' (although Wainwright noticed 'he has a cockney accent!').[18]

The tone of Wainwright's diary is partly the sign of the precociousness of a spoilt only son, but this robustness also emerged increasingly in his public activities – despite what others found to be the intimidating atmosphere of the School. In his second, fourth and fifth years he won School prizes for English Literature and History, as well as the School journal *The Salopian*'s prize for an amusing short story. By his last year, Wainwright was co-Editor of *The Salopian*, President of the Debating Society and an active member of the Halifax Literary Society; and as a Praepostor he was one of the eighteen most senior pupils responsible for the administration of discipline. Although he had made a quiet start – he lost a Hall election in his second term – Wainwright's school reports show that in his third year he 'begins to gain a position' and a year later 'becomes a leader'. The young man who was to register as a Conscientious Objector (CO) three years later was even an Adjutant in the Officer Training Corps. Contemporaries recognised Wainwright's measured response to Shrewsbury's challenges: Williams remembered 'a shrewd and subtle little boy from Yorkshire ... adept at avoiding trouble' and Inglis saw 'the keen political sense that was to make him ... one of the mainstays of the Liberal Party'.[19] Wainwright had the rare combination of a well-stocked storehouse of ideas, with enough good sense to ration their expression.

There seems little doubt that aspects of Shrewsbury helped to shape those ideas. Historically, Shrewsbury was a moderately Tory school: its Anglican chapel was quite high-church, and by tradition the Hall Crier in each House had the task of calling out 'Long live the King and down with the radicals!' However, there was also a tradition of free discussion in the School: though rejected, Irish Home Rule and women's enfranchisement had been formally debated before the First World War, and in the 1930s two of Wainwright's teachers in particular reflected Shrewsbury's tolerance of experiment and argument.

The first was Frank McEachran, affectionately known as 'Kek'. Kek, the model for Hector in Alan Bennett's *The History Boys*, was a product of Manchester Grammar School, and became a legendary figure at Shrewsbury for his dynamism, his sharp intellect and his encouragement of others. 'He was above all', an admirer wrote, 'a goad, an inspirer, a kicker of young imaginations and sensibilities into life'.[20] A.D.C. Peterson, the leading post-war educationalist who taught with Kek at Shrewsbury, called him 'the most inspiring school teacher I ever came across'.[21] Although he arrived at Shrewsbury only for Wain-wright's final year, he came to know him quickly, joining in at Debating Society meetings. In Wainwright's first year at Cambridge, McEachran went to speak to the University Liberal Club.[22] He corresponded with and visited Wain-wright during the War, and afterwards became a friend to Wainwright and Joyce, staying over at Christmas and being 'Uncle' to the children. His books of 'spells' – short literary extracts which he taught Wainwright's children to chant – became treasured possessions of the family; it was partly her ability at interview, to complete Wainwright's recitations from these that Joanna Copsey (later Hannam) secured employment in his office in 1977, as she had been amongst the last few to be taught by Kek in the early 1970s. Most significantly, Kek gave the sermon at the death of Wainwright's second son Andrew in 1974.

McEachran was both a scholar and a radical, a devotee of Henry George, the nineteenth-century American thinker whose proposals for land value taxa-tion brought together resistance to state interference in the market and part-communalisation of property. McEachran's particular interpretation of this doctrine was almost anarchistic, dismissing the value of nations and almost all large-scale organisation, and regarding land tax as sufficient source of any public revenue. Wainwright commended his last work, *Freedom the Only End*, as 'refreshing food, new to the menu of our times'.[23] Kek remained involved in movements for libertarian economic reform until his death in 1975.

Another teacher promoting Georgeism at Shrewsbury was Murray Senior, who came to teach History in 1932. Like McEachran, Senior celebrated non-conformity and raised unusual topics in class. A visiting Inspector, Wainwright remembered to a contemporary, was shocked to be invited by Senior to partici-pate in a vigorous discussion on the ethics of nudism. The same contemporary described Senior's approach to wider political issues:

> In the form room his teaching was wide ranging, encouraging us to think and read outside the syllabus, constantly straying into what was then called Current Affairs, broadly liberal and even radical in his own stance, always with sympathy for the minority and the outsider.[24]

Senior encouraged his students to read Left Book Club publications, and directed their attention to the work of Major C.H. Douglas, a disciple of Henry George, whose Social Credit Party in Canada took control of the Alberta state government in 1935.

Other teachers at Shrewsbury during Wainwright's time were to reappear in his political life, such as A.D.C. Peterson, who went on to be Professor of Education at Oxford, where he stood as Liberal candidate in 1966, founded the International Baccalaureate, and was a senior advisor on education policy to the post-war Liberal Party as a member of the Unservile State Group, of which Wainwright was Treasurer. For Wainwright's final term, Shrewsbury welcomed

Victor Bonham Carter as a modern linguist: cousin of Mark and nephew of Violet, Bonham Carter was later to write a history of his noted political family, rejoicing that 'the wheel has turned, and those who value the liberal tradition can no longer turn their back on Politics. Politics have returned to them.'[25]

Richard Wainwright's ideas at this time were not explicitly attached to the Liberal Party, but certain aspects of his later approach are recognisable in his debating speeches and his work for *The Salopian*. Though as co-Editor Wainwright did not necessarily pen or even agree all its leading articles, *The Salopian* from 1935 to 1936 was consistently internationalist and fiercely critical of Baldwin's foreign policy: as the Rhineland was remilitarised in March 1936, Eden was condemned as 'non-committal'; when, two months later, Addis Ababa fell, *The Salopian* asked gravely, 'has the League failed? It would seem so.'[26] Opposition to conservatism generally was clear, too, in a piece on 'Progress' expressing gratitude that 1930s Britain was not smothered by 'the stuffy and anti-macassared solemnity of a Nineteenth Century or ruled by the caprices and whims of an idle aristocracy'. It went on:

> New ideas can be introduced, digested and criticised without sending people into unbalanced paroxysms of excitement … We take more interest in our surroundings; we can face up to facts (vague it sounds, but yet how gloriously true).[27]

Wainwright had struck a similar note at the Debating Society in November 1935 when opposing the motion 'This House does not believe in reform', saying that 'without reform we have no progress. Reform has curtailed, not encouraged, aggression.'[28] Another *Salopian* editorial under Wainwright's leadership warned against 'the alternatives of Fascism with its sacrifice of morality, and Communism with its sacrifice of religion'.[29] Most obviously, Wainwright took with him from Shrewsbury, from Senior and McEachran, a faith in wider property ownership, expressed in what was to be an abiding faith in co-ownership in industry which his Parliamentary Secretary said he regarded as 'the Holy Grail of Liberalism'.[30] One of the last political posts Wainwright held was the Deputy Chair of the Wider Share Ownership Council, which he retained until his eightieth year.

Wainwright was proud of his association with Shrewsbury. He formed strong friendships, notably with David Gieve of the Savile Row tailors Gieve and Hawkes. He socialised with the Old Salopians at Cambridge, was invited to meet Headmaster H.H. Hardy when he visited the University, and still subscribed to the Salopian Newsletter three decades after he left. Most significantly, he sent his son Martin there in 1963, reading him a satirical poem from *The Salopian* by Paul Dehn, later an Oscar-winning scriptwriter, to help him acclimatise before he went.[31] An indication of quite how firmly Wainwright was prepared to nail his colours to the mast of Shrewsbury and its like – and of his personal politics – came in a Debating Society meeting on 25 October 1935.

Representatives of the Workers' Educational Association had been invited to defend the proposal that the school leaving age should be raised to fifteen, and in a speech carefully typed onto a four-page script, Wainwright objected vehemently.

Firstly, he argued that as the Conservatives supported the measure, it could not be in the interest of working people; rather it was 'one of the sops that they are ready to throw to their enemies when danger threatens. If this extra year of education were to mean the opening of a real pathway to truth, do you think for one minute it would have become part of the program of the propertied classes?' Controversially, he went on to argue that the quality of state education corroborated his suspicion of Tory motives: that 'state education, as presently organised, is no education at all'. Wainwright's attack deftly made simultaneous appeals to Salopian pride and a quasi-Marxist idea of false consciousness:

> With little or no individual attention they are given an uninteresting groundwork in mathematics and their mother tongue which they are not taught to link up with the life in front of them. In their last year they are probably crammed for some diploma to satisfy future employers.

The education thus offered, he reminded Salopians, involved 'thoroughly bad teaching' of 'useless or distorted facts in unfavourable conditions by unfit teachers'.[32] There would be 'no hours on the river, no comfortable library, no thrilling recent novel to look forward to'. History in such schools, Wainwright argued, took the form of Imperialist propaganda comparable to that of the Fascists, and its pinnacle, Empire Day, was 'a very orgy of unthinking national pride'; religious education was reduced to 'an ineffectual watering-down of true religious principles which also helps the master class in their life and death struggle to keep the truth from their proletariat'. The unchallenging character of education outside the public schools, he argued, was 'why the Tories can be prodigal of it'.

His contemporaries were surprised by Wainwright's interweaving of biblical and Bolshevik language. It becomes possible to see why Inglis believed Wainwright had 'strong Communist leanings'.[33] *The Salopian* damned Wainwright with sardonic faint praise as 'fluent and almost cogent. Might we suggest that he might do well to vary his pace?' and the motion was carried against Wainwright by fifty-nine votes to thirty-six.[34]

To modern ears, Wainwright's account sounds a sweeping judgement of a system which back in Yorkshire was honing future Labour intellects such as Harold Wilson and Barbara Castle, and of which Wainwright himself had no direct experience. Certainly there is evidence here of Wainwright's sheltered upbringing and immaturity. Later in life he was to shed this superficial self-assuredness in favour of self-awareness: he acknowledged to Joyce ten years later 'how much the very few women one encounters in life at boarding school unconsciously colour one's outlook'[35] and as a constituency MP he was a keen supporter of early comprehensive state education in Colne Valley. In retirement, he even doubted whether independent education did 'on balance, more good or harm to the principles it claims to serve.'[36]

However, the episode also showed important features of Wainwright's character and politics. He had stuck to unpopular views based on the limited evidence he had, and, in one stroke, he had dismissed the Tories out of hand and challenged the Left to think seriously about the practical consequences of their policy. This was a warning to supposed progressives who made lazy assumptions with Wainwright.

Notes

1 Wainwright, P., *Opposite the Infirmary: A History of the Thackray Company 1902– 1990* (Leeds: Medical Museum Publishing 1997). RSW became a shareholder in Thackray in 1948 and a Director in 1950, which he remained until the 1980s.

2 Assistant Secretary, Institute of Chartered Accountants, to HSW, 6 May 1940, which replies to enquiries about RSW's status taking accountancy exams whilst applying for a Directorship of the Metropole; note of Wainwright's accounts, 7 February 1943, which refers to shares in the Metropole received in October and November 1942.

3 Note of RSW's accounts, 7 February 1943.

4 Wainwright, M., 'Surfing the web for Great-Grandad Fred, and other sons of Abraham', *The Guardian*, 3 January 2002.

5 Hunt, P.R.S., *The Beginner's Garden* (London: W.H. & L. Collingridge 1953).

6 RSW to George Gilpin, 14 July 1932, Wainwright paper file 1/5.

7 Joyce Wainwright, interview, 22 February 2008.

8 Tessa Wainwright, interview, 30 October 2008.

9 Grigg, J., *Lloyd George: The Young Lloyd George* (London: Harper Collins 1997) p. 22.

10 Joyce Wainwright, interview, 22 February 2008.

11 *Streete Court School Centenary*, Streete Court Club 2003; the magazine is in the Wainwright papers file 1/5. The present author is grateful to Mr Nigel Giles of the Streete Court Old Boys' organisation for his advice on the school's history.

12 Joyce Wainwright, interview, 22 February 2008.

13 For general information on Shrewsbury and for access to Shrewsbury's records, the present author is indebted to Dr Michael Morrogh and his colleagues at Shrewsbury.

14 A comparative study of public schools in the 1960s called the Bloxham Project also recognised Shrewsbury's distinctiveness: Leach, C., *A School at Shrewsbury* (London: James and James 1990), pp. 112 ff.

15 Williams, K., *Across the Straits: An Autobiography* (London: Duckworth 1973), p. 68.

16 Inglis, B., *Downstart* (London: Chatto & Windus 1990), pp. 39–42.

17 Charlesworth, M., *Behind the Headlines: An Autobiography* (Wells: The Greenbank Press 1994), p. 38.

18 RSW, personal diary 1932, Wainwright papers File 1/7.

19 Williams, *Across the Straits*, p. 71; Inglis, *Downstart*, p. 46.

20 Le Quesne, L., Introduction to McEachran, F., *A Cauldron of Spells* (Wells: The Greenbank Press 1992), p. xxvi.

21 Peterson, A.D.C., *Liberal Education for All* (London: Liberal Party 1973). This reference is on the opening page.

22 Music Room, St John's College, Friday, 5 March 1937. The title of the lecture was 'Socialism Debunked (by Scientific Economics)'.

23 Wainwright, R., Reviews, *New Outlook*, 1973, No. 4, p. 60.

24 Charlesworth, *Behind the Headlines*, p. 67.

25 Bonham Carter, V., *In a Liberal Tradition* (London: Constable 1960), p. 236.

26 *The Salopian*, 28 March 1936 and 23 May 1936.

27 *The Salopian*, 13 June 1936.

28 *The Salopian*, 9 November 1935. The Debating Society met on 1 November.

29 *The Salopian*, 28 March 1936.

30 Caroline Cawston, interview, 2 June 2008.

31 Correspondence from Martin Wainwright, 6 June 2008. Dehn's credits include *Goldfinger* (1964), *The Spy Who came in from the Cold* (1965), Franco Zeffirelli's *The Taming of the Shrew* (1967) and Sidney Lumet's star-studded 1974 film of *Murder on the Orient Express*. He left Shrewsbury the year before Wainwright arrived.

32 The text of this speech is in the Wainwright papers file 1/4.

33 Inglis, *Downstart*, p. 47.

34 *The Salopian*, 9 November 1935 p. 511.

35 RSW to Joyce Wainwright, 13 October 1947, Wainwright papers file 17/1.

36 RSW to Michael Meadowcroft, 20 November 1989, Wainwright papers file 1/5.

2 Cambridge

During the 1930s, distance from parliamentary and electoral politics was no misfortune for Liberals, for the recovery of 1929 descended into another decade of division and despair. The Party broke into three factions, and was left by the outbreak of the Second World War with fewer than twenty MPs, under 7 per cent of the vote and a perilously weak national organisation. On leaving Shrewsbury, Wainwright surveyed these developments from the detached circumstances of Cambridge University.

Lloyd George's success in leading the Liberals to win nearly a quarter of the vote, fifty-nine seats and the balance of power in the Commons in 1929 had been misleading. *The Liberal Magazine* regarded the result as 'not satisfactory to any party' and 'a disappointment to the Liberal Party'. Though their policy and leadership had been right, its editorial line ran, 'it is evident that a large section of the electorate did not believe us when we said that we could conquer unemployment'.[1] This credibility problem was only amplified by subsequent events. As in 1924, Baldwin left the Liberals with no alternative but to support a minority Labour government or to precipitate another election. Under these circumstances, and with a promise of legislation for electoral reform, Lloyd George committed the Liberals to support a MacDonald Government for the second time.

The hardly healed wounds of the Liberal Party were soon torn at by its own members and its opponents. Almost immediately there were defections by Liberal MPs to the two main parties, and by the end of 1929 Liberal MPs split over individual Labour government measures such as the Coal Bill. In 1930 there emerged clear division over the general competence and direction of the government, and over the Liberals' strategic approach to it. It was the introduction of a Land Value Taxation scheme proposed by Lloyd George and Labour Chancellor Philip Snowden which those Liberals critical of the Labour government chose as their occasion to resign the Whip in June 1931, but the rift was formalised with the creation of a National Government in August, after which Sir John Simon formed the Liberal National group of MPs, who were fully supportive of the new partnership between elements of all parties;

Herbert Samuel led the 'official' Liberal Party, which took part in the National Government reluctantly; and Lloyd George and his family group gave the administration only cursory acknowledgement. The election called to endorse the National Government split these factions apart, leaving them with thirty-five, thirty-two and four MPs respectively. According to Trevor Wilson, 'by the end of 1931 the Liberals had entirely lost their bearings',[2] but worse was to come a year later, when the Government's adoption of protective trade measures following the Ottawa conference led Samuel to withdraw his Liberal ministers from it and, the following year, join Lloyd George on the Opposition benches. This was, for David Dutton, the point at which the Liberal Party lost the Liberal Nationals for ever, and simultaneously confirmed its minor party status.[3]

At the General Election of 1935, Samuel's official Liberal Party fielded only 161 candidates against the Government, and of these only twenty-one won (two-thirds of these being given a free run by one or both of the main parties). In Leeds, Wainwright saw the Liberals fight only one of the six seats in 1931 (coming a poor third), and gain much of their representation in Yorkshire by the restraint of the Conservatives. Tory agents in the County were indignant by 1932 at the Liberals' break with the National Government after 'they did their best to upset us in South Leeds, Penistone, Keighley and Holderness' and took pleasure that 'they were at the bottom of the poll in the first three cases'. In 1935, the Liberals contested no seats in Leeds, and the lack of a Liberal candidate led to an unusually low turnout in other parts of Yorkshire.[4] On Leeds City Council, the Liberals had by this time been reduced to a solitary member of the Council for three years.[5] Nationally, most of the Party's leading figures, including Samuel himself, lost their seats, and there were again almost immediate defections to the Conservatives and Labour.

The remaining Liberal MPs chose as their new Leader the MP for Caithness and Sutherland, Sir Archibald Sinclair. A new constitution was prepared by Lord Meston which swept away the National Liberal Federation and created the Liberal Party Organisation with its later familiar features including the Headquarters, Council and Assembly. Even a sympathetic historian such as Roy Douglas concludes, however, that its approval in 1936 owed most to the need 'to avoid the risk of Liberal National infiltration' – to keep people out rather than to recruit new members in.[6] Four months before the establishment of the new constitution, the Liberals came a dismal fourth in a by-election at Ross and Cromarty, the previously safe Liberal seat which was later represented by Charles Kennedy. Little wonder that when Sinclair came to speak to the Liberal Club at Cambridge during Wainwright's time there, one of those present recalled that 'there wasn't much humour to his speech'.[7] Yet it was at this point that Richard Wainwright joined the Liberal Party.

Just before Christmas 1935 Wainwright received a telegram at Leeds from friends bearing only the words 'Oxford heartbroken'.[8] His offer of an Open

Scholarship to study History at Clare College, Cambridge the following autumn meant that the opportunity to make contacts in the political world, and thereby begin the career in public life which was his father's ambition for him, was laid open to him. Wainwright took it, and despite the difficulties of the Party at national level, committed himself formally for the first time to the Liberals. On arrival at Cambridge in autumn 1936, he joined the Liberal Club, thereby beginning a commitment he was to maintain for over fifty years until the Party's merger with the SDP, and a further fifteen with the Liberal Democrats. Within a year he was Assistant Secretary of the Club, writing for its journal *The New Radical*, and in his final year Wainwright became its President.

Wainwright liked to joke to his wife that the Liberal Club at Cambridge University had only two active members including himself, but this was unduly modest.[9] Like all political clubs at Oxford and Cambridge, it was regarded by its parent party as a nursery for future parliamentarians, and as such attracted an impressive array of visitors, which in turn attracted a substantial membership. The Liberal Club at Cambridge University attracted audiences of between thirty and seventy to its public meetings,[10] claimed 340 undergraduate members by 1939,[11] and though not all of these would be active or even Liberal, involvement in the Club put Wainwright in contact with some of the leading Liberals of the 1930s and notable figures of the post-war world from all fields of public life.

The list of visiting speakers gives a taste of the company with whom Wainwright rubbed shoulders: in 1937–38 these included Viscount Samuel, Sir Archibald Sinclair, Lord Pentland, Lady Rhondda, Professor Gilbert Murray, W.H. Auden, and a string of MPs including Sir Geoffrey Mander, Graham White and Dingle Foot, who came to debate the ethics of pacifism with Bertrand Russell. Amongst Wainwright's contemporaries in the Club were students who were to go on to have high public profiles. On a delegation of undergraduate political activists to investigate French politics in March 1938 he was joined by three future Liberal parliamentary candidates as well as Derek Ezra, Sam Silkin and Abba Eban, who by the 1970s had respectively become Chairman of the National Coal Board, Attorney General in a Labour Government and Israel's Foreign Minister.

As well as hosting a dozen visiting speakers each year, holding social events and organising foreign delegations, the Liberal Club sent resolutions to the Liberal Party Assembly[12] and maintained links with the Cambridgeshire Liberal Association, nominating candidates for the University seat.[13] They also carried out substantial political work amongst other students: in February 1938 the Club ran a survey to test opinion on their proposition that women undergraduates (or 'undergraduettes' as Wainwright addressed them in encouraging them to join the Liberal Club) should have full Cambridge Union membership.[14]

Wainwright was also a member of the 'Eighty Club', a dining club through which the Liberal Party nationally sought to recruit aspirant political leaders.

The corresponding branch in Oxford at the time, for example, included young Liberal and future Prime Minister Harold Wilson; Derek Ezra, who was a member of the Cambridge branch along with Wainwright, remembered it as part of an important political network with links to London.[15] Its meetings offered a less inhibited setting for political discussion and gossip, and attracted a wider range of members, than the Liberal Club. At their meeting at the Lion Hotel in October 1937, for example, Wainwright dined with guest of honour Major Gwilym Lloyd George; others apparently present included the Editor of *The Daily Herald* Francis Williams and Desiree Meyler, who in the 1970s became a prolific romantic novelist. G.R.W. Brigstocke, who went on to be a senior civil servant after the War, and some of the Cambridge teaching staff such as History don Frank Salter, were also there.

University life leaves its imprint on most who experience it, and Wainwright made lifelong friends such as Denis Henry, an historian who was Joyce and Richard's best man ten years later, and who, writing from Stonyhurst College in Lancashire where he had become a master, to commiserate on the death of Wainwright's mother in 1962, fondly remembered drinking sessions in the University Arms 'at least three worlds ago'.[16] Another friend, Derek Ezra, remembered that Wainwright in particular 'acclimatised extremely well' to the University. Ezra was not even aware at the time that Wainwright was a Yorkshireman: 'I never associated him with anything other than Cambridge.'[17]

The strength of Wainwright's attachment to Cambridge is reflected in a letter he wrote a year after graduation, giving advice to a relation applying there. Wainwright reassured the applicant that he had 'already won half the battle' by rejecting Oxford: 'that provincial university is now largely a Fish and Chip shop, with the Potato Marketing Board in one college, the Ministry of Fisheries in the next; and of course Lord Nuffield has all the rest'. Even within Cambridge, Wainwright gave a 'black-list', first presented to him at Shrewsbury, of colleges 'that are really undesirable', including Fitzwilliam, Downing, St Catherine's, Jesus and Pembroke. To dine in Hall at these colleges, Wainwright warned, was 'to gain an impression of life at a low level!'[18] This disdainful tone was – as it had been with his love of Shrewsbury – not a sign of attitudes Wainwright would retain, as his recruitment of staff from all academic backgrounds, and his association in retirement with Huddersfield Polytechnic, demonstrate. Even Wainwright's contempt for Oxford did not prevent him giving a memorable address at the Liberal Club there in 1955.[19] Like his boldness at Shrewsbury, however, it displayed a toughness and self-confidence which were to last a lifetime.

Cambridge was vital to Wainwright's political development, too. It strengthened ideas which were already present in his mind and gave him an attachment to the Liberal Party which he was never to lose. However, it cannot be argued that it was easy to fall into the Liberal Party through inertia or ambition: nobody aware of public affairs in the 1930s could believe that a Liberal membership card was a political meal ticket. Wainwright must have known that, as Wilson's biographer says of him at Oxford, Liberal Club membership 'offered the smallest future opportunity'.[20] Wainwright had been introduced to Labour politicians in his youth and, being fiercely critical of inequality and of the incompetence of the National Government's foreign policy, could easily have found a home in Labour circles had he been prepared to subdue certain of his beliefs; but he did not.

Moreover, an undergraduate motivated chiefly by political ambition would have done better to seek office in the Cambridge Union. Its recent Presidents, after all, included noted inter-war Liberals such as economist J.M. Keynes, Judge Norman Birkett, Hugh Foot, the senior diplomat born into the Liberal dynasty led by Sir Isaac, and Geoffrey Shakespeare MP, who was a government minister from 1931 to 1942. Many of the post-war politicians who would sit in the Commons with Wainwright took the same route: a string of Tory heavyweights including Rab Butler, Kenneth Clarke and Michael Howard; Labour's Jack Ashley and Chris Smith; and the future Acting Liberal Democrat Leader Vince Cable – all were Cambridge Union Presidents. Wainwright's friend Derek Ezra was a regular speaker at the Union, and Wainwright himself reported on Union meetings for *The New Radical*,[21] and was invited to Union Committee dinners, so that fuller involvement would have been natural enough. The promise of such success did not attract Wainwright, however: so we can say that his decision to join a political club might have arisen from general aspiration towards political office; but his decision to join the Liberals was one of conviction.

The convictions which drew Wainwright into the Liberal Party are reflected in his work for the Club publicly and internally, and in his own private writing. These sources do not all emphasise the same strengths of Liberalism, but at the heart of them is the nucleus of the beliefs that were to sustain Wainwright throughout his career.

In appeals to potential recruits, Wainwright was prepared to adopt the 'soft centre' approach which was already becoming part of the stock-in-trade of the Party. This is the point at which, according to one Liberal historian's account, the Party 'shed its provincial radicalism and Nonconformist zeal in favour of a bland, middle-of-the-road sogginess'.[22] Though partly caused by the pounding of internal battles, this sogginess also arose from the convergence of the other parties' leaders and policies on Liberal territory: Keynes had warned the Liberal Summer School in 1925 that the Party had no distinctive themes left except free trade and temperance, and one of its own MPs complained in 1927 that the Liberal Party 'is a *pis-aller* – a kind of shelter for timid passengers in the middle of a busy street. It rouses no enthusiasm. It enlists no zeal.'[23]

The formation of the National Government in 1931, and the moderate tone of Labour and Conservative leaders, squeezed the Liberals' room for manoeuvre still further. Lord Lothian wrote in 1933 that 'Liberalism is in an almost hopeless position, so long as Baldwin is leader of the Conservative Party and Arthur Henderson the leading figure in the Labour Party';[24] and the following year Liberal President Ramsay Muir opened his restatement of Liberal principles by recognising that the younger generation 'have never seen liberalism in action' and 'scarcely know what it stands for'.[25] Lloyd George privately agreed that 'the Party has missed its opportunity as far as the present generation is concerned'.[26]

Jo Grimond, who joined the Liberals at Oxford in the 1930s, recalled that it was a time when Liberalism 'seemed to many too vague, too pallid, to be effective politically'; some were attracted to it, he admitted, 'because they felt a vague urge to do good without taking any precise steps to do it'.[27] Alan Sykes concludes more brutally that 'Liberalism was either so broad a stream that it failed to distinguish one party from another, or it was so narrow, deep and dark that no-one could tell what it was and everyone just ignored it'.[28]

This nebulous, negative recruitment strategy, painting the Liberals as the voice of reasonable, moderate opinion between extreme alternatives, had some currency in the era of the General Strike at home and the conflict between Bolshevism and Fascism abroad. At Cambridge, this polarisation had led in the early 1930s to the recruitment of the infamous spy ring of Blunt, Burgess, Philby and Maclean. Though it was open to the accusation of splitting the difference between the main parties, of unprincipled moderation for its own sake, Wainwright used the 'middle-of-the-road' appeal to get a foot in the door with new undergraduates. On behalf of the Club Committee, he wrote to Freshers in October 1937:

> In recent years people coming up to Cambridge with a reasonable interest in everyday affairs have been faced with three courses. Those who are extremists can join up with a group of Conservatives, or with a brand of Socialism interested in the monthly output of the Left Book Club, rather than the relief of actual human suffering. But for those who feel unsympathetic to both these extremes there has always been another course – to join a moderate yet progressive group of graduates and undergraduates who come together in the meetings of the Cambridge University Liberal Club.[29]

This was clearly an effective recruiting tactic, as Wainwright's contemporary Ezra acknowledged – he even believed it to have been the motivation for Wainwright himself to become a Liberal:

> What attracted him to the Liberal Club? The same things that attracted me: that the alternatives were so appalling. The Socialist Club was extreme Left: it was run, basically, by the Communists. The Conservative Club was extreme Right. The only Club with a sensible viewpoint was the Liberal Club.[30]

Wainwright seemed to confirm this negative motivation – and his greater attraction to Labour – in a conversation after he retired with Tony (now Lord)

21

Greaves. Greaves recalled that 'he said he'd decided at an early age that he wasn't a Conservative: his background wasn't Conservative; he just didn't stand for what the Conservatives stood for, which was basically personal selfishness. On the other hand his background meant he never considered joining the Labour Party.'[31]

For Wainwright, however, this line was mainly propaganda for public consumption: he would be ready to use it again for campaigning purposes in the future, and he did not disagree with it, but it was not this middle-of-the-road Liberalism which really motivated him.

In more serious publications, Wainwright was forthright on particular issues of party organisation and outlook: his contribution to the report of the University delegation to France, for example, expressed approval of the French Radical Party's willingness to adapt its ideology to the demands of the present day, noting that it 'does not appear to believe in constant lip-service to certain "fundamental principles" revealed in the past to the "chosen few" by some semi-divine political hero. There is always of course "La France", but there is no "what Gladstone said in '84", no Cobden, and no Asquith.' He went on to warn fellow Liberals about the conduct of their all-too-frequent internal battles: 'the [Radical] Party conference, in fact, provides a combination of instruction and inspiration for the Executive and rank-and-file alike. It is not a holiday at a seaside resort, nor a non-stop wrestling match. British political parties might learn a lesson from the French Radicals.'[32]

The fullest explanation of Wainwright's Liberalism as an undergraduate, however, is set out in a personal essay on the subject written by hand in 1937.[33] This article, not being annotated by anyone else and still in Wainwright's possession when he left Cambridge, appears to be an entirely private expression of his thoughts on the state of Liberal politics at the time. Here he highlights three radical and distinctive themes which are for him the important, positive features of the Liberal tradition. Firstly (and despite Wainwright's suspicion of lip-service to forbears) there is a brief, almost assumed, wistful backward glance to the honourable history of liberal social reform and its end in the First World War. 'The War came before the Liberal Party had finished its job. It lost its chance to carry on the work after the War, and when bad times arrived, people received the impression that Liberalism meant only liberty for the few, a liberty that was to be a privilege.' Trade unionists and intellectuals, wrote Wainwright, sought liberation by the Socialist road, but there was already renewed hope: 'there are signs that some of them have already found the road a cul-de-sac.' Wainwright stressed the difference between Socialism and Liberalism with a metaphor drawn from his favourite pastime:

> The Liberal does not liken himself to an architect, who can condemn a building and have it demolished, to rebuild it with plans from his own brain, with dead and uniform bricks. He is rather a gardener, dealing with living things which grow

according to their nature. He can discover the necessary conditions for their full growth and ensure that these are present, but more than this he cannot do.

The second of Wainwright's themes pointed to what Liberals needed to do to finish the job that was started before the War, and to build his ideal garden: to complete the land tax reform Lloyd George had prepared in 1912, which the Liberal Party had promised in the 1920s and tried to deliver in 1931, and which Wainwright had learned of from McEachran. 'Statesmen have not yet succeeded in establishing that essential basis for a free society – a scheme whereby those who occupy land return to the rest of the community the annual value of their site.' This, Wainwright believed, was what would make Liberalism distinctively radical and would bring about an end to poverty:

> The community has never received back the values which it creates by its very presence and its labours. The essential source of wealth has not been open at a fair rent to those who could best use it … The monopoly of the earth's surface was the main factor in producing the squalor of what might have been an entirely glorious Industrial Revolution, and Liberalism has not achieved its end until this flaw is righted.

Wainwright was to remain interested in land taxation as a solution to fiscal issues throughout his life, and wrote publicly about it as a form of local government finance whilst an MP in the 1970s.[34]

Lastly, in the international field, there was the distinctive and vital Liberal approach to foreign affairs: free trade, and the internationalism which for Wainwright remained the only antidote to war. 'The refusal of nations to trade freely with one another is a form of war, springing from the same root as actual war, the distrust of nation by nation, and the desire of one nation to profit at the expense of another. There is,' he went on, 'a close connection between tariffs and war, between free trade and peace.' And he issued a stern warning against the doctrine of regime change by war which was at least as seductive in the shadow of Nazi Germany as it has been to some statesmen in recent years: 'by its very nature Liberalism is not prepared to force its creed on foreign nations, or to ally with other centres of Liberalism against such nations. Atrocities perpetrated by one nation on another may call for protest, but the Liberal spirit is not one to allow foreign policy to be dictated by ideological considerations.'

It had become fashionable by the time Wainwright was at Cambridge for intellectuals to declare the Liberal Party finished. As well as George Dangerfield's symbolic but highly personal *The Strange Death of Liberal England*, a clutch of books, particularly from left-wing writers including Labour Party Chairman Harold Laski, the poet Stephen Spender, and Fabian historians G.D.H. Cole and Raymond Postgate, argued that Liberalism had lost its client class amongst the Victorian radical bourgeoisie, and had failed to find another.[35] Wainwright's liberalism, like the subsequent success of the Liberal

Party to which he contributed, undermines such determinism. Even in its darkest hour – or hours – and when it was least willing to voice its beliefs, there remained a long-term role for a separate radical party to promote this distinctive appeal and approach. Wainwright was to personify both the necessity and the limitations of that role.

This was the genuine, radical voice of Wainwright's Liberalism, and reflected the Party's unfinished business – the work which was to occupy him for the rest of his life. These beliefs were doubtless also held by others in the Party who sometimes gave the impression of being 'soggy'. They touched on ideas and values which had characterised the Liberalism of Gladstone and Lloyd George, and which remained dear to the hearts of their successors even after the formation of the Liberal Democrats: individual freedom from the state, wider property ownership, and internationalism; and it was the fullest development of this last principle which was to dictate Wainwright's personal response when, after he graduated two years later, war did come.

Notes

1 *The Liberal Magazine*, Vol. XXXVII, No. 429, June 1929, p. 1.
2 Wilson, T., *The Downfall of the Liberal Party 1914–35* (London: Fontana 1968), p. 398.
3 Dutton, D., *A History of the Liberal Party in the Twentieth Century* (Basingstoke: Palgrave Macmillan 2004), p. 130.
4 Stannage, T., *Baldwin Thwarts the Opposition* (London: Croom Helm 1980), pp. 28 and 238.
5 Meadowcroft, M., 'The Years of Political Transition, 1914–39', in Fraser, D., *A History of Modern Leeds* (Manchester: MUP 1980), p. 425.
6 Douglas, R., *Liberals: the History of the Liberal and Liberal Democrat Parties* (London: Hambledon & London 2005), p. 239.
7 Lord Ezra, interview, 28 July 2008.
8 'Eric' and 'CT' to RSW, 20 December 1935, Wainwright papers file 2.
9 Joyce Wainwright, interview, 22 February 2008. He told the Cambridge University Liberal Club in 1985 that there had been six active members who 'had to cart bottles of poor sherry from college to college to give an impression of more widespread Liberal strength than really existed' (RSW to Kate Arnheim, 18 November 1985, Cambridge University Archives, Records of Cambridge University Liberal Club, SOC 86.3).
10 Lord Ezra, interview, 28 July 2008.
11 *Manchester Guardian*, 15 March 1939.
12 *The Times*, 7 April 1937, p. 18. The present author is grateful to Seth Thevoz of Cambridge University Liberal Club for pointing out this report and for advice on RSW's service to the Club.
13 Cambridge LA to CULC, 13 May 1938; *Manchester Guardian*, 5 March 1939. The Club committee resolved in March 1939 that University representation in the Commons could only be justified by the election of Independent candidates, and supported the

candidature of Sir Ralph Wedgwood.

14 *The New Radical*, February 1938. Most students (826–572) were against, including a majority of those at the all-female colleges Girton and Newnham.

15 Lord Ezra, interview, 28 July 2008.

16 Denis Henry to RSW, 3 November 1962, Wainwright papers file 2/12.

17 Lord Ezra, interview, 28 July 2008.

18 RSW to Uncle Jim, 1 October 1940, Wainwright papers file 3/5.

19 Lord Russell to RSW, 9 June (undated – probably 1989). Wainwright papers file 12/2.

20 Pimlott, B., *Harold Wilson*, London: Harper Collins 1993, p. 48.

21 See for example RSW's report on the debate on Confidence in the Government, Vol. 1, No. 1 of *The New Radical*, 18 October 1937.

22 Bradley, I., *The Strange Rebirth of Liberal Britain* (London: Chatto & Windus 1985), p. 84.

23 Keynes published this lecture, 'Am I a Liberal?' in *Essays in Persuasion*, 1931; the MP was Alexander McCallum Scott, cited in Bradley, I., *The Strange Rebirth of Liberal Britain*, p. 84.

24 Lothian memorandum, 7 September 1933, cited in Wilson, T., *The Downfall of the Liberal Party*, pp. 407–8.

25 Muir, R., *The Liberal Way* (London: Liberal Party Publications 1934), p. 7.

26 Lloyd George to Goronwy Owen, February 1934, cited in Stannage, *Baldwin Thwarts the Opposition*, p. 105.

27 Grimond, J., *The Liberal Challenge* (London: Hollis & Carter 1963), p. 1.

28 Sykes, A., *The Rise and Fall of Liberalism 1776–1988* (London: Longman 1997), p. 255.

29 RSW, CULC open letter to new students, October 1937, Wainwright papers file 2/11.

30 Lord Ezra, interview, 28 July 2008.

31 Lord Greaves, interview, 8 April 2009.

32 Ezra, D. et al., *Politics in Paris: The Report of a Cambridge Delegation* (Cambridge: Cambridge University 1938), p. 16.

33 RSW, 'Liberalism', Wainwright papers file 2/9.

34 *Oldham Evening Chronicle*, 25 May 1977.

35 Dangerfield, G., *The Strange Death of Liberal England* (London: Constable 1935); Laski, H., *The Rise of European Liberalism* (London: Allen & Unwin 1936); Spender, S., *Forward from Liberalism* (London: Victor Gollancz 1937); Cole, G.D.H., and Postgate, R., *The Common People 1746–1938* (London: Methuen & Co. 1938).

3 Wainwright's War

'War', Winston Churchill observed prophetically in 1906 'is fatal to Liberalism.'[1] Churchill had already witnessed the damaging effect on liberal values and Liberal fortunes of the Boer War: the Party had been split between 'Liberal Imperialists' supporting the Conservative Government's campaign in South Africa, and those such as Lloyd George who were bitterly opposed, resulting in a heavy defeat at the 1900 General Election. The First World War caused a fundamental schism amongst Liberals, with Cabinet resignations and back-bench rebellions from the outset and, emerging from the War, two separate Liberal organisations which struggled to reunite throughout the inter-war period. 'They were the party of liberty' wrote Conservative historian Lord Blake, 'and liberty is the first casualty of war.'[2] The requirements of modern warfare for state control of industry, communications and ultimately for compulsory military service challenged core liberal beliefs about individual freedom. Some Liberals were prepared to suspend these liberties in order to defend them; others – especially the Non-conformist pacifists – regarded this as a betrayal of their faith. In the next War, Wainwright joined the latter group. It was a decision which reflected his courage, and which shaped both his character and his career.

The spectre of war hung over Wainwright and his contemporaries throughout the second half of the 1930s. His friend at Cambridge Derek Ezra remembered that it even inhibited politically active students from talking about parliamentary ambitions:

> Nobody was thinking of that at that time – the War was imminent. I don't think it ever arose with any of us, because there were the clouds of the War ahead ... from the time of the re-occupation of the Rhineland and the rise of the Nazi Party. I was convinced it would come in '38.[3]

The most recent study of Liberal Party foreign policy between the Wars identifies it with 'pacific-ism', or the belief that 'war can be prevented and eventually abolished by reforms, with defence justified as a way to protect reforms.'[4] Liberals retained a significant minority of supporters who rejected war as a device of foreign policy: future Labour Leader Michael Foot, at the time President of the Oxford University Liberal Club, took pride that 'I am a Liberal first of all because of the unfaltering resistance which Liberalism is pledged to offer to those twin dangers of fascism and war'.[5] These coexisted with other Liberals who were convinced that the League of Nations and the doctrine of collective security could prevent war: 'a passionate belief in the League of Nations was the *leitmotif* of inter-war Liberal internationalism' concluded Grayson; 'Liberal policy in the 1930s aimed at preventing war, perhaps through a show of force; perhaps through actually using force'.[6] This commitment to the League was shared by Party Leader Archibald Sinclair, who spoke to the Liberals at Cambridge in 1937, and it 'earned him the admiration of the pacifist movement'[7] according to his biographer, even though he later joined the Churchill Government. As late as the debate over the September 1938 Munich agreement, Sinclair could tell the Commons, 'I am not a pacifist, but I respect the pacifist point of view'.[8]

The Liberals, like the other parties, were divided and bewildered by developments on the Continent, and Wainwright could sit comfortably enough in this tolerant coalition ranging from principled pacifists to optimistic diplomats. When war came, however, he declared his personal position of refusal to fight.

Wainwright was later to claim that he had been considering his duty in time of war since 1933, when he was fifteen. This is broadly supported by his activity at Shrewsbury and Cambridge: at school he had heard sermons on the arms race in chapel, and condemned British foreign policy and all national aggression in the pages of the *Salopian* and from the floor of the Debating Society. His early essay on liberalism at university had attacked the 'folly' of 'the "Crusade" type of foreign policy which has become connected with "-isms" and ideologies of today'.[9] At Cambridge, this scepticism about war grew into fully fledged pacifism, partly under the guidance of Canon Charles Raven, Regius Professor of Divinity. Raven had since 1932 been Chairman of the Fellowship of Reconciliation, which brought together pacifists from various Christian denominations. He published *Is War Obsolete?* in 1935, *War and the Christian* in 1938 and *The Starting Point of Pacifism* in 1940. Wainwright said he had been 'greatly helped' by Raven, 'whose reasoning helped to confirm my own conviction'.[10] Extracts from *War and the Christian*, written whilst Raven was lecturing Wainwright, give a taste of the former's rhetoric:

> As all history of religion shows, it is by the protest and, if need be, the martyrdom of individuals standing alone against public opinion that God's will has been made plain. No Christian will claim he is a prophet: every Christian accepts the prophet's responsibility to listen to the voice of the Lord and to proclaim what he hears in his life, if not upon his lips ... Jesus, while He accepted the Old Testament, is in the succession not of its warriors but of its prophets. From the Temptation onwards, His rejection of war is unquestionable.[11]

In February 1937 Wainwright accepted the pledge in the Covenant of the Methodist Peace Fellowship, a solemn undertaking 'to renounce war and all its ways and works, now and always'. This was a year after renowned Methodist preacher Donald Soper had founded the Peace Pledge Union to encourage 100,000 others to sign a similar promise; a year later a PPU activist at Cambridge invited Wainwright to join the organisation, saying he had been talked of as a possible recruit and 'lively member'.[12] At this time and throughout the War Wainwright received literature from the PPU, the Fellowship of Reconciliation and a range of other anti-war bodies including the War Resisters' International, the Parliamentary Pacifist Group, the International Voluntary Service for Peace, the Council of Christian Pacifist Groups, the Quakers and the publishers of *Peace News*.

When war broke out in September 1939, 'no important Liberal voice was raised against the declaration of war', in the words of one Party historian;[13] and when Churchill became Prime Minister in 1940, Sir Archibald Sinclair joined the Cabinet as Air Minister. It was only later that a minority of Liberals questioned the wartime electoral truce and the coalition. For Wainwright, however, the course was crystal clear from the beginning: he would refuse to go to war.

Wainwright had begun to seek out opportunities to serve the public without taking part in military activity before the War began. The day after the declaration, Councillor Paul Cadbury of the leading Liberal Quaker family sent Wainwright a circular with details of how to apply for training camps of the Friends' Ambulance Unit at Manor Park in Birmingham.[14] These proved to be heavily oversubscribed, and though Wainwright had an interview with Cadbury at the Station Hotel, York in October, a training place at Birmingham did not become available until January 1940.[15] He appealed to Leeds National Service Committee for work but was told that a man of his age could only enrol as a Special Constable.[16] In the meantime, Wainwright joined the Blood Transfusion Service, was interviewed by a civilian Ambulance Unit and worked in an air raid shelter run by the International Voluntary Service for Peace under St George's Church in Leeds.[17] In November he submitted his application for registration as a Conscientious Objector (CO), and he appeared before the Board in Leeds on 22 December 1939. His submission set out in the strongest terms his convictions about participation in war, and was supported by legal representation in the person of Donald Wade, Wainwright family friend and future Liberal MP for Huddersfield. Wainwright declared in his submission that 'gradually, through prayer, thought, reading and discussion, there grew within me a spiritual conviction that I must take no part in military activity'.[18] Two days after Christmas Wainwright learned his application had been successful.

Wainwright spent the first half of 1940 training and working in hospitals for the FAU. As well as qualifying as an ambulance driver with the St John's Ambulance Service at one of Cadbury's training camps in Birmingham by

February, he worked as an Emergency Hospital Orderly in Gloucester, where a local minister had asked the FAU to send help because of growing local opposition to his work arranging placements for Conscientious Objectors at the City Hospital. The Leader of the FAU later described the Gloucester operation's reputation as 'the Unit's Siberia', where duties consisted of 'general portering work, emptying pig-swills, dustbins, coal-buckets, cleaning down corridors and acting as general scavengers. The work was hard and long and the hospital was hostile.'[19] Before the official opening of the Gloucester section in May, Wainwright had already been at Whitechapel Hospital in the East End for a month, but his health was suffering from overwork, and – presumably following medical advice – he drew up notes of an alarming array of symptoms including swelling of the glands, widespread rashes, hair loss, septicaemia and even madness, to which he may have thought himself vulnerable. In August, Wainwright was given indefinite leave with pneumonia and suspected tuberculosis, though the latter was later discounted.[20]

Though it was naturally frustrating to Wainwright to be separated from the service of the FAU, this extended pause in his work – during which he returned to Leeds to recover – sheds some light on Wainwright's attitude to the relationship between Conscientious Objectors and the state. Amongst those who would not fight, there existed a spectrum of opinion about the approach they should take towards the state: some believed that it was both politic and proper for Conscientious Objectors to show the Government gratitude for its recognition of their unusual status, and not to stir up controversy by advertising their position or their convictions to sceptical non-pacifists. The co-operation of the London County Council, the Ministry of Health and the Red Cross, for example, was necessary to allow training and field operations to continue. Paul Cadbury, keenly aware of what might be lost if a backlash were provoked against the FAU, wrote to its staff in the early stages of Wainwright's leave, stressing that 'our service is a service of deed and not of word. This has been emphasised again and again, and all argument and discussion must be avoided both inside and outside the hospitals in which we are working.'[21]

On the other hand, the most hardline FAU members took the view that their moral principle was being patronised by a brutal Government, and that they had a duty to resist as far as possible co-operation, and to proselytise their cause. Amongst Wainwright's correspondents these included his Cambridge friend and future best man Denis Henry, who wrote to Wainwright mocking the incompetence of the evacuation programme, dismissing Fenner Brockway's Central Board of Conscientious Objectors and complaining that broadcasts by FAU leaders presented their work as 'a big adventure' which 'sounded far too reminiscent of "Exciting Experiences of the Great War" by Lieutenant-Col Snooks'. When Henry refused to seek exemption from military service and 'the idiotic business of attempting to call me up has begun', he anticipated that 'in a few weeks I shall have to be detained with all the primitive and barbaric accompaniments of gaol life'. A hint of where Wainwright's position was on this spectrum can be gleaned from Henry's remark that 'I quite agree with you that any meaning to talk about humanitarian treatments for COs, and indeed any meaning to governmental talk at all has almost vanished.'[22]

Others of Wainwright's friends were similarly righteous. A former colleague at Gloucester – which in the view of the FAU's Leader 'typified the difference in view within the Unit as to the value of "humble service" for its own sake'[23] – wrote to say that the 'specifically Christian' spirit there was in decline and that 'the key-word of our work and personal relationships in the hospital is "humility". It took us a long time to accept the idea that daily self-criticism is necessary before the birth of the Christian spirit is possible, and many of the people have still not accepted it.' In a reference to their leadership's vanities, it was bitterly remarked that 'the staff meeting becomes a Reichstag where Cadbury efficiency may be applauded, and the rest of us are to act as raw material'. Wainwright was again assumed by his correspondent to share his rigour, and it was cheerfully remarked that a starch collar he had left behind at Gloucester was 'the embodiment of the spirit of Richard Wainwright.'[24]

Others wrote for a sympathetic hearing from Wainwright about the difficulty of securing work for COs, or about the 'stooges' in the FAU Headquarters; Wainwright himself was also writing to other pacifist organisations such as the George Lansbury Fund, to which he sent a donation to support the establishment of a farm where COs could work.[25] However, whilst he retained the trust and confidence of radical elements of the pacifist movement, Wainwright showed in this matter an ability which was to serve him as a politician, and his Party, repeatedly over many decades – the capacity to build bridges between remote leaders and hasty or unrealistic purists. Wainwright wrote to FAU Headquarters in autumn 1940 expressing some of the concerns he had heard and seeking reassurance. For good measure, he added a £100 donation to the letter (a sum worth nearly £3,000 at 2010 prices). The reply he received indicates the ability Wainwright had already developed to wring concessions from officialdom:

> I was a little upset by your comments about Gloucester, because I know that coming from you, such criticisms will not be unfounded. However, you have already heard that two 'Holy Men' have been appointed – John Bailey and Freddy Temple, one of whose jobs will be to see that spiritual stagnation does not spread any further through the Unit.[26]

The exact date of Wainwright's recovery is unclear: medical records show his leave ended in April 1941, but friends understood that he was confined to The Heath for at least a year,[27] and it was not until the last month of the year that he was working at FAU Headquarters in Gordon Square, London, where over the next three years he held various senior executive posts including Assistant Officer for Overseas work, and later Personnel Officer. These positions put him in contact with high-profile political figures within the FAU and outside, and they honed his considerable natural skills for managing organisations under pressure, and for handling the media.

In only his first six months, Wainwright's duties ranged from organising a social for the families of FAU men serving overseas hosted by Brandon Cadbury, to 'traipsing' around Fleet Street visiting the *News Chronicle*, *Star*, *Liverpool Echo* and *Yorkshire Post* to promote the FAU's work; he learned the value of sending items early to *The Times* and the *Manchester Guardian* because they expected preferential treatment, and was proud to have gained favourable coverage in *The Economist* and later the *Yorkshire Evening Press*. He also wrote regularly for the FAU's own publications. Even when Wainwright undertook active service in the last year of the War, he continued sending reports to newspapers and monitoring broadcast coverage of the FAU's efforts. He was frustrated to find that a piece for *The Times* on displaced persons in Europe had had all his careful caveats removed – 'very annoying for a precise thinker' one of his colleagues remembered – and concluded from radio broadcasts he had heard that 'pushing public opinion was best done not by headline stories, but by accurate selected information'.[28]

Wainwright travelled to an FAU unit in Dover and a Quaker settlement in East Ham, and again continued this work whilst on the Continent.[29] He heard from friends and colleagues in Africa, Asia and the Far East about the FAU's work and the nature of the War, and organised the reception of a delegation of forty Ethiopian dignitaries including deposed Emperor Haile Selassie; and he found time to take up the case of a soldier detained at Northallerton and disciplined for refusing to obey orders. This range of activities and the skills they required were, entirely by chance, an excellent apprenticeship for a campaigning politician, and Wainwright was an appreciated apprentice: just before his stint at Headquarters came to an end, the Deputy Chairman of the FAU Executive wrote to Wainwright expressing his thanks for Wainwright's 'unsparing work for the unit'. He continued: 'While you were looking after the affairs of the Unit in this country they were in good and safe hands'.[30]

Wainwright's most dramatic experiences came in his last two years with the FAU, on active service in Europe. In the first week of September 1944 his parents received notification that he had left for the Continent 'in very good form' and 'with a grand party'.[31] He landed on the beach at Arromanches in Normandy on the evening of 6 September 1944 in a party of twenty-three members split into two sections with eight vehicles. Protracted negotiations between the FAU and the authorities in London had delayed this landing, and 'in Normandy the immediate crisis was past', leaving hospital overcrowding and housing, and the distribution of food, clothing and medicine as the chief problems to be tackled. 'For five weeks the small trucks and one ambulance plied throughout Calvados and into the Manche and Orne', says the FAU description of Wainwright's section's work, 'moving patients and materials, and linking one regional relief headquarters with another, in lieu of the precarious post and telegraph services.'[32]

In mid-October, Wainwright's section moved into Holland behind the troops who had arrived with the D-Day landings, attached to the 12th Corps Refugee Detachment. The work remained piecemeal, the section's location shifting rapidly between nunneries, furniture factories and concentration camps. In the week before Christmas, Wainwright was stationed in Antwerp, the main Allied base port, and still the target of German rocket-fire and flying bombs, in charge of three FAU teams. During January 1945 they transported five hundred patients.[33] Within a month, Wainwright was appointed Deputy Officer-in-Charge of all FAU work in Germany, based in Brussels at the right hand of Gerald Gardiner, later Lord Chancellor in the Labour Government of 1964.

Wainwright left few records of his work on the Continent and was painfully reluctant to discuss his experiences: there can be no doubt that this was because of the profound significance of what he saw, rather than its insignificance. He certainly saw suffering and faced danger during this period: those who knew him after the War, such as Trevor (now Lord) Smith became aware that 'the Friends' Ambulance Unit was on the front line. They weren't cowards – they were the stretcher-bearers and they tried to restore civil society in occupied and released places. So he was certainly no physical coward; quite the contrary – it took as much guts as if you were an infantryman.'[34]

The closest testimony of Wainwright's service in the FAU is left by his colleagues. Tegla Davies describes the problems of managing displaced persons, 'newly liberated forced workers, mostly young, most of them heeding nobody in their determination to secure what spoils there were, and to avenge themselves on the German population'. The grimmest job in Germany, according to Davies, arose in April 1945, when Allied advances revealed a camp of 23,000 prisoners: 'apart from the smaller numbers involved, this was a replica of Belsen'.[35] Grigor McLelland, another FAU worker who later became Director of Manchester Business School and a Professor at Durham, saw Wainwright managing visits of Tegla Davies and Paul Cadbury, and heard of his meetings with one of the Nuremburg prosecutors. He visited refugee camps at Diepholzstrasse, Visbek and Goldenstadt with Wainwright, and learned from him of the horrific problems being caused by the movement of millions of refugees in the East. Lastly, McLelland heard with Wainwright first-hand reports from FAU members who had intervened at the destruction at Hitler's mountain retreat, Berchtesgaden:

They had been in at the end of Berchtesgaden, where they found five grand pianos, all wrecked, also a library of gramophone records, likewise broken. They stayed three weeks in the area and the troops looted and raped and burned down houses. The FAU got themselves billeted one separately in each house to save it from the French, and thus earned some unpopularity.[36]

These experiences must have confirmed for Wainwright the capacity of war for the release of our worst instincts and the destruction of our greatest potential. To his own family, he revealed an example of an atrocity he himself had witnessed:

> There was a terrible occasion at the end of the War when they occupied Germany, and there was some huge barn that there were a lot of Germans in, and it was blown up, and it crushed them. Once, people were asked to give experiences at chapel, and he found it very difficult: he felt he ought to tell people about it, but he found it almost impossible to talk about.[37]

Wainwright probably had more stories to tell of this ugly type, but the feelings they provoked were not ones which a man who was reserved about the most ordinary matters would wish to be open about. They would stay with him and drive his scepticism about militarism; his loyalty to internationalism and especially European integration; and his abiding awareness of the problem of human wickedness. His daughter Hilary, born three years after Wainwright left the FAU, believes that Wainwright's sense of duty to the disadvantaged was strengthened by his wartime experience:

> He was kind. Even though he was from a privileged background, his experience in the Ambulance Unit meant that at a formative time of his life he was dealing with real, raw problems of people dying, so he had a deep kindness, deep humanity, deep empathy with people who were suffering.[38]

As with those who undertook military service, there were for Wainwright positive aspects of his experience, too: he shared with his colleagues a bond strong enough that he continued to attend FAU reunion weekends in York until the later years of his retirement. Perhaps it was in this company that he could remember his experiences less painfully.[39]

There were other, more tangible, effects on Wainwright of his wartime experience: many friends and colleagues attribute his penchants for strong cigarettes and reckless driving to his time in the FAU: his secretary at Westminster obliged Wainwright to smoke his Senior Service out of an open window in their office.[40] His driving led colleagues to avoid conversation whilst he was driving so as not to distract him,[41] and eventually Wainwright's children refused to let his grandchildren share a vehicle in which he was behind the wheel. More than once the West Yorkshire police had to show leniency to a local Member of Parliament hurtling around dark moorland roads as if still in charge of an emergency vehicle.[42]

More seriously, Wainwright had to deal with the stigma which inevitably marked a Conscientious Objector in post-war elections at which candidates habitually identified themselves by former military rank. It may have been his anticipation of this which made Wainwright, as Lord Smith learned later, agonise about his decision to seek exemption from service in 1939. The stigma was worsened by court proceedings after the War, in which Wainwright was brought before a tribunal in Leeds in April 1946 for failure to comply with the terms of his exemption. The breach was overlooked as a technicality, given the disbandment of the FAU earlier in the month, until which point he had been in their service, but another court appearance in his home city must have strengthened Wainwright's sense of his vulnerability.[43]

That vulnerability remained real for the next forty years: at General Election campaigns until the 1980s he was challenged at public meetings and on the doorstep to justify his failure to do military service. Sometimes, according to his supporters, these campaigns were orchestrated by his opponents – the Colne Valley Labour Party were usually believed to be the culprits – and took root amongst war veterans, as former Councillor Barry Fearnley remembers:

> He was a Conscientious Objector, and this didn't go down well with some of the British Legion members, but once Richard had spoken to them … He'd meet people, he'd talk to them on the doorstep, and he wasn't frightened of saying he was in the First Aid section. He had to break some resistance, but they admired him for it. He didn't hide it.[44]

Wainwright's Assistant Joanna Copsey (later Hannam) says, 'I remember there was a really nasty slur in the '79 election about him being a conscientious objector. I watched him front all that stuff at those public meetings when people would throw this at him, and he was brilliant. He didn't duck away.'[45] Wainwright always answered his critics frankly, factually and proudly. Unprompted, he set out his record with the FAU in print in every address to the electors of Pudsey and Colne Valley. Of course, those who challenged Wainwright on this issue were probably committed opponents before they learned of his pacifism, but if their actions lost him any substantial number of votes, they cost him victory at Colne Valley in 1964, where a hundred switched votes would have put Wainwright in.

Some of Wainwright's potential contribution to politics was inhibited by his uncertainty about the effect of his status in the War. Lord Smith attributes Wainwright's rigid adherence to economic parliamentary portfolios in part to a desire to avoid foreign affairs, in which he remained nonetheless keenly interested, as his visit to Guinea-Bissau in 1972, and occasional later public speeches, demonstrated. It is noteworthy that whilst he was opposed to the idea of a British nuclear capacity,[46] and particularly the SDP-Liberal project of a European nuclear deterrent, he supported the Party's pro-nuclear defence policy in public – though he told his Whip he had done so 'very reluctantly' at Assembly,[47] and wrote a monthly letter to David Steel for some time asking him for reassurances about it.[48] Similarly, he retrospectively criticised 'the way the Liberal Party and the Alliance drifted into support for the Falklands War'[49] in contrast to their opposition to the Suez adventure a generation earlier, but he did not stand out against the leadership over it at the time.

Several of Wainwright's colleagues – including Emlyn Hooson, who stood for the Liberal leadership in 1967 – also believe that his status as a Conscientious Objector is what ultimately meant he would never consider seeking the leadership himself. Wainwright set out his reasons for refusal to fight at the end of his parliamentary career, and the almost casual tone he adopted suggests that he had grown both less dogmatic and more sensitive to his audience about the issue since his tribunal appearance in 1939. On the central issue, however, he remained consistent:

> I felt, and I feel now, on a personal basis, that warfare is now, and was then in 1939, so indiscriminate that it was both immoral, and, in the end, counter-productive. I would never have any hesitation in shooting somebody who was about to attack my wife or whatever, nor have I any great objection to professional soldiers fighting each other if that's what they want to do, but bombing cities, whether it be Coventry or Dresden, seems to me to be wide of the mark.[50]

Wainwright's response to his detractors in campaigns should have won him more votes than the cause of the controversy lost: it is a cliché to say that it took courage to refuse to fight; but it took a different kind of courage to serve in the field as Wainwright did as a young man; and yet more courage to defend his decisions publicly to a doubtful audience. All this reflected Wainwright's principle and individualism – there were, after all, only 1,314 FAU members in total. His work with the FAU entailed experiences and brought contacts in politics, the media and charitable institutions (such as with the Rowntree family, two of whose prominent members were amongst his commanding officers) upon which he was to build in the post-war era. Serving in the FAU had been the right decision for Wainwright for moral reasons; even for most of those who disagreed with the decision, it demonstrated what was right about Wainwright's character. It so happens that it also made him even more right to be a successful parliamentary candidate.

Notes

1 Winston Churchill, St. Andrew's Hall, Glasgow, 11 October 1906.
2 Blake, R., *The Conservative Party from Peel to Churchill* (London: Fontana 1972), p. 96.
3 Ezra, interview, 28 July 2008.
4 Grayson, Richard S., *International Relations and Appeasement* (London and Portland: Frank Cass 2001), p. 1.
5 Michael Foot, *News Chronicle*, 4 April 1934.
6 Grayson, *Liberals, International Relations and Appeasement*, p. 154.

7 De Groot, Gerard J., *Liberal Crusader: The Life of Sir Archibald Sinclair* (London: Hurst Co.; New York: NYUP 1993), p. 107.

8 Ibdi., p. 144.

9 RSW, 'Liberalism', Wainwright papers file 2/9.

10 Application for entry in Register of Conscientious Objectors, case no. NE583, 4 November 1939.

11 Raven, C.E., *War and the Christian* (London: Student Christian Movement, May 1938), pp. 87 and 125.

12 Unknown PPU supporter at Gonville & Caius college to RSW, 24 June 1938.

13 Cook, C., A *Short History of the Liberal Party 1900–84* (London and Basingstoke: Macmillan 1984), p. 125.

14 Paul Cadbury, FAU circular, 4 September 1939. Cadbury remained a member of Birmingham City Council until 1953, when he was its only Liberal councillor.

15 Paul Cadbury to RSW and FAU circular, both undated. RSW was invited to York on 22 October 1939.

16 Leeds National Service Committee to RSW, 8 September 1939.

17 Donald Bentley to RSW, 3 October 1939, Wainwright papers file 3/4.

18 Application for entry in Register of Conscientious Objectors, case no. NE 583, 4 November 1939.

19 Davies, A. Tegla, *Friends Ambulance Unit: The Story of the F.A.U. in the Second World War 1939–46* (London: George Allen & Unwin 1947), p. 331.

20 RSW's medical notes are in the Wainwright papers file 3/6.

21 Paul Cadbury, circular to FAU, 24 June 1940.

22 Denis Henry to RSW, 27 October and 9 November 1940, Wainwright papers file 3/5.

23 Davies, *Friends Ambulance Unit*, p. 331.

24 'David', Gloucester, to RSW, 28 January 1940, Wainwright papers file 3/5.

25 Ruth Fry to RSW, 22 December 1940, Wainwright papers file 3/5.

26 'Peter', FAU HQ, to RSW, undated; probably September 1940, Wainwright papers file 3/5.

27 Denis Henry to RSW, 27 October 1940, Wainwright papers file 3/5.

28 McLelland, G., *Embers of War: Letters from a Quaker Relief Worker in War-torn Germany* (London: I.B.Tauris 1997), pp. 41–2 and 99.

29 McLelland, ibid, p. 89 reports that in November 1945 RSW was sent to speak to a conference of teachers at Hanover about Quakerism.

30 Ralph Barlow, Deputy Chairman FAU Executive, to RSW, 11 August 1944, Wainwright papers file 3/6.

31 Ronald Joynes to Henry Scurrah and Mrs. Wainwright, 5 September 1944, Wainwright papers file 3/14.

32 Davies, *Friends Ambulance Unit*, pp. 422 and 426.

33 Ibid., p. 428.

34 Lord Smith, interview, 22 June 2009.

35 Davies, *Friends Ambulance Unit*, pp. 431–2.

36 McLelland, S.S., *Embers of War:*, pp. 41–2, and for preceding material, 61, 76, 89 and 99.

37 Joyce Wainwright, interview, 22 February 2008.

38 Hilary Wainwright, interview, 22 February 2008.

39 See for example Wainwright's personal diaries for Septembers of 1990, 1993 and 1996, Wainwright papers file 1/26.
40 Caroline Cawston, interview, 2 June 2008.
41 Lord Rennard, interview, 30 July 2009.
42 Martin Wainwright, interview, 17 June 2008.
43 Tribunal case 5545, 29 April 1946, County Court, Albion Place, Leeds.
44 Barry Fearnley, interview, 30 October 2008.
45 Joanna Hannam, interview, 19 January 2009.
46 *Liberal News*, 27 April 1982.
47 RSW to David Alton, 25 September 1986, Wainwright papers file 8/23.
48 Lord Rennard, interview, 30 July 2009.
49 Speech to the Liberal Movement conference at Wolverhampton, 17 July 1988. *Liberal Movement News*, No. 3, p. 1.
50 RSW, 'Profile: Richard Wainwright', *The House Magazine*, 6 March 1987

PART TWO: OUTSIDE PARLIAMENT

Introduction

By summer 1946 Wainwright, aged twenty-eight, had returned to Leeds and to civil society with characteristic purpose and careful planning. The way in which this happened reflects not only Wainwright's personality but also the traditional flavour of his upbringing, and the dynamic relationship between these two aspects of his life. The foundations of his adult life laid during the next two years were vital in Wainwright's political career.

Firstly Wainwright resumed his position at Beevers and Adgie, the Leeds accounting firm in which his father was a partner. This had not been inevitable, nor was it work for which he felt any special enthusiasm; he even reflected that 'in some ways the boredom of chartered accountancy drove me into changing my occupation,'[1] and tried to lighten the dry atmosphere of his profession by setting accountancy exams featuring characters with facetious names such as 'Rudolph Rottenpaws'. At Shrewsbury he considered a career in Law, at university he looked into taking examinations for entry into the civil service, but he acknowledged later that 'I took, in a sense, the easy way.'[2] Nonetheless, he applied himself diligently to the accountancy exams, and qualified in 1950, when he also became a partner in Beevers and Adgie. He remained a partner until 1968 when the firm was taken over by Peat, Marwick and Mitchell, of which he was a partner until 1970. This gave Wainwright access to a network of Yorkshire business and professional contacts from which he learned, and with which he built up trust. In 1965 he served as President of the Leeds and Bradford Society of Chartered Accountants. Between 1948 and 1952 Wainwright also became Director of two local firms, and shareholder in three, a situation which subsequently led to political controversy.

For Wainwright, these investments, and his professional position, were convenient and somewhat lucrative; they gave him a training which he was to put to good use in his economic portfolios and on the Treasury Select Committee; and they added strength to his analysis of Party finances in the report he was called upon to write in 1975. At another level they served the same function as his membership of the Leeds Group 'B' Hospital Management committee for ten years from 1948, his Trusteeship of the Leeds Savings Bank from 1955 onwards, and his membership of the Joseph Rowntree Social Service Trust from the following year until 1984. That was a duty of social engagement. Wainwright saw no distinction between commercial, professional and charitable activity: it could all contribute to the health of the community if managed in the right way by the right people. That conviction was to mark his campaigning style and his political beliefs on everything from welfare policy to industrial strategy.

Secondly, Wainwright married. This proved to be the central relationship of his life not merely for its personal fulfilment but because of its political dimension, too. Joyce was to be an unstinting supporter, advisor, campaigner and partner to Wainwright throughout their forty-five years together. As with his professional life, however, Wainwright's marriage was originally founded upon an old-fashioned acknowledgement of society's expectations. The Wainwrights' relationship developed at a disconcerting pace – only eighteen months passed between their first introduction and their wedding – but the brevity of their engagement reflects not a whirlwind romance so much as the deferral of courtship which many of their contemporaries had suffered because of the War, and the support and encouragement of their respective families.

Joyce was a daughter of the Hollis family, prosperous owners of a firm of Yorkshire auctioneers. Two years Wainwright's junior, she had been educated at Harrogate Ladies' College before going on to a career in nursing, working after the War at Foremarke, the preparatory school at Repton. The Hollis and Wainwright families had known each other before the War in Leeds professional circles, and Henry Scurrah had given Joyce's father use of his land to shoot pigeons.

After the War, Hollis actively encouraged Joyce's engagement by arranging social functions at which she met eligible men, amongst whom Wainwright was an obvious candidate, and swiftly stood out as the favourite. He was invited on a holiday to Point of Ardnamurchan in Scotland with the Hollis family, where, after cementing the relationship with Joyce on regular morning walks to the shops, he proposed on the banks of Loch Shiel. She accepted immediately. He also wrote her a passionate letter concerning the political significance of their life together, about the changes which needed to be made in the world and how together they would bring them about.[3] By the autumn of 1947 they had bought most of the furniture for their home,[4] and on January 3rd, 1948 they were married.

Without Joyce's contribution, Wainwright's political fortunes would never have risen to the heights they did, and he might on more than one occasion have fallen back from his position never to return but for her support. Their marriage confirmed Wainwright's status as a pillar of the Yorkshire bourgeoisie, but it did far more. In many ways, as Lord Greaves observes, Joyce played very effectively the traditional role of a Tory MP's wife, hosting coffee mornings, opening bazaars and welcoming visitors to the gardens at the Heath, accompanying her husband at public events, and giving appropriate interviews and family photographs with their children to the local press.[5] This was especially important in a constituency parts of whose electorate had conservative social values, and with a husband not always at ease with spontaneous social exchange. Many of those who saw the Wainwrights at work noted that he regularly relied upon her to whisper discreetly the names of approaching constituents as he stretched out his hand in familiar welcome.

This was only one aspect of Joyce's contribution: a formidable personality with a sharp mind, she took the reins of the Colne Valley Women's Liberal Council, strengthening it to become a vital organ of Wainwright's constituency organisation; she took a parallel part in campaigning on the doorstep, arguing the case with voters rather than being a silent companion, and being his representative in Colne Valley whilst he was at Westminster; and though there was little occasion for disagreement between them on policy, Wainwright consulted his wife on questions of strategy throughout his life. At key points such as the resignation of Jeremy Thorpe, she helped prepare notes and speeches for Wainwright. This part of the record makes Joyce and Richard's relationship look less like that of old-fashioned Conservatives and more like a Clinton-esque modern political couple. The values of the time and place in which they worked did not give it full expression, but to Wainwright's staff the integral role of Joyce in the Wainwright story was indisputable:

> Joyce was the best possible for Richard in every way, shape and form: magical. She was the oil in that engine. I used to think he didn't give her enough credit for doing that sometimes. She was the perfect constituency wife: she wasn't doing it because she was a constituency wife, because she had those beliefs herself, so for Joyce it was a passion as well.[6]

Wainwright was fully aware of Joyce's vital role, even if he did not say so frequently. He closed an account of his parliamentary career written as he retired by saying: 'She's the one that gets me in, every election. She's the one people like to see.'[7]

This was the starting point for Wainwright's political career, and despite his talents it would be fatuous to deny a great deal of the credit for Wainwright's remarkable success to the people and institutions around him. Assessment of the role is the purpose of Part 2. In a fiercely debated book written ten years ago, American social scientist Robert Putnam argued that the recent decline in political participation is the result of a decline in social capital – those groups, organisations and relationships which used to give the public a sense of common identity, interest and obligation. Putnam says that 'television, two-career families, suburban sprawl, generational changes in values' have undermined our willingness to join churches, sports clubs or even go on picnics together. 'Our growing social-capital deficit threatens educational performance, safe neighbourhoods, equitable tax collection, democratic responsiveness, everyday honesty, and even our health and happiness.'[8]

Five months before the 1970 General Election, Wainwright instructed his constituency organiser to update his 'Record of intimate contacts': a list which Wainwright regarded as 'a key tool' for campaigning, it detailed the names and home addresses of community leaders whose co-operation would be particularly useful in organising campaign activities, but also in understanding local opinion and dispersing news about Wainwright's work. As well as local Headmasters and the Association's own bank manager, Wainwright insisted that the following be included: the officers of all Liberal Clubs, 'whether they are active Liberals or not'; all senior newspaper staff living in the constituency; and lastly the Superintendent of the Huddersfield Methodist Mission, who lived at Linthwaite.[9] It was a telling insight into Wainwright's awareness of the need to keep trust and keep in touch with the villages and their electors, and of the arterial system by which he knew this could be done, and which still sustained Colne Valley society.

Wainwright's political career, which finished as Putnam set down his ideas, illustrates both the strength of Putnam's diagnosis and the danger of accepting his pessimistic prognosis too uncritically. Wainwright's success relied upon his personality and his Party, but also, as Putnam suggests, on his ability to motivate the less politicised through religion, the popular press, social clubs and other public organs which nowadays are thought quite separate from politics. Moreover, contrary to Putnam's expectations, he restored and increased the effectiveness of these relationships. This is a story, therefore, which has uses for politics today.

Notes

1 RSW, 'Profile: Richard Wainwright', *The House Magazine*, 6 March 1987
2 Ibid.
3 Although still held in private, the content and significance of this letter were confirmed to the present author by Tessa Wainwright, interview, 30 October 2008.
4 Joyce Wainwright to RSW, 28 October 1947, Wainwright papers file 1/16.
5 Lord Greaves, interview, 8 April 2009.
6 Joanna Hannam (nee Copsey), interview, 19 January 2009.
7 RSW, 'Profile: Richard Wainwright', *The House Magazine*, 6 March 1987.
8 Putnam, R., *Bowling Alone* (New York: Simon and Schuster 2000).
9 RSW to Maurice Burgess, 10 January 1970, Colne Valley Divisional Liberal Association papers.

4 Liberal Clubs

One of the institutions which nourished the Liberal Party's roots in the community during its darkest days was the local Liberal Club – and Wainwright was aware of the support it could provide. Re-opening one Club in 1981 he declared that 'if it wasn't for Clubs such as this, the whole Liberal movement would die, for they embody the momentum and spirit of the Party.'[1] In Colne Valley political clubs had been vital to the survival and growth of Labour and the Liberals,[2] and Wainwright helped to revive both the fortunes of the Clubs and their relationship with the Liberal Party in a way which was vital to his political career.

Liberal Clubs were established in Victorian and Edwardian times as gentlemen's or working men's social clubs committed to supporting the cause by raising funds, hosting meetings, providing committee rooms and staff for elections, or simply offering a congenial social base all year round for people sympathetic to the Liberal Party. Most were members of the National Union of Liberal Clubs (NULC), which had representation on the Liberal Party Council, and whose rules confirmed their objective 'to carry on, both amongst its members and the general public, propaganda in support of the Liberal Party.'[3] The Yorkshire Liberal Federation reiterated in annual reports of the 1940s and 1950s that 'for the continued support of the Liberal Clubs and the Federation of Liberal Clubs we are most grateful and we appreciate the loyalty and help of all Club members.' In the Federation's Golden Jubilee booklet of 1953, a full-page advertisement by the National Union and the Yorkshire Federation of Liberal Clubs reflected this support.[4]

These bodies were a useful but wasting asset during the post-war period, and their decline undermined sources of both the Party's support and its identity. Many Clubs sold their premises or distanced themselves from the Liberal Party. The substantial Clubs at Bristol, Birmingham and Newcastle all ended political conditions for membership before closing between 1957 and 1967. Ten miles from Colne Valley, Manchester Reform Club, founded in 1867, merged with the Engineers' Club on its centenary.[5] On the Yorkshire side of Colne Valley, the Bradford Liberal Club was negotiating its merger with the local

Conservative Club by 1955, and the Huddersfield Borough Liberal Association acknowledged that 'there seemed to be room for improvement' in the attitude of local Liberal Clubs.[6]

Wainwright and his father were members of the Leeds and County Liberal Club where family friend Donald Wade was the Chairman. Its building in Quebec Street was founded by Sir James Kitson, one of Wainwright's predecessors as MP for Colne Valley, in 1890, when it had 1,650 members. By the 1920s membership was falling, and the Club began to rent out space for offices. By the Second World War, Wainwright was one of only 178 members, and the Club was abandoned in 1947.[7] Other Liberal Clubs in Leeds complained in 1954 that they were made to feel unwelcome at the city's Liberal Federation meetings, and the issue of co-operation between Clubs and Party was a running sore in Leeds in the 1950s and early 1960s.[8] Wainwright was also a member of the only major Liberal Clubs to survive and maintain any link with the Party: the National Liberal Club in Whitehall with over 3,000 members, and the Reform Club in Pall Mall where Liberal Peers held their annual dinners in the 1950s.[9]

This decline in numbers and Party activity in Clubs was part of a national picture which saw the National Union's number of affiliates fall from around 400 to just over 200 between 1945 and 1962.[10] By 1981 the National Union could not gather a hundred delegates to its conference.[11] The Liberal Party Executive took stock of the situation in a report commissioned in 1956 with the assistance of Yorkshire Liberal Agent and mentor to Wainwright, Albert Ingham. It pointed to the work done by many Liberal Clubs, especially in the North, West Midlands, and Devon and Cornwall, and argued that 'if there had been no Liberal Clubs in some parts of the country there would have been fewer candidates for both Local and General Elections. Politics being very much a social thing, if other parties have clubs in an area where there are no Liberal Clubs, they have an advantage.'[12]

Wainwright shared this concern, and asked his Cambridge contemporary D. Fletcher Burden – Secretary of the National Union of Liberal Clubs – to prepare a confidential report about the most effective ways to strengthen links between Liberal Clubs and the Party. Burden stressed the valuable services performed by Clubs, the contrast in strength between Clubs in different parts of the country, and the need to guard against politically unreliable stewards and proprietors. He also proposed the Party offer NULC members legal advice.[13]

Wainwright's enthusiasm for Liberal Clubs was rooted in his upbringing, but it was nourished by his experience as the candidate in Colne Valley. Yorkshire was the stronghold of Liberal Clubs: the office of the National Union of Liberal Clubs was in Devon Mount, Leeds; but even here there was evidence of a pattern of decline. In Yorkshire, however, it was less advanced; and in Colne Valley, with Wainwright's help, it was reversed.

In 1953 the Colne Valley Liberal Association Executive was discussing reports that 'the Kirkheaton Club had ceased to be a Liberal Club and that the Holmfirth Club was meeting shortly to consider their future'.[14] Kirkheaton was lost to the Liberal cause, and though the Holmfirth Club had over a hundred members in the early 1930s, receipts suggested this figure had fallen into double figures after the War, when the Club Executive set up a sub-committee to consider a change of name and policy 'with a view to increase its field of activity and enrolling more members'.[15] A proposal to wind up the Club was voted down by a General Meeting of just twenty-six members in 1953; the subscription fee was cut by another of seventeen in 1957 and the following year the auditors complained that the membership register 'could not be considered as reliable'.[16] During all this time, and as Wainwright began his first parliamentary campaign, the Holmfirth Liberal Club had no formal contact with the Colne Valley Liberal Association, though efforts were made by the Deakin family, established local Liberals, to save the Club.[17] By 1960 the Committee hardly met, and the following year the Holmfirth Liberal Club finally closed.[18]

Nonetheless, when Wainwright became parliamentary candidate for Colne Valley in 1956, there were still eleven clubs available in the constituency as venues for social functions, meetings and as campaign rooms, and listed in the Colne Valley Liberal Association Yearbook as 'Our Liberal Clubs'. Joyce Wainwright remembers that, though old fashioned, 'most of them' – especially at Marsden, Golcar and Linthwaite – were supportive of the Party.[19] The clubs in Delph, Marsden and Golcar had officers who were also Councillors. Wainwright immediately saw the vital function the Clubs could play, particularly amongst an electorate divided into distinct villages, in extending the Party's roots in the community. As well as holding rallies, dances, supper clubs and whist drives at Golcar and Linthwaite Liberal Clubs, the Association used Marsden Liberal Club as its Headquarters for Wainwright's first parliamentary contest in 1959, and in the 1963 by-election Wainwright also established campaign offices at Liberal Clubs in Golcar, Meltham and Skelmanthorpe; at the Reform Club at Delph in the west of the constituency, and at the old Club premises in Victoria Street Holmfirth, which the Association retained until 1970. Until he won the seat, Wainwright used the Clubs for week-night accommodation whilst campaigning in the constituency;[20] in 1966, the Clubs at Skelmanthorpe, Linthwaite and Honley hosted public meetings addressed by Party Leader Jo Grimond; and once elected, Wainwright used the Clubs to stage his 'Report from Westminster' meetings with the public.[21] Golcar's Club hosted meetings of Liberal Councillors from across the Pennines; Party coffee evenings took place at the Clubs in Honley and Marsden; and Skelmanthorpe Liberal Club was the venue of a Liberal Christmas Party entertained by the Barnsley Salvation Army Band.[22] David Whitwam, who joined the Colne Valley Liberals in 1956, remembers the Clubs 'kept Liberalism going':

I can remember in Golcar where I was born, Norman Richardson was President of Golcar Liberal Club and he was on as a Liberal. He'd been on since the year dot: he was a survivor. Then in Slaithwaite Heather Swift came and Amy Bamforth, and they got Liberalism going again in Slaithwaite. There was a man in Marsden who came in and got them going. Some clubs were just clubs, but some were involved: so the amount of involvement varied from club to club, but basically in those days you joined a club if that was your politics, and you didn't if it wasn't.[23]

In the 1960s and 1970s the Clubs at Golcar, Springhead, Linthwaite, Marsden and the Liberal Rooms at Holmfirth were the venues of meetings of the Colne Valley Women Liberals. The Colne Valley Liberals held their General Meeting at the Clubs in Marsden in 1963 and 1971 and Honley in 1975, and the Committee met at Linthwaite and Springhead Clubs during the same Parliament.[24] In the 1980s, the Divisional Association Executive met regularly in these and Liberal Clubs at Crosland Moor, Golcar and Lindley.[25] When the seat was lost in 1987, Wainwright remembered that 'immediately after the 1970 defeat, for instance, it was agreed (and carried out) that the Officers visit each Liberal Club in turn, fraternising and running a full-scale monthly public draw with a very wide sale of tickets. That certainly helped morale.'[26]

Golcar Central Liberal Club, established in 1915, was the jewel in the crown of the network of Liberal Clubs in Colne Valley and had six hundred members in 1980.[27] Even when Wainwright fought Colne Valley for the first time in 1959, its active committee of over a dozen men was chaired by Councillor Norman Richardson who was also Vice President of the Liberal Association. Affiliated to the National Union of Liberal Clubs, Golcar's objects were 'the political education of its members and to secure combined and prompt action in favour of Liberal principles in all national and local affairs'.[28] The Club gave the Party rooms at election times and for Association and Young Liberal socials, and maintained a healthy current account which, by the time of Wainwright's election in 1966, stood at more than £1,000 – worth well over ten times that sum at 2010 prices.

These funds were regularly given to support Liberal local and parliamentary election campaigns: starting with six pounds and six shillings made available in 1961 by the Club's cancellation of its subscription to *The Guardian*, this figure rose to forty pounds the following year, when Liberal hopes for the local elections were high. The equivalent of hundreds of pounds today was given to each of Wainwright's campaigns in 1964 and 1966, and to the Liberal local election fund in 1974. In 1970 Golcar's Committee encouraged donations from the Liberal Clubs in Wellhouses and Scapegoat Hill,[29] and several of the Colne Valley Clubs made annual subscriptions of twenty or thirty pounds apiece through the 1970s and 1980s. Golcar doubled its regular subscription to the Liberal Party in 1981, raised it to £200 the following year, and £300 in 1983. That year saw the Club make the most generous contribution to Wainwright's election appeal with a gift of £500, and donations from the Liberal Clubs at Lindley and Marsden almost doubled that sum to make up a third of the overall appeal funds.[30] Association Chairman and future parliamentary candidate Nigel Priestley was careful to thank the Clubs for their continued financial support in his Annual Report for 1984.[31]

Golcar Liberal Club operated almost as a branch of the Colne Valley Liberal Association, endorsing council candidates like Norman Richardson and later Barry Fearnley, and calling its women members' section, established in 1962, the Women's Liberal Association. In 1964, the position of Political Secretary was established on the Club Committee. One of Wainwright's Association Chairmen of the 1980s gave a more dramatic picture of Golcar's role as the cockpit of local Liberal politics on occasions such as the controversial meeting to select Wainwright's successor as Liberal candidate, saying 'there's plenty of blood on the floor there.'[32]

Perhaps the greatest function of Liberal Clubs, however, concerned those outside the Party: they provided a point of contact between politicians like Wainwright and the voting public, whom he met on Friday night tours of the Clubs.[33] Barry Fearnley was a Liberal Councillor from the 1960s onwards whilst being Political Secretary and then President of Golcar Liberal Club: he explains the role of the Clubs as an opportunity for Wainwright to keep in touch with less politically conscious electors:

> I could take him to Golcar Liberal Club, and he knew most people; and he didn't just stand at the bar talking to his own colleagues. He spoke to everybody in the Club – he went out of his way in some cases to talk to people, and they liked that. Since then I've found politicians – local as well as national – stand in the corner.[34]

Those who worked with Wainwright at Westminster were aware that he cultivated this approach somewhat against his nature: his secretary Joanna Copsey (later Hannam) said, 'he trained himself to have small talk, but it wasn't natural. In order to do the Liberal Clubs, two pints of beer and all the rest of it, Richard would always have around him – he knew who they were – people who would ease that path for him.'[35] Another supporter, Robert Iredale, noticed that Wainwright always had a half-pint at the bar in clubs, but 'I bet three quarters of it were still there when he left.'[36] Wainwright himself described the diplomatic skills required in using the Clubs in this way to his organiser Maurice Burgess in the run-up to the 1970 local elections: 'I do not think that any local Liberals would have suggested that you ought to be converting members of the Honley Liberal Club. It is more a question of talking to them, hearing from them what is being said locally, and sorting out who can be relied upon.'[37]

This sort of informal interaction between political activists and citizens is hard for either side to achieve, and its decline is both a cause and a sign of the all-too-familiar modern public disillusionment which would have horrified

Wainwright. The scope of contact this could achieve is reflected in the fact that, as late as 1977, the Huddersfield Liberal Clubs Winter Games League arranged fixtures for over thirty teams at each of snooker, dominoes and All Fours.[38] There was no 'golden age' in which such contact took place effortlessly; but there was a time when politicians like Wainwright made the effort.

Part of the decline in Liberal Clubs was inevitable: they were, after all, attached to two causes in decline – the Liberal Party and social clubs. As long ago as 1968 the Colne Valley Liberal Association Executive called local Club representatives in for a meeting to explore ways in which the Clubs could give more support to the Party.[39] The Clubs which Wainwright used as bases have drifted from the Party: Meltham Liberal Club was one of his recruiting offices in 1963, but today its Steward insists that even his most senior patrons can remember only one visit by Wainwright, when 'he did not receive a political welcome'.[40] The Delph Reform Club, where the Wainwrights opened Christmas fetes, remembered by a Saddleworth Liberal Democrat Councillor as 'a hotbed of Liberalism',[41] was the last point on the election tour of Violet Bonham Carter as Liberal candidate in 1951,[42] but is now merely the Delph Club, divested of any party loyalties. Even Golcar Liberal Club's Steward confirms that it has similarly lost most of its political dimension.[43] Wainwright himself accepted in 1987 that with the formation of a new Party, Liberal Clubs could not expect separate representation in the councils of the Liberal Democrats.[44] To some extent, the replacement of clubs by television for both politics and entertainment could not be resisted.

However, Wainwright's approach in the Colne Valley illustrates the dangers of accepting uncritically this deterministic view of social and technological change. Wainwright chose to invest in, revive and exploit Liberal Clubs as a link with sympathisers, potential sympathisers and constituents. He showed that institutions such as parties and political clubs are not merely inert victims of social and economic trends, but live organisms which have their own part to play in that change, and which with strategic sense and mutual support can prosper against the tide. Wainwright's friend D. Fletcher Burden gave advice to Golcar Liberal Club in 1960;[45] the Liberals in Skelmanthorpe held 'At Homes' to restore the finances of their Club in 1967,[46] and in Delph the Club was rescued by financial support from the village's Women's Liberal Association.[47] This sustained a network of Clubs which helped to build Wainwright's claim to represent the people of the Colne Valley, and it is no coincidence that the Clubs' decline and drift from the Liberal Democrats has run alongside the Liberal Democrats' own difficulties in recovering the seat. Their potential usefulness is less great than in the past, as it was when Wainwright arrived; but, to use the sort of horticultural metaphor of which he was fond, when the weaker roots of a plant wither, it is time to tend the remaining ones more closely than ever, rather than let them rot.

Notes.

1 *Lincolnshire and Humberside Times*, 31 October 1981. The Club was the Barton-on-Humber Liberal Club.

2 Clark, D., *Colne Valley: Radicalism to Socialism* (London: Longman 1981), pp. 182–3 confirms this significance for Labour in the Edwardian era.

3 National Union of Liberal Clubs Ltd. Rules, 1935, p. 1, and revised rules, 1965 and 1998.

4 See for example Yorkshire Liberal Federation Annual Report 1950; this and the Golden Jubilee booklet are in Yorkshire Liberal Federation papers, West Yorkshire Archive Service, Sheepscar, ref. LIB/P.

5 Manchester Reform Club records, John Rylands Library, Manchester, ref. MRC, Administrative History.

6 Bradford Club papers, West Yorkshire Archive Service, Bradford, ref. 50D86; Huddersfield Borough Liberal Association minutes, 17 July 1945.

7 Leeds and County Liberal Club published accounts for 1941; RSW to family, 1 January 1942, Wainwright papers file 3/11, in which RSW urges his father to visit the Club to read a piece he had placed in *The Economist*; Newiss, J. and Grady, K., *Leeds and County Liberal Club: Historical Notes*, Leeds Civic Trust, July 2004. A Leeds Civic Trust plaque was unveiled at the former premises of the Club by Joyce Wainwright, who observed that for most of its life as the Liberal Club she would have been disqualified from membership by her gender. This was an issue she took up with clubs in Colne Valley whilst RSW was the MP.

8 Egan, M., 'Grassroots Organization of the Liberal Part, 1945–64, unpublished thesis, Universit of Oxford, 2000, p. 68.

9 National Liberal Club Bulletin, July 1957.

10 Information from Mr. Bernard Simpson, Secretary, National Union of Liberal Clubs, 18 August 2004.

11 'Yes Liberal Clubs Do Matter', *Liberal News*, 16 June 1981.

12 A copy of the report, written by B.S. White, is in the West Midlands Liberal Federation papers, University of Birmingham Special Collections, Box 25. A Hansard Society study of the 1955 election also showed the main parties' clubs could motivate turnout amongst otherwise inactive supporters (Milne, R.S. and Mackenzie, H.C., *Marginal Seat* (London: Hansard Society 1958), pp. 72–4).

13 Wainwright papers file 8/2.

14 Colne Valley LA Executive minutes, 1 September 1953.

15 Holmfirth Liberal Club Ltd, Annual Report and accounts, 1930–33, 1944–47; Committee minutes 25 October 1945 (the sub-committee abandoned the idea of a name change apparently because of doubts about its legality).

16 Holmfirth Liberal Club AGM and Committee minutes, 25 October 1953, 8 October 1954 and 26 February 1957, including H.N. Bostock & Co. to E.B. Kaye, 7 February 1958.

17 Lise Newsom, interview, 17 April 2009.

18 Holmfirth Liberal Club minutes, 14 October 1960, 21 March and 18 April 1961.

19 Joyce Wainwright, interview, 22 February 2008.

20 RSW to Maurice Burgess, 10 January 1970, Colne Valley Divisional Liberal Association papers.

21 Colne Valley Liberal Association Executive minutes, 11 October 1966 and 3 September 1968.
22 Ibid., 17 June 1964, 7 December 1967 and 22 June 1968.
23 David Whitwam, interview, 15 April 2009.
24 Colne Valley Liberal Association minutes, 13 July 1963, 3 September 1970, 13 February 1971, 16 May 1972 and 8 February 1975.
25 Colne Valley Divisional Liberal Association Executive minutes, 14 August 1984 to 31 October 1985, *passim*; Executive minutes, 4 August 1987.
26 RSW to Councillor David Ridgway, 16 July 1987, Wainwright papers file 5/B/16.
27 Golcar Central Liberal Club Annual Report 1980.
28 Rules of the Central Liberal Club, Golcar (undated, apparently 1983), p. 1.
29 Golcar Central Liberal Club minute book, 1959–88. Election funds were granted or requested on 11 April 1961, 19 June 1962, 13 October 1964, 2 August 1966, 9 June 1970, 12 February 1974 and 10 May 1983.
30 Ibid., 19 March 1981, 21 March 1982 and 24 March 1983; Colne Valley Divisional Liberal Association General Election appeal records 1983. Golcar's contribution was the first one made, on 14 May.
31 Colne Valley Liberal Association General Election appeal records 1983; Chairman's Annual Report, 31 December 1984.
32 Councillor David Ridgway, interview, 31 October 2008.
33 Bradley, I., 'Liberals are Cool towards Pact', *The Times*, 9 February 1981.
34 Barry Fearnley, interview, 31 October 2008.
35 Joanna Hannam, interview, 19 January 2009.
36 Councillor Robert Iredale, interview, 16 April 2009.
37 RSW to Maurice Burgess, 22 April 1970, Colne Valley Divisional Liberal Association papers.
38 *Huddersfield Daily Examiner*, 11 March 1977. This figure includes Clubs from both the Colne Valley and Huddersfield itself, some of which entered 'A', 'B' and even 'C' teams.
39 Colne Valley Liberal Association Executive minutes, 3 October 1968. Similar concerns were expressed by the Executive in 1973.
40 Allen Chapman, interview, 20 October 2008.
41 Cllr Christine Wheeler, interview, 16 April 2009.
42 Pottle, M., *Daring to Hope: The Diaries and Letters of Violet Bonham Carter 1946–69* (London: Weidenfeld & Nicolson 2000), p. 103. In a sign of her difficulties in connecting with local Liberalism, Bonham Carter confided to her diary that she and her friends had gone to the Club 'against our better judgement'.
43 Tim Bolton, interview, 15 April 2009.
44 Wainwright, R., 'What Now?', *Liberal News*, 14 August 1987.
45 Golcar Central Liberal Club Executive minutes, 13 September 1960.
46 Colne Valley Liberal Association Executive minutes, 11 November 1967.
47 Clara Shaw, letter to the present author, 8 May 2009

5 Wainwright's faith

Like most politicians of his generation, Wainwright was raised as a Christian; but Wainwright's faith was a more significant element in his life, his politics and the politics of his Party than for most of those contemporaries. The particular form of his Christianity – Methodism – had practical and electoral implications for Wainwright, and in particular invested him with a sense of duty to do God's work in the mortal world.

The strong links between religious belief – especially Non-conformist Christianity – and the fortunes of the Liberal Party need only an outline re-iteration here. Dissenters, barred from public office until the repeal of the Test Act in 1828 and socially excluded by the Establishment for a century afterwards, found a natural home in the party which argued for open competition for economic and political rewards, for social mobility and self-improvement, and which was driven by the same egalitarian and participatory values in its organisation as they were. Great Liberal families such as the Cadburys and the Levers reflected this link, and Gladstone (though himself an Anglican) famously described Non-conformism as 'the backbone of Liberalism'.[1] The Liberal election victory of 1906 – at which the issues of the Boer War and consequent 'Chinese slavery' in South African mines, state funding of Anglican schools and the reform of licensing laws all motivated Dissenters to vote Liberal – saw no fewer than 200 Non-conformists returned to Parliament.

In Yorkshire Methodism was particularly strong, described in 1837 by the new and somewhat despondent Anglican Vicar of Leeds as 'the *de facto* established religion' of the City.[2] Despite his efforts, thirty-five years later the Church of England still only offered 36 per cent of the accommodation for worshippers in Leeds.[3] Philip Snowden, later MP for the Colne Valley, remembered that during his upbringing in West Yorkshire around this time Anglican prelates were often without congregations and with time on their hands.[4]

In childhood, Wainwright attended the Lady Lane Chapel in Leeds, a leading centre of the Methodist Union which had been open since 1840 and which supported substantial foreign missionary work as well as engaging with the issues of hardship in the local population.[5] Wainwright's father was an officer of the Chapel, and the pastor, Rev. W.D. Lister, was a family friend whose children were playmates with Wainwright. When the Chapel moved its premises to the suburbs in the 1930s, Wainwright's mother opened the Lady Lane Memorial Chapel at Gipton, and Wainwright became its Secretary. The new Chapel maintained its old promise that '"Evangelism" is the word that explains all our activities'.[6] Lister's affectionate recollections in a letter to Wainwright after the move give an impression of the old Chapel's work and of the young Wainwright's role in it:

> I shall never forget the old place and I do miss those lodging-house men. There were some excellent men amongst them and they did seem to appreciate what was done for them and the kiddies! How they did enjoy the cinema. I wish you had been a little older when I was at Lady Lane. You would have been a great help to me. I am glad to hear that you are doing well at the 'Lady Lane Memorial' at Gipton. Glad to hear that you are looking after the poor. I hope that you will go on with this good work which in my opinion is practical Christianity.[7]

The occasion of Lister's writing was to congratulate Wainwright on his trial sermon at Skipton, for Wainwright was by 1939 training as a local preacher, and told his Conscientious Objectors' tribunal in December of that year that 'for the last seven years I have regarded my life as consecrated to the service of Jesus Christ, and subject to the guidance of the Holy Spirit'.[8] The specific obligations which Methodism placed upon its pastors were set out for aspirants like Wainwright in a standard text by a Tutor at the Wesley College in Headingly, Leeds, H. Watkin-Jones. Passages like this describe elemental parts of the duties of Methodists like Wainwright. 'The Christian faith', the author wrote, 'has never lacked social implications' and 'the influence of the Church of Christ needs to be brought to bear simultaneously both on international and social problems':

> It is our duty, as a Church of Christ, to go to those who will not come to us. The Church is Missionary by nature ... Evangelism must be based on convictions, so it is vital that we should be certain of the spiritual essentials which we proclaim to the mass of the people ... Never was there a greater incentive to earnest Christian preaching on the part of those who are prepared to think hard concerning what they preach ... These are days of terrific issues, when the gravest decisions in the spiritual life of the world are being made.

'In the war against the powers of darkness for the salvation of mankind', Watkin-Jones ends, 'has Methodism wounds upon it?'[9] The integral and sincere nature of Wainwright's faith, and its impact on his politics, were noticed by all who knew him. Sir Cyril Smith, a Unitarian who acknowledges the support of Rochdale Methodists in putting him in Parliament, said 'he was a genuine Christian, and behaved like one and thought like one'; Wainwright's Research Assistant in the 1970s, Chris Greenfield, concluded that 'it was his religious background that gave him his political perspective'.[10] Those who came to know

Wainwright later, such as Sir Menzies Campbell, saw immediately that 'his Liberalism was founded on strong Non-conformist Christian beliefs'.[11] Wainwright's daughter Tessa confirms that throughout their marriage, he and Joyce read Bible passages to one another at the start of their day, and his son Martin came to know the Methodist hymnbook comprehensively because 'it was the only thing to read at chapel'.[12]

In the post-war era, there continued to be a disproportionate number of significant members at all levels of the Liberal Party who were Non-conformists, and whose faith partly determined their political outlook. These included leading intellectuals such as Professor of Divinity Nathaniel Micklem, experienced parliamentary figures such as Lord Rochester, Vice President of the Methodist Conference, and seasoned campaigners such as Isaac Foot, former MP and Party President in 1947. Foot's successor to the Presidency, Elliott Dodds, was a Deacon of Highfield Congregational Chapel, and a member of the Huddersfield Council of Churches. Leading MPs of the post-war period, notably Party Whips, have been active Christians, often preachers, usually Non-conformists.[13]

In Colne Valley churchgoing remained strong, and political: the Labour MP for the seat until 1910, Victor Grayson, complained that 'the capitalists owned and controlled the pulpits of their churches, and were the financiers behind the spiritual appeals of their parsons'.[14] In 1922 there were still over two thousand Methodists in the constituency attending chapel, and nearly one voter in ten was a Non-conformist.[15] Today there remain at least nineteen Methodist chapels in the former constituency's area; in 1963 there was that number in the Holmfirth circuit – the eastern end of the constituency – alone, and across the constituency dozens. Every village had its chapel, some had several, and it was said that Wainwright preached in them all. From the 1950s until his retirement, Wainwright accepted invitations to take part in Methodist services throughout Colne Valley and its surrounding area. Some were high-profile occasions attended by other local dignitaries; others were ordinary weekly services.[16] At all of these, Wainwright took the opportunity to demonstrate both his convictions and his talents. These convictions, and their spirit, motivated many Liberal activists. Equally importantly, the chapels formed one of Wainwright's bonds with the less partisan public, and a means by which to strengthen their mutual trust.

The scope and scale of these churches' reach in the community through Sunday schools, choirs and recreational groups should not be underestimated. Uppermill Methodists took regular trips as far afield as Whitby, Grange-over-Sands and Plas-y-Coed, as well as having their own tennis courts and a popular badminton club; the chapel at Scholes in the south-east of the constituency staged annual theatrical productions and a public Christmas Eve carol-singing. It is easy in the age of broadcast and internet communication (and domestic central heating) to overlook the vital role such activities played in binding communities together and serving their needs until some time after Wainwright became an MP. The Wainwrights were aware of this – Joyce remembers that walking behind prominent councillors in church processions meant 'people got to know us',[17] and it was even mischievously rumoured that Wainwright attended funerals of strangers to consolidate his profile – and he was plugged into this network through his preaching.

Wainwright's preaching, like his political speeches, was neither flamboyant nor prosaic, but carefully prepared and thought-provoking. Gordon Ellis, who heard him preach at Slaithwaite from the early 1960s onwards, remembered that 'you came out from the service thinking about what he'd been saying. He'd left something with you to consider as an application of the Christian faith.' David Whitwam compared Wainwright's style to that of a noted Liberal and Non-conformist barrister, acknowledging that his content could be 'political, but not party political'.[18] In an era of controversy over race relations, sexual liberation and the Cold War, and given Wainwright's strong commitment to the struggle against poverty, it would have been difficult for the most conservative of preachers to draw the line between issues of politics and faith. Wainwright did not even try. An outspoken address to a Methodist summer fete during Wainwright's last year in Parliament showed he had lost neither his rhetoric nor his passion. Rebuking as 'un-Christian' Tory Home Secretary Douglas Hurd's attack on a New Age 'Peace Convoy' travelling through the New Forest, Wainwright warned:

> Britain is not automatically immune from the world disease of treating people as trash and others as superpersons. People who have never been on the dole become suspicious of able-bodied unemployed. And a small band of unarmed hippies in the countryside are called brigands by the Home Secretary and treated as a national emergency in parliament ... Every human being is of equal worth to God, and this is the foundation of Britain's way of life. We cannot expect civilised standards to continue if we utterly neglect the faith on which they have been built.

'That', Wainwright concluded, 'is why Almondbury Methodists and their friends from other churches are right to bring their witness into the open air and claim their essential place in the community', before listening to the Holme Silver Band, watching the Marsden Pride Clog Dancers and crowning the Sunday School Queen.[19]

Wainwright made clear the practical political implications of his faith privately around this time, too, insisting to Michael Meadowcroft that Christianity calls for relentless struggle against wrong. He called Meadowcroft to account for a phrase he had quoted in print from Liberal MP Russell Johnston:

> You must have been teased about your quote from Russell Johnston, 'as long as birds sing in unclouded skies, so long will endure the power of the compassionate

spirit.' Russell feeds our philosophical enemies by regularly displaying in senti-
mental terms the Liberal heresy that skies are unclouded and 'all things are bright
and beautiful'.

'Real Liberals', Wainwright went on, 'realise that they have to come to terms
with clouded skies and Original Sin. There are too many Liberals, in my view,
who share Russell's sentimentality.'[20] This interpretation of Christianity had
active political implications, and saw no end to the battle for virtue in the
mortal world. It was another example of Wainwright's unfinished business.

In parts of the country where Non-conformism remained strong, there was
a substantial cross-over between it and the Liberal Party. Electoral studies –
including one in Glossop next to the Colne Valley – confirmed that a larger
proportion of Non-conformists than of Catholics and Anglicans voted Liberal.
Wainwright reminded his supporters that Isaac Foot had blamed his loss of his
Cornwall seat on his Agent's failure to provide cars for the Bible Christians,[21]
and talked wistfully of the West Country, where canvassing could be replaced by
standing outside chapels on Sundays to nurse Liberal support.[22] His preaching
whilst campaigning as a candidate caused little controversy amongst Methodists, Ellis remembers, 'because by and large most of the Methodist communities were of Liberal tendencies, or were open Liberal supporters.'[23] Martin
Wainwright remembers from canvassing for his father in the 1950s with Liberal
activists in Colne Valley that 'independence and Methodism (or sometimes
the Strict and Particular Baptists) united this band'.[24] The delegation of four
who came to The Heath to invite Wainwright to apply to be Colne Valley's
candidate in 1956 were all Methodists; the leading lights of the Saddleworth
Liberals, Allan and Nancy Bradbury, with whom Wainwright stayed on visits
to the Manchester end of the constituency, were trustees of Uppermill Methodist Church, where they had worshipped since the 1920s.[25]

In the nearby village of Delph, a team of women from the Methodist Church
who were not officially registered as Liberal supporters raised funds for
Wainwright's campaigns – but also used the funds to buy hymn books for the
chapel.[26] Teetotaller Maggie Furniss, one of the constituency's longest-serving
Liberals when Wainwright became the candidate, remembered that in the last
decade of the nineteenth century she had been raised in a Christian household
in Slaithwaite, 'and my father believed Liberalism to be the Christian way of
life'.[27] At the 1963 Colne Valley by-election, Wainwright drew support based on
his religion from outside the constituency. A Liberal from Dewsbury rang to
wish Wainwright all the best, saying he hoped 'that the Lord and the votes are
with him', a preacher from Cornwall wrote that 'quite apart from the need for
Liberals, we could do with some Nonconformist Methodists in the House!' and
a message from Wainwright's own Gipton Methodist Church in Leeds came to
'assure you of my thoughts and prayers on your behalf'.[28]

Another stalwart of the Colne Valley Liberal Association, its Chairman from

1978 to 1981, Harry Senior, was described in a tribute by Wainwright as 'liberalism personified. A deep concern for his community, and for people everywhere, was underpinned by his cheerful Christian faith.' Wainwright noted: 'His local patriotism centred on Linthwaite Methodist Chapel.'[29] Wainwright recognised the work of his Methodist supporters by organising trips for them to meet MPs of their faith at Westminster, presided over by Lord Soper.

Wainwright's opponents soon noticed the impact of his religious work. The Colne Valley Labour Party's Agent claimed that poor local by-election results in 1958 had come about because 'the Liberals and the organised Churches have ganged up on us.'[30] Amongst the Tories Andrew Alexander, Conservative candidate in 1963 and 1964, found indignant activists saying, 'You know about Wainwright – he's been preaching all round the area.' 'They thought he was only preaching in the area because he had been the candidate before', Alexander recalls: 'they thought he was exploiting his Methodist credentials.'[31] David Clark, Wainwright's Labour opponent in 1970 and 1974, pointed to the significance of his association with 'the bastions of the Wesleyan Methodist church.'[32]

After the 1983 General Election, Wainwright wrote to *The Guardian* correcting the impression given in an editorial that Liberal MPs survived because of their personalities. There was, Wainwright insisted, more importance in the correlation 'between Liberal survival and England's main strongholds of the liberal, democratic strand of Methodism', especially in the West Riding:

> These democratic Methodists perfected and enshrined a pattern of regular obligation which transferred naturally and automatically to rebuilding the Liberal movement in the Grimond era … The key note has been a sense of perpetual obligation, not reliant upon paid officials or hierarchy. And whereas the Wesleyans timidly forbade the use of their premises by political organisations, the liberal Methodists welcomed it. At every kind of public election in Colne Valley, a central committee room is entered under a headstone – carved too deeply for church bureaucrats to obliterate – 'United Methodist Free Church.'[33]

In retirement, too, Wainwright continued to encourage those whose Liberalism and faith went hand in hand. As the battle over merger between the Liberals and Social Democrats raged, Wainwright was trying to help Bishop Stephen Verney to establish a Christian group for the new Party;[34] Wainwright had been impressed by the preaching work of his successor as candidate for Colne Valley, Nigel Priestley,[35] and also actively encouraged a young Methodist minister, Geoff Reid, who became the Liberal candidate in the Yorkshire seats of Rother Valley in 1974 and Barnsley in 1983 before fighting Eccles in 1992. Supporting Reid's candidature Wainwright told Liberal Democrat Headquarters that 'his Methodism and his politics blend well together, partly because he is not a stuffy clergyman; he knows he must address the problems and the human nature around him.'[36] Reid remembers of Wainwright:

As a Methodist, of a somewhat non-establishment bent, he seemed intrigued by the thought of a young Methodist minister standing for the Party. At regional meetings, including pre-election candidates' meetings, both Richard and the formidable Albert Ingham were thoroughly supportive, and insisted on reminding people of my Methodist background.

In 1998 one of the Wainwright charitable trusts supported Touchstone, an urban interfaith project in Bradford led by Reid, with a grant which 'proved to be crucial to the development of Touchstone.'[37] To Wainwright, the dividing line between convictions of religion and politics remained as insignificant as the need to put them into practice was vital.

Wainwright's political views remained informed by the church community, too: he warned Liberal Democrat Chief Whip Archy Kirkwood in 1993 that 'my Methodist colleagues tend to think the Libs have gone Thatcherite.'[38] In the same year, Wainwright reacted when the *Yorkshire Post* published an article on Methodism describing its female adherents as 'pained women', insisting that 'women leaders in Methodism are today helpfully developing a notable tradition in their Church, starting with the Bible Christian Methodists whose women preachers were treated as equal with men in their ministry.' He looked back upon seven decades' experience of the positive practical impact of Methodism and in particular of its women:

> Some of us have been blessed, life long, by the ministry of deaconesses, women ministers, and now by a woman President of the Conference – the more effective for being unpretentious, undogmatic and unbureaucratic. The darker parts of West Riding towns have for generations been lightened by their sensitive and perceptive service.[39]

All of the evidence above should be set in its context: in West Yorkshire, as in Britain generally, organised Christianity was in decline throughout this period, as even inter-war descriptions of the Colne Valley had noticed;[40] the Labour Party also had strong connections with the Non-conformist sects and benefited from the companionship amongst them; moreover, this was truest in Oldham and Huddersfield, where Methodism was in fact more predominant than in the Colne Valley. On those issues which might have reflected Non-conformist influence – licensing of premises for gambling and drinking, abortion, voluntary-aided education and the curriculum more generally, and defence and foreign policy in the Middle East especially – the Liberals did not have a policy distinctively closer to the Methodist standpoint than that of other parties. Indeed, Wainwright himself, though often reported to be a teetotaller, drank regularly if modestly, and regarded drunkenness in other MPs merely as amusing.[41]

It would be mistaken, therefore, to attribute Wainwright's political impact chiefly to his chapel connections or to imply that he sought to impose his religion through political measures. 'I never found him to be judgmental' said Eric Flounders, who worked for Wainwright but did not share his faith: 'he never condemned other people who didn't do the same thing.'[42] His connections did, however, give Wainwright an important platform from which to build his local profile, and they gave voters a shorthand signal of his character and convictions which could only otherwise be demonstrated at greater length. Most important, religion helped to guide and consolidate Wainwright in his own views, in his belief that there was wickedness, that he had a duty to confront it, and that this was a confrontation which would never be over. This wickedness included poverty, ignorance and inhibition from using the talents given to us to the fullest possible extent. 'That supported him in the things that he had to do because he had a faith that was behind him', remembered Gordon Ellis: 'that's why he wasn't afraid sometimes to be unpopular. Where's the highest authority? He was a believer in the highest authority.'[43] That combination of piety without piousness is one upon which few politicians can draw today.

Notes

1 Cited in Glaser, John F., 'English Nonconformity and the Decline of Liberalism', *American Historical Review*, Vol. 63, No. 2, p. 352; originally used in Gladstone, W.E., 'The County Franchise and Mr. Lowe Thereon', *Nineteenth Century II*, November 1877, p. 552.

2 Rev. Dr W.F. Hook to S. Wilberforce, July 1837, cited in Pelling, H., *Social Geography of British Elections 1885–1910* (London: Macmillan 1967), p. 291.

3 *The Nonconformist*, 8 January 1873.

4 Snowden, P., *An Autobiography* (London: Nicholson & Watson 1934), Vol. 1, pp. 29–30.

5 *United Methodist Magazine* (October 1913), pp. 340–45.

6 Lady Lane Chapel Annual Report, 1923; Lady Lane Memorial Chapel Annual Report, 1942.

7 Rev. W.D. Lister to RSW, 13 January 1939, Wainwright papers file 1/1.

8 Application for entry in Register of Conscientious Objectors, case no. NE 583, 4 November 1939.

9 Watkin-Jones, H., *Methodist Churchmanship and Its Implications* (London: Epworth Press 1946), pp. 33, 37, 47 and 54. The book was based on an article by Watkin-Jones, 'Implications of Methodist Churchmanship', in the November 1943 edition of the *Methodist Recorder*, to which Wainwright was a subscriber.

10 Chris Greenfield, interview, 1 December 2007.

11 Sir Menzies Campbell, interview, 23 July 2009.

12 Tessa Wainwright, interview, 30 October 2008; Martin Wainwright, 'Torrington '58', Liberal Democrat History Group/LSE seminar, 14 June 2008.

13 See, for example the following Whips: David Steel (1970–75, Scottish Presbyterian); Cyril Smith (1975–77, Unitarian); Alan Beith (1977–85, Methodist); David Alton

(1985–88, Roman Catholic); and more recently Andrew Stunell (2001–5, Baptist).

14 Cited in Lockwood, E., *Colne Valley Folk* (London: Heath Cranton 1936), p. 142. Here Grayson seems by his terminology to have in mind the Anglican Church, but his remarks confirm the political significance of faith in the Colne Valley.

15 Kinnear, M., *The British Voter: An Atlas and Survey* (London: Batsford Academic 1981), p. 128.

16 Significant services RSW addressed included the centenaries of Parkwood Methodist Chapel in Huddersfield in 1969 and Greenfield Chapel in the west of the constituency in 1983.

17 Joyce Wainwright, interview, 22 February 2008.

18 Ellis, G. and Whitwam, D., interviews, 15 April 2009. The barrister was Gilbert Gray QC, who had been a Liberal candidate, and spoke in support of RSW at one of his adoption meetings.

19 *Huddersfield Daily Examiner*, 19 June 1986.

20 RSW to Meadowcroft, 10 February 1988, Wainwright papers file 11/5.

21 RSW, letters page, *The Guardian*, 17 June 1983.

22 David Wheeler, interview, 26 July 2009.

23 Gordon Ellis, interview, 15 April 2009.

24 Wainwright, M., 'Reliving the Liberal Party of the 1950s', *The Guardian* website http://www.guardian.co.uk./politics/blog/2008/jun/13/tomorrowsat14junetheres (accessed 15 September 2008).

25 Bob Birse, interview, 16 April 2009. Birse was recruited to the Liberal Party by what he called 'the Bradbury effect' in the early 1970s, and quickly became a local Councillor. See also Ashton, W., *The Story of Methodism in Uppermill* (Uppermill: Uppermill Methodist Church 1996), pp. 60 and 65.

26 Dorothy Shaw, interview, 16 April 2009.

27 *Colne Valley Guardian*, undated cutting in Wainwright papers file 13/1, apparently 1963–65.

28 Mr Allsop to RSW, telephone message; Rev Oliver Beckerlegge to RSW, 19 March 1963; Deaconess Sister Gertrude Wright to RSW, 20 March 1963, Wainwright papers file 6/7.

29 Cited in Bradley, *The Strange Rebirth of Liberal Britain* (London: Chatto & Windus 1985), p. 244. This tribute originally appeared in *Liberal News*.

30 Colne Valley Labour Party Agent's Report on Urban District Council by-elections, 9 December 1958.

31 Andrew Alexander, interview, 13 March 2009. Alexander distanced himself from these accusations, doubting whether Wainwright had preached in the constituency itself, because 'that *would* look wrong'. When told that the story was true, he said: 'Oh *did* he! No wonder they thought that he was exploiting his religion.'

32 Lord Clark, interview, 3 June 2008. In fact Wainwright was not a Wesleyan, but an independent Methodist.

33 RSW, letters page, *The Guardian*, 17 June 1983. RSW was emphatic about the significance of the differences between 'Free' and 'Wesleyan' Methodists, the former being in his view more democratic and less deferential to the Establishment.

34 RSW to Bishop Verney, 26 October 1987, Wainwright papers file 12/1.

35 RSW to Heather Swift, 1 August 1983, Wainwright papers file 5/B/2.

36 RSW to Liberal Democrat candidates' office, 29 April 1991, Wainwright papers file 12/1.
37 Reid, G., letter to the author, 24 May 2009.
38 RSW to Kirkwood, A., 26 April 1993, Wainwright papers file 12/2.
39 RSW to *Yorkshire Post*, 1993 (undated, Wainwright papers file 12/2.
40 Lockwood, *Colne Valley*, p. 142. Lockwood argued, however, that there were signs of a recovery in numbers at chapels at the time he wrote.
41 Caroline Cawston, interview, 2 June 2008.
42 Eric Flounders, interview, 18 May 2009.
43 Gordon Ellis, interview, 15 April 2009

6 The press

In an era when newspapers were the chief source of political information, the support of the press at national and local levels was often a significant factor in winning elections. Editorial support for the Liberal Party amongst major news titles went into decline after 1945, and was effectively non-existent by 1962. However, Richard Wainwright was keenly aware of the importance of communication, and particularly of press support: he had contributed to the student press at Shrewsbury and Cambridge, and had briefed the nationals as part of his duties for the FAU. Later he wrote occasionally for Party publications such as *Liberal News* and *Radical Quarterly*. In different circumstances, Wainwright might have made his living as a journalist; he certainly invested considerable effort in cultivating the goodwill of journalists in the Colne Valley. Though this was an uphill struggle, and the significance of the printed word was being eclipsed by television during Wainwright's political career, this work almost certainly made Liberal victory in Colne Valley possible.

In 1945, two major national newspapers – the *Manchester Guardian* and the *News Chronicle* – retained a tradition of support for the Liberal Party, and a joint circulation of over one-and-a-half million copies daily between 1945 and 1960. The share of national circulation this represented declined from more than one in eight of daily newspaper sales to under one in ten during that period, and these were wasting assets. The *Manchester Guardian* argued in 1945 that 'Liberal successes are an essential means of averting the great danger of an overwhelming Conservative majority', but when the results of the General Election came in, it was obvious that the Labour Party would for the immediate future be the vehicle of the paper's values, and this in the assessment of the paper's historian, 'ended the official link between the editor of the *Manchester Guardian* and the Liberal Party'.[1] The *Manchester Guardian* continued to give Liberal activity more coverage than other papers, but at elections it dismissed the Party's pretensions to power. The only national title to remain loyal to the Liberal Party – the *News Chronicle* – went out of business in 1960. With daily sales of over a million, it was owned, edited and largely written by Liberal sympathisers, but found it difficult to recruit advertising.

The result was that Liberals were barely noticed by the national press when Wainwright came to contest Colne Valley. The *Daily Mirror* even announced solemnly after the Orpington by-election victory of 1962 that it would resume reporting Liberal statements as a public service. Even most of the significant Liberal local papers had been merged with larger rivals favouring other parties, including the *Yorkshire Observer* in 1957, at which the Yorkshire Liberal Federation expressed regret for 'the closing of that fine and forthright Liberal newspaper'.[2]

As with the chapels and Clubs, Wainwright was fortunate that this decline had not advanced as far in Colne Valley as elsewhere, but he had to work hard to reverse it. At both ends of his constituency Wainwright had local newspapers with Liberal sympathies, and at its heart was a smaller one opposed to Labour and ready to support a promising Liberal opponent.

The local paper in the east of the Colne Valley was the *Huddersfield Daily Examiner*. Its proprietors, Joseph Woodhead and Sons, were Non-conformist Liberals, and it was described by one of its journalists as 'an acknowledged Liberal newspaper' in the 1930s.[3] Its Editor from 1924 to 1959, Elliott Dodds, was President of the Liberal Party and on his death a colleague wrote that 'the Liberalism he espoused in the paper's leading articles went hand in hand with his activities for the Party at all levels.'[4] He continued as Chairman of the Board until 1969 and a Director until 1974. Dodds campaigned personally for Wainwright, and his paper followed suit, arguing at the by-election of 1963 that he was 'a worthy successor on personal grounds to Mr. Glenvil Hall as Colne Valley's MP' and that the big two Parties 'must make way for the Liberals, who are in tune with the times, who are the representatives of no sectional interests and who have the ideas and energy to make Britain into a lively, go-ahead and prosperous nation'.[5] From Wainwright's point of view the limitation of this advantage was that the paper served several constituencies, and so its endorsement tended to be a general party preference rather than having specific reference to the Colne Valley: in 1979 it argued that 'Mr. Steel's considerable and increasing personal appeal has lent attraction to his notion of a Liberal wedge' and that 'if there were a definite chance of breaking the Labour–Conservative stranglehold on politics then many more might opt for it. Apparently that chance is indeed there.'[6]

At the Manchester end of the constituency Wainwright had the support of the *Oldham Chronicle*, also serving several constituencies and sensitive to the varied opinions of its readership, but also in sympathetic hands, and prepared to make a special case for Wainwright as well as offering generally approving comment on the Liberals. At Wainwright's first successful campaign the *Chronicle* told its readers that 'Liberals improve the quality of debates, and the quality of some of the legislation that comes out of debates; and they have a salutary effect on the junior wings of the major parties' and that 'wherever

Liberal victory is more than a remote possibility, it is worth thinking about and voting for, too.'[7] In Colne Valley, the paper concluded, 'there is a definite prospect of change. We make no secret of the fact that we would like to see that change take place.'[8]

At the next contest the *Chronicle* insisted that 'if ever there was a time to vote Liberal, this is it,'[9] and when David Clark took the seat for Labour the *Chronicle* omitted the result from its list, which included every other constituency in the country. Clark was told on his first meeting with the *Chronicle*'s Editor at a social function 'that his objective was to lose me the seat at the next general election.'[10]

However, the *Chronicle* seems to have felt its fingers had been burned, and was in future less partisan, promising to 'provide its usual impartial forum for all candidates fighting in local seats' in 1974.[11] It continued to compliment Liberal policy, to celebrate Liberal success retrospectively and to give Wainwright regular opportunities to report on his work in Parliament, but the endorsement was muted and editorials only gave non-committal encouragement to turn out.[12] In 1983 the *Chronicle*'s readership was removed from Colne Valley by boundary revisions.

Geographically in between the *Examiner* and the *Chronicle* sat the *Colne Valley Guardian*, a paper with a more old-fashioned format and more right-wing politics. Focused exclusively on the constituency, it faithfully gave detailed coverage to Liberal activities – and those of any other organisation – in each village and was clearly a vital ally, but Wainwright had to win its Editors over to gain positive approval. At Wainwright's first contest, the *Guardian* gave no recommendation on how to vote, but its reaction to the Conservative victory nationally gave an indication of how it regarded the Labour Party:

> Nationalisation can now be considered as dead as the dodo … By their votes last Thursday they [the people] decided not only that they wanted no more nationalisation, but that they detest bribes, regulations and unofficial trade union strife that holds the country to ransom.[13]

At the 1963 by-election the *Guardian* was again nominally non-partisan, and its main concern was about the tone of the campaign. After the result, it took the view that Wainwright had fought well, but that the Conservatives had performed badly because of Government unpopularity, and that the Liberal opportunity had gone.

Only in the run-up to the 1964 General Election did the *Colne Valley Guardian* decide that Wainwright was the horse to back to beat Labour and that 'the only party that can beat Labour are the Liberals'[14] and that 'Mr. Wainwright is in with a real chance of winning.'[15] In 1966, with a Labour landslide in prospect and Wainwright 187 votes from victory, the paper declared in phraseology remarkably similar to the *Oldham Chronicle*'s that 'we make no secret of the fact that we hope Mr. Richard Wainwright will be returned to Westminster next week as the Member for Colne Valley.[16] From then on the *Colne Valley Guardian* gave more or less open support to Wainwright, either by emphasising in weaker years his claim to be the chief challenger to Labour and calling for 'independently-minded representatives, untied to the apron strings of vested interests'[17] or more boldly by calling for 'a rich leavening of Liberal MPs pledged to support radical new thinking' and reiterating that 'we hope that the electors of the Colne Valley division will play their part in bringing in a new, more constructive political era by returning Mr. Wainwright to Westminster.'[18]

The weakness of the *Colne Valley Guardian* was its precarious financial existence, and in 1976 it was merged with the *Huddersfield Daily Examiner*. According to Wainwright's Assistant, 'Richard was concerned that the Colne Valley hadn't access to community news or voice especially when there was so much going on' such as the decline of the textile industry.[19] This emphasises that Wainwright's interest in the media was not wholly cynical, but was part of his wider view of society in his constituency. Despite that, he knew the dangers of the trend in decline of local newspapers which had caught up with him.

Wainwright's good relations with the press were not achieved without effort. His staff all remember being instructed in detail in writing press releases and newspaper articles which would appear under his name:[20]

> I can remember when I first went to work for Richard it was like being back at school, because I would write stuff and it would come back literally red-penned. There were no niceties: spare words would go. Concise – he hated flowery.[21]

'He really courted the local media and understood its value in communities'[22] continues Joanna Hannam, to whom Wainwright wrote on his retirement that 'I am only just fully realising that you and I will no longer be scheming and writing to keep the Colne Valley show on the road.'[23] He took the trouble to write to the local press when he had been re-elected that 'I look forward to resuming what I found a very pleasant relationship with the paper when I was last in Parliament.'[24] He even courted the Conservative *Yorkshire Post* light-heartedly, congratulating its new Editor on his more balanced approach because his father had taken the *Post* for ninety years and declared that the births, marriages and deaths were the only reliable part.[25] When Joanna Hannam married a journalist with the *Post*, Wainwright joked at the wedding that it was part of a guerrilla campaign on his part to improve his profile. Wainwright monitored the press carefully, and even apologised for not seeing the death notice of a supporter's father in the papers 'which I usually examine fairly carefully.'[26]

Given their support from the county and national press, Wainwright's Conservative opponents were more philosophical about his success with local papers than they might have been. Andrew Alexander, Conservative candidate in 1963 and 1964, was a journalist with the *Yorkshire Post*, and felt that 'the *Huddersfield Examiner* was perhaps a bit over-enthusiastic about Wainwright but otherwise the local press I found was fine'.[27] His successor in 1987 was told by Colne Valley Tories to expect no coverage from the *Examiner*, and was disappointed by their refusal to use an early press release on capital punishment, but found that some of the editorial staff were Conservative Party members and concluded: 'I have no complaints about the *Huddersfield Examiner* at all. I used to send them a lot of press releases, wrote lots of letters to the Editor; they published them'.[28]

The Labour Party in Colne Valley was more indignant. After poor local election results in 1961, their Agent complained that 'we have been up against an almost uniformly hostile press'.[29] 'It was a unique situation in that both the local daily papers were Liberal-controlled', Labour's candidate in 1970 and 1974, David Clark, remembers: 'so Richard was very, very lucky in a sense'.[30] The local Labour Party's awareness of this is reflected in the dossier of Wainwright's press coverage which they kept after he lost the seat to Clark: though not the MP, Wainwright managed to keep up roughly weekly appearances in the *Examiner* with reports of everything from speeches to the annual opening of Wainwright's gardens, to picturing him swimming in a stream at Eastergate in Marsden to disprove Clark's claims that the river serving it was running dry.[31]

Wainwright made excellent use of the press in his campaigns for Colne Valley, and his endeavours suggest he thought this important for the retention of his seat. This sort of impact became harder to achieve as the nature of the press and its ownership changed, and competition grew from television. Wainwright was no Canute in a futile battle against change, however: he made the press more useful than it had been, and than it quickly became afterwards. He managed to reverse the decline, if only for a time.

Notes

1 Ayerst, D., *The Manchester Guardian: Biography of a Newspaper* (Ithaca: Cornell UP 1971), p. 564.
2 Yorkshire Liberal Federation Annual Report 1957. Other Liberal papers to close or merge in the 1950s included the *Birmingham Gazette* and the *Nottingham Journal*.
3 Lockwood, E., *Colne Valley Folk* (London: Heath Cranton 1936), p. 89
4 Cited in Wade, D. and Banks, D., *The Political Insight of Elliott Dodds* (Leeds: The Elliott Dodds Trust 1977), p. 6
5 *Huddersfield Daily Examiner*, 20 March 1963.
6 Ibid., 1 May 1979.
7 *Oldham Chronicle* 11 March 1966.
8 Ibid., 30 March 1966.
9 'The End of Deadlock', ibid., 17 June 1970.
10 Lord Clark, interview, 3 June 2008.

11 *Oldham Chronicle*, 11 February 1974. Editorials of the non-committal type included 'Many Issues: One Vote', 25 February 1974, and 'It's Your Vote', 10 October 1974.

12 See for example 'Refreshing', editorial on Liberal industrial policy, 13 February 1974; 'Revival' on Liberal success, 25 February 1974; 'Realignment' on prospects of coalition, 23 September 1974; and 'Ending Age of Confrontation' on the Lib-Lab Pact, 2 May 1979. Wainwright had a regular 'Westminster Report' column in the *Chronicle* from 6 November 1974.

13 *Colne Valley Guardian*, 16 October 1959.

14 Ibid., 20 March 1964.

15 'Liberal Challenge', ibid., 18 September 1964.

16 'The Liberal Impact', ibid., 25 March 1966.

17 Ibid., 22 May 1970.

18 'Battling for Votes', ibid., 22 February 1974.

19 Joanna Hannam, correspondence with the author, 21 January 2009.

20 Chris Greenfield, Caroline Cawston and Joanna Hannam, interviews, 1 December 2007, 2 June 2008 and 19 January 2009.

21 Joanna Hannam, interview, 19 January 2009.

22 Joanna Hannam, correspondence with the author, 21 January 2009.

23 RSW to Joanna Hannam, 21 July 1987, Wainwright papers file 5/B/25.

24 RSW to the *Oldham Chronicle*, the *Colne Valley Guardian* and the *Bradford Telegraph and Argus*, 4 March 1974, Wainwright papers file 6/17.

25 RSW to John Edwards, 9 June 1972, Wainwright papers file 4/7.

26 RSW to J. Beardsell, 14 January 1980, Wainwright papers file 5/B/23.

27 Andrew Alexander, interview, 13 March 2009.

28 Graham Riddick, interview, 16 March 2009.

29 Colne Valley Labour Party Agent's report, 15 May 1961.

30 Lord Clark, interview, 3 June 2008.

31 This file is kept in the Colne Valley Labour Party records at Huddersfield University Library Archives, file CV3. Wainwright's bathing at Marsden was reported in the *Huddersfield Daily Examiner*, 1 August 1973.

7 The Party in the country

As his retirement approached, Wainwright received a letter from a supporter recalling the first time she and her husband had seen him, speaking at a meeting in Leeds before he was married, 'a very young man who made a simply wonderful speech. Neither of us could get you out of our minds.' She recalled her husband saying on the way home, 'there is a young man who is going far in the Liberal Party'. 'What wonderful times we all had. The excitements, often very hard work – but, the splendid friendships! It has all added to the colour of life.'[1]

Wainwright had a special affection for Liberal activists, saw himself as their voice in Westminster and in the higher councils of the Party, and devoted more of his time to the Party organisation than most Liberal MPs. Yet he was ambivalent about the Liberal Party Organisation (LPO) and often critical of its effectiveness: Wainwright liked to quote Jo Grimond's remark that he was grateful to represent an offshore constituency as it meant that at elections he could throw the official Liberal Party propaganda from London into the harbour as soon as it arrived. Wainwright was much more attached to the Liberal Party in the country than to its organisation outside Parliament.

Wainwright was first elected on to the Liberal Party Executive in 1953, and held several significant positions in the Party, including leading its Organisation Department from 1955–58 and being a member of the Committee on the contentious issue of industrial co-ownership in the 1950s and its Campaign Committee from 1959 onwards.[2] He was a Vice President of the Party between 1959 and 1966, Chairman of the Liberal Research Department from 1968 to 1970, and finally Party Chairman between 1970 and 1972. His speeches were a regular feature in Assembly debates, and he topped most polls he contested for internal positions in the Party. Wainwright came to know from tours of constituency Liberal Associations around the country the state of the Party and the motivations of its members.[3] He also saw the Party's mixed fortunes in different election campaigns, notably at parliamentary by-elections and local elections. The roles Wainwright played were vital ones, and exploited his gifts for organisation and motivation. Through them he strengthened the effectiveness of the Liberal machine on several fronts.

In 1975 he was invited to write a report on the LPO's structure and finances which concluded that 'the LPO is heading for a financial breakdown.'[4] Wainwright's solution was to decentralise the functions of Headquarters to the regions and, most controversially, in the words of Sir Hugh Jones who was soon to be General Secretary, 'Party Headquarters should be decapitated by abolition of the post of Head of LPO.' Though many parts of the report were accepted, this last was, on the casting vote of the Executive Chairman, the only one rejected. Nonetheless, the Head of the LPO resigned, much to Wainwright's satisfaction, as he later confided to Sir Hugh Jones that the proposed abolition 'had been conceived as a device to get rid of the incumbent'. Wainwright had made an impact on attitudes to the LPO even if he had lost the vote: on taking over, Jones found that 'the whole affair had left the reputation of Party Headquarters in tatters.'[5] The Rowntree Trust also diverted its funds to various special funds rather than the LPO.[6]

Some of Wainwright's misgivings about this work – particularly his time as Party Chairman – can be attributed to the fact that it substituted unsatisfactorily for being an MP after his 1970 defeat, and he was frustrated by what he was not rather than what he was. His daughter Hilary remembers a lunch with him at Oxford after his defeat at which even the minor details of the meal made him cross in an uncharacteristic way.[7] Partly his unease was simply a reflection of his distaste for London, which contact with the LPO required him to visit more often; but mainly it was that, to Wainwright, the titles in themselves meant little. It was the opportunity they gave to support, inspire and send away others in their own autonomous parts of the Party to carry on the work that he valued, and for which he was valued by others. Such was Wainwright's popularity in the Party that one senior politician warned Michael Meadowcroft that the Liberals would never get anywhere until they got rid of the 'Wainwright problem' – the overriding need to keep faith with all parts of the Party, and to lose touch with none. As Meadowcroft added, however, when Wainwright went to speak to 'three people in a shed in Goole', it was not to win popularity; it was because one of the three might be mad, one bored and the third a great Liberal activist.[8]

Young Liberals

Wainwright was aware from his own experience of the importance of the youth wings of parties as recruiting organisations: colleagues in Parliament including Cyril Smith, Michael Meadowcroft and David Penhaligon were former officers of the Young Liberals (YLs), and most others had joined the Party as students. He was also aware from his campaigns to enter Parliament of the useful work which energetic young supporters could do in canvassing, stewarding at meetings and carrying out challenging publicity stunts. Young supporters are the public proof of a party's future prospects, and therefore a vital asset in vote-winning – especially for a Party which, like Grimond's Liberals in the 1960s, stressed its modernity and freshness. This was exemplified by the emergence of the 'New Orbits' group in 1959, from which many long-serving activists and policy-makers were recruited to the senior Party.

Yet elements of the youth wings of all parties have also periodically presented a problem for their senior partners, having a high turnover of membership, a tendency towards unrealistic expectations, an unwillingness to compromise and a penchant for direct action. Both of the main parties have had to disband their youth organisations in recent years in order to flush out extremists, and the YLs showed themselves equally capable of embarrassing their Party leadership during Wainwright's time. Wainwright showed in his handling of the Young Liberals a talent for appealing to young voters as strong as his determination to tell them when he thought they were wrong. Even then, however, he did not shut them out. He was, as ever, a bridge-builder.

Wainwright's first post-war position in the Liberal Party was as Vice Chairman of the Leeds Young Liberal Federation, and he continued to hold office in the Yorkshire Young Liberals when he was an MP. As a member of the Party's National Executive and Council in the 1950s, Wainwright was especially supportive of those who represented the YLs: he struck up conversation between Party Council sessions with Roy Douglas, Chairman of the YLs in 1955, and was 'gentle, firm, quietly determined, and very sincere';[9] Trevor Smith, who joined the National Executive as Chairman of the Liberal Students in 1958, said 'he took a particular interest in younger people.'[10]

On becoming candidate for Colne Valley, Wainwright used this charm to recruit young supporters to the campaign. By the early 1960s, the Colne Valley Young Liberals had four separate branches in the constituency, ran the hardware stall at the Divisional Association's autumn fair, and Wainwright opened their garden party at the home in Wilshaw of Major Kirby, one of the Association's senior members. They also took trips to Blackpool illuminations and boasted 'the finest skiffle on the Yorkshire–Lancashire border' at their mixed grill socials in Saddleworth. One who was a Young Liberal in Linthwaite at the time remembers being in a team of a dozen YLs in the village who canvassed in harness with the senior Party branch.[11] As the General Election of 1964 approached, a tour party of Liberal Students spent a week campaigning in Colne Valley.

After Wainwright's defeat in 1974, the Colne Valley Young Liberals undertook survey work in the constituency, organised a sponsored walk between their constituencies with YLs in Hazel Grove constituency, where Wainwright's former parliamentary colleague Michael Winstanley was standing, and ran a welfare advice stall in Meltham with materials supplied by Wainwright. Wainwright also recruited young workers from Edge Hill constituency in Liverpool in exchange for visits he made to speak there. These activists stayed with Colne Valley members for days at a time: Dorothy Shaw had 'absolutely wonderful parties' at her home in Diggle with her visitors;[12] Chris (now Lord) Rennard remembers joining carloads of YLs to do survey work by day, and at night to enjoy Chinese takeaways and playing drunken games of 'Murder in the Dark'. Wainwright would take the dozen or more Liverpudlian apprentices – including two future MPs, one of whom became a Member of the European Parliament and the other a Peer, a future Chief Executive of the Party and a clutch of Liverpool councillors – out for a meal and was 'always very generous, very motivational; you were really well thanked'.[13] At the same time, in his own constituency Wainwright was cultivating the next generation of supporters like David Wheeler, who as a teenager asked for help with a school project which turned into days of work experience in the Commons, including nights out in London and floor space in the home of Wainwright's staff. 'He was always so amenable,' remembers Wheeler.[14]

There were, however, signs that Wainwright's ability to reach out to young supporters was waning: the new recruits were coming from within families of existing Colne Valley activists (David Wheeler's mother was a Councillor) or were brought from Liverpool precisely because 'there were very few young people who were deciding to be Colne Valley Liberals'.[15] This natural process of increasing distance from youth added to what had always been a potentially turbulent relationship between youth and experience in the Party: even in 1949, the Yorkshire YLs had objected to the Party's failure to fight by-elections at Sowerby, and Batley and Spen,[16] and condemned the Liberal pacts with the Conservatives in Huddersfield and Bolton, where the national YL Executive even threatened to put up a candidate against the Tories to sabotage the deal.[17] Wainwright shared their misgivings about such deals, but he bided his time before bringing them to an end by funding the Liberal Local Government Department which exposed their weaknesses in councils, and by his involvement in the 1960 Bolton by-election, at which he insisted the Liberals stand.[18] He was aware for the time being, however, of the short-term benefits of the deals – not least in returning his friend Donald Wade to the Commons as one of only six Liberal MPs.

This tension over YL hot-headedness was at its greatest during the so-called 'Red Guard' phase of the YLs' leadership.[19] The YLs from the late 1950s onwards had recruited members on issues of social change, one future Leader remembering how 'we plagued our elders with resolutions on disarmament, homosexuality, capital punishment and other "radical" topics'.[20] But in the second half of the 1960s the YLs adopted positions including British withdrawal from NATO and workers' control of nationalised industries which strayed too far from Party policy for the comfort of many senior members. Some YL leaders, including future Labour minister Peter Hain, took to using direct action to publicise their views, sabotaging cricket grounds to object to a tour by the South Africans in 1970.[21] Even former YL Chairman Roy Douglas described his successors as 'a small and very noisy band of young "Liberals" whose opinions and attitudes bore no relation to the views of any substantial section of the Party – but who alarmed a number of potential Liberal voters'; Chris Cook regards the difficulties they caused as 'perhaps the most pronounced' of Thorpe's leadership.[22]

Wainwright was fully aware of the difficulties this raised, because he addressed the YL conferences in 1966 and 1970, at the latter of which Tony Greaves beat the incumbent Louis Eaks, closely linked to the direct action which had taken place, to the Chairmanship of the YLs. More than this, his daughter Hilary was part of the radical leadership of the YLs. At first there was some evidence Hilary might follow her father's career more closely than she did: as he was elected to Parliament, Hilary won a mock election as Liberal candidate amongst 800 teenagers on a school trip aboard the SS *Devonia* off Algeria.[23] She had, however, always been a Left-leaning Liberal – she attributes her first introduction to these ideas to a teacher at The Mount School in York – and at Oxford she established a radical ginger group within what she preferred to think of as the Liberal movement, before drifting out of the Party altogether. She later explained her disillusionment as being linked to the failure of the promise held out by Jo Grimond's leadership:

> He talked of breaking the two party monopoly; he conveyed very publicly the sense of voices being deprived of political expression. This sort of appeal led many young radicals who would never before have given the Liberals much of a thought, to join the Young Liberal Movement. They did not think they were joining a conventional political party. They/we believed we were creating a new movement to break up 'the system'.

After Grimond, she argued, too many of the Liberals engaged in wishful thinking about inequality because they were uncomfortable about appealing to the working class, and instead engaged in the very government institutions and procedures – for instance through the Lib-Lab Pact – which they had previously condemned.[24]

There was no decisive breaking-point in Hilary's departure, and therefore no traumatic break with her father, though he was surely disappointed and suffered some political embarrassment during the process. At the tender age of eighteen Hilary had written to the Conservative *Yorkshire Post* complaining at a critical editorial on the YLs. The Editor replied in sarcastic tone, accusing Hilary of irrelevance and incoherence, and saying 'I am returning your letter for you to read, for I can hardly believe you read it before posting it':

We do not get many letters from Young Liberals, but what we do get are extremely poor, barely literate and full of enthusiasm and indignation and platform propaganda, which no newspaper (except perhaps *The Guardian*) has room for. Someone ought to take the Young Liberals in hand and teach them how to compose short and effective letters. My regards to your esteemed Parliamentary parent.[25]

Wainwright was angered when Hilary arrived late at a meeting of the Liberal Executive to defend a resolution she had submitted, following her involvement in a demonstration which had ended in confrontation with the police; after one discussion he sent her a postcard at Oxford insisting that he would 'fight to the death against Marxism';[26] and when her split with the Party had become public, he testily corrected opponents who taunted him that 'she has not joined Labour; she's become a socialist.'[27] Most directly, Wainwright felt the backlash against YL radicalism in his own constituency, when in 1970 the Colne Valley Liberal Association passed two separate resolutions attacking 'recent destruction of cricket grounds' and YL direct action aimed at sabotaging that year's 'Miss World' competition.[28]

Throughout all of this, however, Wainwright maintained his faith in young recruits to the Party and never wholly dismissed even those who were the source of bad publicity or what he saw as bad ideas. Peter Hain recalls that, in contrast with some other Liberal MPs, 'he was always a mixture of firmness where he disagreed with policy, but never confrontational or patronising towards us. He would say if he disagreed, but he didn't do it in a vitriolic or patronising way.'[29] In 1968, Wainwright even funded a move by the Young Liberal office out of the Liberal Headquarters to protect the group's independence, and on another occasion provided an unexpected three-figure sum in response to an appeal from the Union of Liberal Students.[30] He accepted Tony Greaves's invitation to address Manchester University students, even though on his previous visit he had noticed Greaves's predecessor putting up publicity for the meeting as he arrived and had spoken to an unsurprisingly small group (though he did point this out to Greaves).[31] He put his position to his constituency organiser when reporting some correspondence with Steve Galloway, who later became a leading York councillor and parliamentary candidate, and was then the Yorkshire Young Liberal Federation leader: 'I have not always seen eye to eye with them, but I have remained a Vice President.'[32]

In the early 1970s, Wainwright persuaded David Mumford, who with a group of YLs had taken over the moribund Association of Liberal Trade Unionists, to withdraw; he also conciliated when Thorpe demanded of Tony Greaves that YL policy on the Middle East be modified following complaints from Party backers. Hilary had shown the same talent for restraint, telling the YL conference at Great Yarmouth that one of their proposed policies was a 'toytown dream'. The fact that the proposal – votes at sixteen years old – is now the policy of the UK Youth Parliament and is seriously canvassed as an idea in the Liberal

Democrats, and that votes at eighteen were achieved at the end of the decade in which Hilary said this, perhaps reflects why Wainwright was cautious to condemn youthful excess: he knew that from somewhere within its output, the mainstream ideas of the future would somehow flow.

Women Liberals

It is a characteristic of the Women's Liberal Federation (WLF) nationally and locally that it maintained a more consistent existence than some other elements of the Party, and the same was true in Colne Valley. Wainwright recognised this, but it was Joyce who exploited the organisation's potential to the full.

The WLF had existed since 1887, and whilst the fortunes of the Party nationally went into freefall in the inter-war period, the Women's organisation retained 100,000 members in the late 1920s, and its conference still attracted 800 delegates in 1935. It had adopted a progressive position on women's enfranchisement, social reform and disarmament before other elements of the Party, and in the words of Richard Grayson, 'the WLF had a clear role within the Liberal Party as a source of radical ideas.'[33]

At local level, the role of Women's Liberal Associations was more often concerned with organisation and fund-raising, but in this again the national organisation had led the way, re-establishing regional Federations quickly in the late 1940s: the Yorkshire Women's Liberal Federation was already contributing a sum equivalent to about £500 a year at 2010 prices to the Yorkshire Liberal Federation accounts.[34] The first post-war WLF conference separate from the Liberal Assembly was a Yorkshire affair, held at Harrogate in 1955.

In Colne Valley, individual women activists were the thread which linked the Liberalism of the previous century to Wainwright's time, and their organisation had survived the downturn in Liberal support. Four months before Wainwright's adoption as candidate for the Colne Valley, the Slaithwaite and Linthwaite Women's Liberal Association held a celebration to mark the eighty-ninth birthday of Mrs. Shaw, a life-long Liberal described by WLA Secretary Miss Furniss (herself a member since Edwardian times) as 'an example of a living faith in Liberalism'.[35] Two years later the Slaithwaite and Linthwaite WLA won the national Women's Liberal Federation Silver Tea Pot awarded for the year's most original fund-raising idea, a commemorative 'At Home' organised by Miss Furniss.[36]

As with other parts of the Liberal organisation and its support, Wainwright – or rather in this case, Joyce – took the existing structure and strengthened it by personal endeavour and charisma. Joyce became President of the Colne Valley Women's Liberal Council in 1958,[37] and ensured that it performed three important functions: fund-raising, campaigning and political education. The Colne Valley Women Liberals organised an annual fair raising between

£250 and £370 a year (the lower of which is worth well over £3,000 in 2010),[38] and contributed £900 to the campaign to restore Wainwright to Parliament in February 1974.[39] Even local branches such as Crosland Moor could add as much as £80 to the campaign appeal of 1983, and the Colne Valley Women's Liberal Council would occasionally, if slightly disapprovingly, give a donation of £20 or £25 – hundreds of pounds at 2010 prices – to the Divisional Association 'who are in the red'.[40]

This revenue was clearly valuable to the Divisional Association, but so was the activity which raised it, drawing into the Party whole households rather than individuals, and engaging them in common activity with a clear purpose. Where most – but not all – of the initial political recruits from a home were men, their wives were encouraged to become active in the Women's Council, and according to Wainwright's assistant 'all of these people's wives were in love with Joyce'.[41] Certainly, some of the most consistent activists were the wives of leading Liberal councillors. The numbers involved were not great, usually reaching an attendance of twenty at regular meetings and forty at an AGM, but for an outing to the Commons, the theatre or Wedgwood Pottery over fifty would turn out. Team spirit is difficult to measure, but the Women's Council undoubtedly brought more than money to Liberalism in Colne Valley.

However, the business of the Women's Council was not all outings and bring-and-buy stalls, useful as these were: an input to the political character of the Party was a regular feature of the Council's activity. Richard Wainwright, or sometimes Joyce deputising for him, gave regular reports on his work at Westminster, and could face greater challenges than were dared (or at least recorded) at Divisional Association meetings. The minutes of discussions following his defeat in 1970, and during the Lib-Lab Pact, betray a tension which was surely greater in the meetings. Following these reports, there were sometimes letters written to the Chancellor on Selective Employment Tax proposals; there were resolutions submitted to the Annual national WLF conference on mental health, employment incentives and the treatment of young offenders; and there were political rallies and meetings with panels of speakers on themes such as 'Are our schools democratic?', 'Juvenile crime – whose fault?' or on more prosaic issues such as local government finance. For this sort of activity, the Colne Valley Women's Council was made runner-up for the WLF's national Baerlin cup for political work.[42]

Wainwright was not a social conservative on the role of women. His speeches at adoption meetings made reference to the obstacles faced by working women, and in his private life he recognised the limitations his own upbringing had imposed upon his views of women, and he expected as much of his daughters as of his sons, and admired his female as much as his male employees and colleagues. Similarly, the Colne Valley Women's Liberal Council performed certain traditional and very significant functions effectively, as a result of both its historic strength and the leadership of Joyce Wainwright. At the same time, it gave some limited opportunities to voice women's views and to encourage their participation. Wainwright always respected those views when he heard them.

Liberal councillors

Wainwright neither served nor stood as a councillor yet he recognised the vital role of success in local government in a way which only became fashionable in the Liberal Party a decade later. Supporters and critics alike acknowledge that Liberal success in Colne Valley's local elections was the precursor and the precondition of Wainwright's election to Parliament. Wainwright knew it too, and preached the same message outside Yorkshire.

When Wainwright was selected to fight Colne Valley, the Liberal Association was rare in being able to boast four councillors between the five Urban District Councils (UDCs) which served the parliamentary constituency. Three of these were in Saddleworth and the last was Norman Richardson, a member of Colne Valley Urban District Council since 1937.

The number of Liberal candidates for the thirty-two wards was gradually increased from fourteen in 1960 to twenty-four in 1963, and the dramatic improvement in Liberal local government representation following the arrival of Wainwright and his Agent Edward Dunford is made clear in the table below.

Liberal councillors in Colne Valley Division	
1957	4
1958	5
1959	12
1960	16
1961	19
1962	20

Underneath these overall figures lie stories from individual UDCs: in Saddleworth the Liberals had half the seats by 1961; in Labour's stronghold of Denby Dale the Liberals had their first post-war victory in 1961 and on Holme Valley Council they held the balance of power between Labour and the Independent group after winning a second seat in 1963; and in 1961 the Liberals claimed their only County Council seat in Colne Valley. The Colne Valley Labour Party were at first indignant that 'we have been too ready to regard the Liberals as some sort of semi-allies',[43] and later concerned that 'the future at present does not look promising, especially in the light of the advances of the Liberals.'[44]

The local Labour Party's history of these events shares this view of the importance of Liberal local government success: 'the parallel between the local Liberal surge in the Colne Valley UDC in the 1960s and Labour's loss of the Parliamentary seat in 1966 is there to be seen'; Wainwright's team won 'by virtue of the base given them by local government successes'.[45] Wainwright himself said that the Party's image 'rests largely with our 24 Liberal Councillors all of whom were carefully and democratically chosen by their Ward Association' and that 'if Liberals make good councillors ... the inference is drawn that the rest of Liberal policy is likely to be sound'.[46] Success bred success as in 1968 the Liberals became the first party to ever hold a majority on Colne Valley UDC, and claimed thirty-eight seats in total across the constituency, with a clutch on each council.

This was no spontaneous development, for Wainwright had been promoting the expansion of Liberal representation in local government since the late 1950s. In January 1960 he funded the establishment of a Local Government Department in Liberal Party Headquarters, staffed by Michael Meadowcroft and Pratap Chitnis, who was to be the Agent in the 1962 Orpington by-election victory. Modestly, Wainwright later told another champion of municipal Liberalism, Tony Greaves, that 'we smuggled Pratap Chitnis into a broom cupboard in the basement of Victoria Street!' but Greaves sees the significance of the development:

> There is no way that the people running LPO wanted a local government unit, but Richard saw the importance of local government, and although it was in London it was from his perspective as a person out in the country who saw the importance of building the Party up. Where he'd been candidate there was a continuing tradition of Liberal councillors and Aldermen in Pudsey, and there was a continuing tradition of Liberal local government involvement in Colne Valley and in Huddersfield.[47]

The Department worked to establish reliable records of numbers of Liberal councillors, to give support and guidance in election campaigns and in carrying out municipal duties, and also sought deliberately to break up pacts with other parties – Conservative and Labour – which still persisted in some parts of the country, notably in Yorkshire. Wainwright explained the purpose of the Department as threefold: to encourage public interest in council work and politics generally; to increase the number of younger councillors; and to encourage Urban District Councillors to press for their constituents' interests by 'camping out in front of County Hall'. He acknowledged, however, a partisan interest, pointing out that 'the crowning process already illustrated by the return of Orpington Councillor Eric Lubbock as Orpington's MP is the linking of the Liberal Council force with a growing Liberal Parliamentary force.' Local government success, he insisted, was 'a basic part of the political engine'.[48] The Colne Valley Liberal Executive apparently agreed, congratulating him on the success of the Department.[49]

Wainwright also supported the development of the Association of Liberal Councillors, helping with Councillor David Shutt to arrange the purchase by the Joseph Rowntree Social Services Trust of the Birchcliffe Centre, a former Baptist chapel in Hebden Bridge, West Yorkshire as their Headquarters in 1977. Looking back on this at the Centre's tenth anniversary – and in the midst of the debate about the merger of the Liberals and SDP about which he was concerned – he paid lavish tribute to the independence the ALC had developed since the time the LPO Local Government Department had been established, and said, 'I believe Birchcliffe has played, and will play, a crucial part in maintaining the credibility and integrity of the Party, and I think this decentralisation gives us a great advantage over our opponents.' He pointedly called the Association of Liberal Councillors 'the Liberal Party's most authoritative body of elected public representatives.'[50] A year after the Liberal Democrats had been formed, when Wainwright was still feeling ambivalent about the national Party, he made a personal donation to the Birchcliffe Centre.[51]

As well as helping to get Wainwright into Parliament, a healthy body of Liberal councillors helped him to carry out his constituency duties, passing on queries and grievances of Wainwright's constituents, some of which he referred on to councillors to tackle. Wainwright's constituency casebook suggests that he made greater use of this relationship in his last Parliament, and documents at least four Liberal councillors fulfilling this role in one year alone from 1983–84.[52] There were surely more occasions when this happened on a less formal basis, as Councillor Robert Iredale confirms: 'that's almost standard practice now, but later on if something came up, we'd feed it through if it had a national slant on it.'[53]

Councillors could also be Wainwright's eyes and ears on the political climate in the Colne Valley, and their fates at elections could forewarn him of threats such as the growing success of the Conservatives during the Lib-Lab Pact. The achievement Wainwright made partly to underpin his own ambitions survives in Liberal Democrat success in local elections in the Colne Valley constituency. More than two decades after Wainwright's retirement, the Liberal Democrats still hold all the Oldham and Kirklees council seats in Saddleworth, Golcar and Colne Valley itself, as well as others elsewhere in his old constituency. That, Councillor Iredale argues, is an enduring part of Wainwright's legacy.

Notes

1 'Ivy' to RSW, 21 December 1986, Wainwright papers file 5/B/25.
2 Douglas, R., *History of the Liberal Party 1895–1970* (London: Sidgwick & Jackson 1971), p. 272. The Campaign Committee controversially assumed what Douglas calls 'sweeping powers' to reorganise the Party structure. RSW was its only member who had not sat in Parliament.

3 See RSW's Interim Report on Visits to Constituencies, 1956, Wainwright papers file 8/6.

4 RSW, Report to LPO Executive, 20 March 1975.

5 Jones, Sir H., *Campaigning Face to Face* (Brighton: Book Guild 2007), p. 59.

6 Kavanagh, D., 'Organisation and Power in the Liberal Party' in Bogdanor, V., (Ed), *Liberal Party Politics* (Oxford: OUP 1983), p. 133.

7 Hilary Wainwright, interview, 22 February 2008.

8 Michael Meadowcroft, interview, 17 June 2008.

9 Roy Douglas, interview, 11 July 2008.

10 Lord Smith, interview, 22 June 2009.

11 Councillor Robert Iredale, interview, 16 April 2009.

12 Dorothy Shaw, interview, 16 April 2009.

13 Lord Rennard, interview, 30 July 2009.

14 David Wheeler, interview, 26 July 2009.

15 Lord Rennard, interview, 30 July 2009.

16 Chairman of Yorkshire Young Liberal Federation to Albert Ingham, Yorkshire Liberal Agent, 21 February 1949, Yorkshire Liberal Federation Records, West Yorkshire Archive Service.

17 Rasmussen, J.S., *The Liberal Party: A Study of Retrenchment and Revival* (London: Constable 1965), pp. 104–5.

18 RSW's role in the by-election was confirmed by the daughter of the candidate Frank Byers, Luise Nandy, interview, 18 January 2009.

19 The nickname was coined by the press in reference to the young followers of Chairman Mao.

20 Steel, D., *Against Goliath: David Steel's Story* (London: Weidenfeld & Nicolson 1989), p. 25.

21 The 'Stop the Seventy Tour' campaign led to Hain being put under surveillance by security authorities. The tour was cancelled on 22 May 1970.

22 Douglas, R., *The History of the Liberal Party*, p. 286; Cook, C., *A Short History of the Liberal Party 1900–84* (London and Basingstoke: Macmillan 1984), p. 148.

23 *Liberal News*, 22 April 1966, p. 7.

24 Wainwright, H., 'Why I Am Not a Liberal', address to Liberal Summer School, 12–14 July 1985.

25 J.E. Crossley to Hilary Wainwright, 29 March 1967, Wainwright papers file 13/1.

26 Hilary Wainwright, interview, 22 February 2008.

27 Lord Greaves, interview, 8 April 2009.

28 Colne Valley Divisional Liberal Association, AGM 31 January 1970 and Executive meeting 25 November 1970.

29 Peter Hain, interview, 30 January 2009.

30 Lord Greaves, interview, 8 April 2009.

31 Ibid.

32 RSW to Maurice Burgess, 26 November 1969, Colne Valley Divisional Liberal Association papers.

33 Grayson, R.S., *Liberals, International Relations and Appeasement* (London: Frank Cass 2001), p. 96 Grayson makes particular reference to the WLF policy on colonial development passed in 1942.

34 Yorkshire Liberal Federation accounts, 1946 and 1947. The sums were £11 10s and £18 7s.
35 *Colne Valley Guardian*, 6 January 1956. Another member who had been Secretary of the Colne Valley WLA before the First World War, Miss O'May, was congratulated on her long service at the age of ninety, ten years later.
36 Colne Valley Divisional Liberal Association Executive minutes, 4 June 1958.
37 Joyce was elected at the Women's Liberal Council AGM at Honley on 1 July 1958, reported in the Colne Valley Divisional Liberal Association minutes, 30 July 1958.
38 Colne Valley Women's Liberal Council AGM minutes, 17 March 1964 and 10 July 1973.
39 Colne Valley Women's Liberal Council AGM, 13 July 1974.
40 Colne Valley Women's Liberal Council meeting, 13 July 1965. See also minutes of 22 November 1977.
41 Joanna Hannam, interview, 19 January 2009.
42 This recognition was reported at a Women's Liberal Council meeting on 11 July 1972. The preceding activities are recorded in the Women's Liberal Council minutes variously in March and July 1966, July 1968, July 1970, October 1973, November 1977, and March and June 1978.
43 Colne Valley Labour Party Agent's report, 9 December 1958.
44 Ibid., 15 May 1961.
45 Pearce, C., *Colne Valley Labour Party Souvenir Centenary History 1891–1991* (Colne Valley: Colne Valley Labour Party 1991), pp. 46 and 49.
46 *Liberal News*, 7 April 1966.
47 Lord Greaves, interview, 8 April 2009.
48 Wainwright, R., 'Now there are 1,600 Fighters for the People', *New Outlook*, No. 9 (June 1962), pp. 27–8.
49 Colne Valley Divisional Liberal Association Executive minutes, 16 May 1962.
50 'Richard Wainwright's Message to the ALC', *Liberal News*, 3 July 1977.
51 Association of Social and Liberal Democrat Councillors Chairman to RSW, 12 March 1989, Wainwright papers file 1 2/10.
52 RSW's constituency casebook 1974–84. The Councillors were Barry Fearnley, Heather Swift, Basil Kaye and James Crossley.
53 Councillor Robert Iredale, interview, 16 April 2009.

8 Colne Valley

It is common in the biographies and autobiographies of politicians with a national profile to make only a handful of passing references to their constituency; the people who send politicians to Parliament are too often regarded as incidental to the things those politicians do once there.[1] No serious account of Wainwright's life could give other than a vital role to his constituency, for he chose it as much as it chose him, and both sides of the relationship were strengthened by it.

All constituencies can claim to be distinctive, but Colne Valley truly deserves to be called unique. Its history, its composition and its character all mark it out. In Wainwright's time, the constituency lay across the southern Pennines between south-east Huddersfield and north-western Manchester. Stretching some thirty miles end to end and covering 230 square miles of territory, it had a remarkable history of independence and industry, and a striking landscape of close-knit villages set in wild moorland. Ted Hughes, raised a few miles north of Colne Valley, romanticised the area as part of the ancient Kingdom of Elmet, 'the last British Celtic Kingdom to fall to the Angles. For centuries it was considered a more or less uninhabitable wilderness, a notorious refuge for criminals, a hide-out for refugees.'[2] In his last Parliament, Wainwright congratulated the new Conservative MP for the constituency of Elmet on having 'the good fortune to represent part of the ancient kingdom.'[3]

By the early eighteenth century, Daniel Defoe was reporting that the cloth trade so dominated the steep hillsides of the West Riding that 'not a thing above four years old, but its hands are sufficient to itself,'[4] and the mills remained vital pillars of the economy and social order of Colne Valley when Wainwright arrived in the 1950s. The hardships of textile production and the breathtaking topography of this part of Yorkshire were reflected together in the work of the Brontë sisters, and more recently, if less seriously, Colne Valley featured in the long-running television series *Last of the Summer Wine*, filmed at Holmfirth since 1973.[5] To describe Colne Valley as quaint or charming is a patronising understatement; the term 'inspiring' would hardly be hyperbolic.[6]

Colne Valley embraced five population centres, around which were clustered thirty villages, each with its own independent life. That life was reflected in the existence of dozens upon dozens of sporting clubs, musical societies, political clubs and churches. Wainwright's reliance upon the Liberal elements amongst these is detailed earlier in Part 2; but their more general preponderance made the society of the Colne Valley distinctive: its citizens were active, community-spirited amateurs. The Colne Valley Urban District itself, only one of five municipal divisions of the constituency, there were more than twenty recreational groups, including fishing, football and rugby clubs, a theatre company, the Colne Valley Male Voice Choir and the Slaithwaite Philharmonic orchestra. Joyce Wainwright remembered particularly that 'it was a great place for brass bands: it was called "the land of puff and blow"'. The connection was strong enough that some of the players reassembled at Wainwright's home as 'Vintage Brass' to help him celebrate his eightieth birthday.[7] There was also a strong tradition of Beagling in the constituency, with as many as thirty packs active. At Denby Dale there was a tradition of baking gigantic village pies to celebrate historic events, including the end of the First World War, Queen Victoria's Golden Jubilee, the repeal of the Corn Laws and the Battle of Waterloo.

The isolated citizens of late twentieth century society had yet to dominate this part of Yorkshire. David Alton, who canvassed Colne Valley in the 1970s before becoming MP for Edge Hill in Liverpool, remembered the way that the Liberals embedded themselves in these 'vibrant little towns and villages which genuinely had strong local branches and Associations and Clubs, all of which fed into the life of the community'.[8] Wainwright's Conservative opponent in 1963 and 1964 was seduced by 'going to Diggle and Delph and all these places, each one was a little gem in itself. I'd quite like to have lived there.'[9]

It was necessary to march many streets in many villages to contact the constituents of the Colne Valley; but when engaged, they were positive, active and critical. In Colne Valley, community was more than just a politician's slogan, it was a way of life. 'The peculiar nature of the constituency', remembers Nigel Priestley, who became involved in the Liberals there in the 1970s, 'was that whole sense that you still had village meetings in different townships in a way that you can't do now'.[10] This nourished a healthy suspicion of outsiders, from which Wainwright, though not himself from the constituency, profited politically, and which even led his supporters from one side of the Pennines to query visiting Party colleagues from 'over the other side' with the challenge, 'you're not from round here, are you?' Philip Snowden, the MP for Colne Valley from 1924–31, noted the enduring character of the local population, who were 'typically Yorkshire. I know no part of the West Riding where the sterling qualities of the moorland race have been better preserved.'[11] Violet Bonham Carter, the Liberal candidate in 1951, immediately characterised its people as 'hard-headed and warm-hearted – the country is wild, bleak, bare and rather Brontë-ish and beautiful.'[12] Wainwright himself described the distinctive features of the communities there in a tribute to both Colne Valley and the adjacent seat of Penistone:

> A deep understanding of the needs of the individual citizen, as against the state and big business, is fostered by life in small towns and villages, each with its own means of livelihood. The people of Penistone, like the people of Colne Valley, do not live on state subsidies. On the contrary, the state sends back to the area far less wealth than the people of Penistone pay over to Whitehall.[13]

Wainwright reiterated his gratitude at the privilege of representing 'the wonderful people of these tremendously strong communities' when re-elected in 1974.[14]

This explains Wainwright's ability to present himself to the constituency as a native candidate, even though he never lived within its boundaries. Opponents from David Clark to Graham Riddick were indignant to find canvassers for the man from Leeds (by way of Shrewsbury, Cambridge and London) dismissing them as outsiders. Riddick pointed to his own Yorkshire origins, and Clark – whose move to Skelmanthorpe in Colne Valley was mocked by Wainwright – painstakingly calculated that even when his home address was in Manchester, it was marginally nearer to the western boundary of the constituency than Wainwright's at Adel was to the east. Yet Wainwright was an honorary native of Colne Valley, partly because of the time and money he invested in it, but mainly because he was manifestly a Yorkshireman in ways which his opponents found it hard to match. In election literature, he emphasised his status as 'born and bred in the West Riding' or 'born in Leeds, of Yorkshire folk', and his speeches and articles were marked by arcane idioms such as 'arsy-versy'[15] or the assertion that 'there is no room on the political menu for milk pudding and barley water', a phrase which David Steel's assistant regarded as 'perhaps only intelligible to fellow Yorkshiremen.'[16]

Wainwright was keenly sensitive to the significance of accent, the ability to adapt which he had learned at Shrewsbury, and which his own children were amused to notice him modify in telephone conversations once he had learned the identity of the caller. He countered his family's gentle mockery by teasing Joyce about the prim voice she acquired at Harrogate Ladies' College, stressing the second word of her school's name. He once joked to Nicholas Budgen, successor to Enoch Powell's seat, that 'Wolverhamptonspeak is so different to Yorkshirespeak that we find it difficult to communicate.'[17]

When Trevor Smith went campaigning with Wainwright in Yorkshire he was surprised to hear how far the MP's accent changed, particularly in delivering his signature doorstep introduction 'Wainwright's the name!': 'he didn't have that broad Yorkshire accent, but he put it on for the punters.'[18] Sir Alan Beith agrees that 'he was more of a Yorkshireman in Yorkshire, but', stressing the short 'a' in northern speech, says 'he was always a "bath, grass and castle" man.'[19] Wainwright's secretary Caroline Cawston was firmly restricted to canvassing Conservative districts of Colne Valley at elections until her metropolitan received pronunciation accent had softened.[20]

Wainwright could even overplay the part of the robust, simple Yorkshireman: when Alan Beith accepted an invitation to speak to a Colne Valley Liberal dinner, Wainwright scoffed at the idea that formal dress would be expected, only for Beith to find that he and Wainwright were the only ones not in dinner suits on the night. Even when study and work took him away, Wainwright returned as often as possible to Yorkshire; though he travelled widely in retirement, he never thought of making his home anywhere outside Yorkshire, and nobody who knew Wainwright thought he could represent anywhere outside the county. One of Wainwright's researchers in the 1970s, Christopher Greenfield, said simply that Wainwright regarded being from Yorkshire as 'a sort of nationality'.[21] The typical Yorkshire folk of Colne Valley recognised the typical Yorkshireman that Wainwright represented. One follower called him 'the man next door who could get things done'.[22]

The economics of the Colne Valley were also unusual. It was heavily industrial, with woollen mills the key employers, and had only a small professional population, mostly teachers; there were also many small businesses. This limited the extent of inequality, and strengthened Colne Valley's suspicion towards the trappings and vanities of ostentatious wealth. The constituency was politely described by one of its former MPs as 'an area known for its dislike of the frivolities of life'.[23] Though heavily industrial, with nearly half the population engaged in manufacturing even in the recession of the early 1980s, it had a very high level of owner-occupation, including nearly three-quarters of the population constituencies, a higher figure than any neighbouring seat, and a higher proportion than in all but forty-three other seats in the country.[24] Wainwright liked to repeat the Yorkshire nostrum of Colne Valley that 'everyone owns their own home – and the one next door!' The Colne Valley was thus more resistant than neighbouring Yorkshire seats to the stirring of class consciousness. David Clark has recognised the significant absence of trade union activity in the early success of the Labour Party in Colne Valley, and this distaste for class conflict was cited as an explanation of Wainwright's success in Colne Valley by David Whitwam, who joined the Liberals there in the late 1950s:

> Colne Valley was a Liberal area. In this area, there wasn't envy for people who succeeded, there was admiration. It was non-Socialist in that way. There wasn't class envy. It's never existed really. If you got on, if you started from the bottom and succeeded, you were admired. It goes right back to Victorian times and self-help.

Whitwam remembers that the President of his Cub Scout group in the post-war period was a local Slaithwaite millowner, who was not regarded with 'abject terror' for his status, but rather admired. 'The local millowners were regarded as men who succeeded and brought wealth and prosperity to the area. The same applied to solicitors or teachers or anything.'[25] The professional, the employer, the waged labourer, the aged and the disadvantaged, all were part of the same community, and Wainwright was welcomed into it, too.

Wainwright fitted the distinctive social and economic climate of Colne Valley closely, and some of his core characteristics were ideal: he was educated and professional, but provincial and unaffected in his tastes. Though wealthy, he was unextravagant for himself and quietly generous to others; though a national politician, he relied upon personal charm and a reputation for being approachable to maintain his political base. His most consistent and sincere attributes included a strong distaste for London life and an absence of snobbery or inverted snobbery. It is a measure of Wainwright's ability to blend in that David Ridgway, who worked closely with Wainwright as an officer of the Colne Valley Liberal Association, was surprised to learn that Wainwright, like him, had been to public school.[26] This was not because Wainwright made a secret of his privileged background; it was simply irrelevant.

Recollections of Wainwright's disdain for social affectation are legion: his successor as Liberal candidate Nigel Priestley was disconcerted by Wainwright's insistence upon wearing the same striped tie, blue blazer and plimsoll shoes to all functions,[27] and his secretarial staff had to intervene when they noticed he had worn the same tie for a month;[28] enquiries from colleagues at a meeting of Liberal MPs about Wainwright's particularly severe, if inexpensive, new haircut were rebuffed with the response 'twice a year, twice a year', to which David Penhaligon asked, 'yes, Richard, but why on the same day?'[29] Sir Alan Beith dined with him regularly at the Commons and noted that Wainwright smothered his food with unpalatable quantities of salt, and both Councillor Christine Wheeler in Saddleworth and Lord Tony Greaves,who met Wainwright when Greaves was a student at Oxford, remembered that he was as happy to eat fish fingers as a formal meal after canvassing or speaking to a meeting.[30] Wheeler described Wainwright as capable of being 'at home anywhere'.[31] Lord Smith remembers that 'he wouldn't have wanted fancy airs and graces' and that 'he was a Yorkshireman, a Methodist and a Chartered Accountant, and that particular alchemy meant that he looked after his brass.'[32]

It would be naive to regard Wainwright's image as completely unstudied, for he was sharp enough to know that the details of political communication mattered vitally to his fate. Like all MPs, he found some duties and colleagues tiresome, but restrained himself from advertising the fact. He played shamelessly on his Yorkshire credentials to win public trust. However, this was no cynical act, and his credentials were as genuine as his admiration for the Colne Valley. If there was any performance involved, it was one which came naturally and usually with pleasure to Wainwright. He maintained his demeanour too long and too consistently for anything less honourable to be true, and he showed on other occasions his willingness to offend by not humouring behaviour he disliked. His close friend William Wallace, who knew the constituency well and was the Liberal candidate in Huddersfield, describes Wainwright's relationship with the Colne Valley as distinctive, close and sincere, though he points to its vulnerability:

> By today's standards, he was a very old-fashioned politician, and Colne Valley and Huddersfield were very old-fashioned places still. I can remember being introduced to a meeting in Huddersfield in 1968–69 as 'Dr William Wallace, M.A., Ph.D.' with a real old-fashioned reverence for learning which has completely gone now. The Liberal Party was a very old party, with the Liberal Clubs in the Colne Valley and the Methodist Churches, which Richard was very closely linked to – it was part of what gave him his standing in the community.[33]

One personification of this old-fashioned, community-based Liberalism was Maggie Furniss. Born in the 1890s, she had lived almost her whole life at Hill Top in Slaithwaite, where her father, the manager of the Gas Works, member of the local School Board and leading Liberal, had helped down-and-outs. Miss Furniss was secretary of the Colne Valley Women's Liberal Association from 1913 to 1963, as well as a teetotaller supporting the White Ribbon and the Band of Hope. 'I came from a Christian home, and my father believed Liberalism to be the Christian way of life', she told the local newspaper in the 1960s, aged 71. 'I disapprove of young people going into public houses and have no use for bad language. Hooliganism has reached a deplorable stage and sometimes I wonder whether the cane ought to be brought back', she added, saying also that 'more money should be spent on educating people abroad instead of them coming over here'.[34] Furniss welcomed Wainwright as the new Liberal candidate, hosting coffee mornings and other money-raising events; and there are still those who remember her reaction when Wainwright won Colne Valley in 1966:

> The one thing that sticks in my mind is seeing Maggie Furniss walking up from the count to Hill Top – and she was well into her seventies then – absolutely bursting with pride because at long last we'd got a Liberal MP. I can see her now absolutely full of it.[35]

It took a special candidate to rekindle this historic and distinctive strain in Liberal politics so as to win Colne Valley, and to build a link between Maggie Furniss's father, Miss Furniss, and those who remember her today. Wainwright was that candidate.

Colne Valley's political history

Most immediately important for Wainwright was the distinctiveness of Colne Valley's political history. Robert Waller's survey of British constituencies in the 1980s confirmed that 'for many years now Colne Valley has been the only true Liberal-Labour marginal in the country.'[36] From the time Tom Mann fought the seat as its first Labour candidate in 1895 to the date of Wainwright's retirement, it was held by these two parties for almost exactly equal periods of time, and had changed hands between them no fewer than eight times. Its MPs matched the distinctiveness of the seat in their own personalities: its first Labour Member was the mercurial Victor Grayson, winner of a by-election in 1907, who disappeared in mysterious circumstances. The Liberal who defeated him was Rev. C.R. Leach, who insisted he was 'an evolutionary socialist'[37] and was removed from office under the Lunacy Act in 1916. Between the Wars, two men of each Party represented Colne Valley: the Liberals were F.W. Mallalieu, a millowner from Delph who joined Lloyd George's Liberals when the Party split and was defeated in 1922. The seat was recovered nine years later by Mallalieu's son, who held the seat only until 1935, and later joined the Labour Party. In between these, Colne Valley was held by Philip Snowden, Chancellor of the Exchequer in the first Labour Government of 1924 who left the Party to join the National Government of 1931. The seat was recovered for Labour by Eric Marklew, after whose death in 1939 it was retained at a by-election by William Glenvil Hall, who remained the MP until his death in 1963, by which time Wainwright was his Liberal opponent.

The unusual activity in Colne Valley during the post-war period was concentrated in the opposition parties. After 1945, strenuous efforts were made by some leading Conservatives, including Macmillan, Quintin Hogg and most notably Churchill, to draw the Liberal Party – by this stage reduced to twelve MPs and in decline – into a formal electoral pact, and these efforts bore fruit in Colne Valley. Churchill held a string of meetings with Liberal Leader Clement Davies, and addressed meetings of his own MPs, to seek common ground on which the two non-Socialist parties could agree, and to get agreement in principle to a pact whereby between three and sixty seats would be left free by the Conservatives for Liberal candidates in exchange for a similar gesture from the Liberal Party. Most members of both parties resisted the idea, but a small number of local arrangements at council level – particularly in the north, as in Halifax – did exist, and a number of parliamentary constituencies were fought by Liberal candidates with no Conservative opponent. In the Parliaments of the 1950s, these included five of the six Liberal MPs. In two cases these Liberal MPs had made formal arrangements to secure Conservative withdrawal, including reciprocation by Liberals in a neighbouring seat. In Huddersfield, Wainwright's family friend Donald Wade became Liberal MP for Huddersfield West without a Tory opponent, whilst the Liberals gave the Conservative candidate in the east of the town a free run. At the other end of the Colne Valley, Bolton was divided up in the same way in 1951 to allow Arthur Holt to become Liberal MP for Bolton West in a straight fight with Labour.

At the same election, Churchill tried to set up another Liberal-Conservative deal in Colne Valley. Using the bait of his close confidante and intense admirer Violet Bonham Carter – the daughter of Asquith and grand-dame of the Liberal Party – as Liberal candidate, the Conservative Leader persuaded Colne Valley Conservatives to withdraw from the contest. He went further and travelled to Huddersfield to speak in Lady Violet's support. The Liberals had come third in Colne Valley in 1945 and 1950, but their strength on the ground, and the fact that the Tories had never won more than 35 per cent of the Colne Valley poll, made the seat seem a promising prospect to unite the majority of voters who opposed Labour behind a single Liberal candidate. The local Labour Party's own assessment was that 'the Colne Valley cannot be regarded as an easy seat for Labour.'[38] In the event, the project failed: Bonham Carter lost to Labour by over 2,000 votes, and in fact secured a lower vote than the Liberal and Conservative candidates combined at the previous year's contest, though the turnout had risen. It was obvious that a significant number of Liberal and Conservative voters had refused to support the arrangement; that, as one of Bonham Carter's supporters commented afterwards, 'the oil of the die hard Tory and the vinegar of the extreme Radical would not mix.'[39]

Bonham Carter declined the Executive's offer of readoption as their candidate, leaving the Colne Valley Liberals exposed to righteous criticism from Labour, Conservatives and their own doubters. Executive members reflected philosophically, and prophetically, that 'a good candidate of more humble origin might get a lot more votes than we should expect',[40] but the Association Secretary's Annual Report for 1952 expressed his 'unhappiness at the state of affairs in the division'.[41] The following March, word reached the Colne Valley Liberal Executive that the Conservatives had adopted their own candidate.[42] Spirits must have been low in the Association in April when their delegate A.D. Nichols went to the Liberal Annual Assembly at Ifracombe in Devon; but the following month he returned with a report identifying the high points of the conference, and foremost of these was a speech on Site Value Rating made by the candidate for Pudsey, for whom the occasion was described as a 'personal triumph'. His name was Richard Wainwright.[43]

Wainwright's selection

Wainwright fought Pudsey on the Colne Valley side of Leeds in 1950. He was adopted in 1949, leaving little time to nurse the constituency before a General Election was due in 1950: 'With all due respect to the Liberal Party and their supporters', Conservative candidate Colonel Cyril Banks patronised Wainwright, 'they have come into the field at far too late a date to make an impressive showing.'[44] To make matters worse, Pudsey was a knife-edge marginal contest between the two main parties, with Deputy Prime Minister Herbert

Morrison visiting to boost Labour, and Banks eventually getting home by only sixty-four votes. The Liberal candidate at the previous election had won only 16 per cent of the vote, and this, along with an anticipated national photo-finish between the two main parties, placed Wainwright's potential supporters under intense pressure to choose between the two front runners and thus squeeze the Liberal vote. Wainwright was infuriated when Liberal Headquarters published a list of thirty-two target seats, of which Pudsey was of course not one: he later told Michael Meadowcroft that when he heard the Conservatives' loudspeaker van gleefully announcing this news 'everything dropped'.[45] He later admitted he had come to the conclusion that 'it was obvious I was not going to win it.'[46]

Despite these circumstances, Wainwright raised the Liberal share of the vote in Pudsey by just over a percentage point whilst the average Liberal share of the vote per candidate across the country fell by nearly 7 per cent.[47] Wainwright was already developing the central electioneering techniques which would prove successful in Colne Valley: he set up base in the Liberal Club at Farsley and recruited support through Clubs elsewhere; he re-established the Young Liberals at a meeting at Horsforth[48] and had the help of the Yeadon Women's Liberal Association on loudspeaker tours;[49] and, with Edward Dunford as his Agent and press officer, he claimed equal space to that of the other parties in the *Yorkshire Observer*[50] and the *Wharfedale and Airedale Observer*[51] to put his case, and won the recognition of the *Pudsey and Stanningley News*, a passage from which he quickly reprinted on election flyers:

> The fight put up by that cheerful, smiling young man from Horsforth, Mr Richard Wainwright, has won universal admiration: the audiences he has attracted to his meetings have proved their claim that the Liberal Party certainly is not dead in this Division, nor is it so numerically weak as some people thought. If Liberalism be dead, then Mr Wainwright is a very active 'zombie'.

The paper foresaw that Wainwright 'may provide a very unpleasant surprise for his opponents'.[52] The energy and enthusiasm of Wainwright's apparently hopeless campaign came to be his hallmark. He addressed nine meetings a week, sometimes three each evening, and took part in public debates with Labour candidate A.G. Collingwood which the *Pudsey and Stanningley News* reported were 'grand fun'.[53] Lord David Shutt, who was to be candidate for Pudsey himself forty years later, was a schoolboy when Wainwright fought Pudsey in 1955, and remembers his dynamism and charm:

> A mate of mine and I both had bicycles, and we followed Richard's wagon – he had an open wagon and a driver … Richard had the presence of mind to tell the driver to stop the wagon. He said: 'Lads, don't waste your breath pedalling; come on board the wagon.' That explains, in a way, the start of my involvement in the cause. He was an active person who was doing far more than just the rudimentary: he was obviously trying hard.[54]

Wainwright was also indefatigably upbeat about the Party's prospects, reassuring Young Liberals like Shutt that their Party would be in power within ten years: 'the Liberal Party is in fine form today – better than it has been for twenty years. Those who vote Liberal at the General Election will be voting for a going concern. This division can be won for Liberalism.'[55] By the time of the 1950 local elections three months after Wainwright's campaign, Miss Winn, the Women's Liberal Secretary, and Mr Smith, who had been the agent for forty years, were prepared to say publicly that 'they should not be without hope of some day returning a Liberal Member of Parliament for Pudsey'.[56]

The impending birth of Andrew, his third child in three years, a month after polling day meant that Wainwright did not fight Pudsey at the next election in October 1951; in fact the Liberals fought only 109 of the 630 seats in the Commons that year, and won only six, of which only one had been contested by the Conservatives. The Party had reached its nadir, and Churchill had threatened to extinguish it at the parliamentary level by offering Liberal Leader Clement Davies a Cabinet post as Education Secretary. In an act of self-denial which rescued the Liberal Party from hibernation if not extinction, Davies refused. The years which followed were dark ones for the Liberal Party: most by-elections were not fought, and where they were, the results were disastrous.

Wainwright was effectively head-hunted for the Liberal candidature in Colne Valley, but he was happy to receive the call. He was visited at Leeds in early 1956 by four notables from the Colne Valley Divisional Liberal Party – Wainwright later described them as representing the Yorkshire Liberal Federation – who included Denis Deakin from Holmfirth, Keith Haigh, the owner of Dobroyd mills, and Councillor A.G. Holland from Saddleworth, who invited him to apply to the Association for nomination as their parliamentary candidate.[57] Wainwright was familiar with the constituency, had already spoken there, but also undertook careful analysis of its electoral politics before taking up this invitation. Advised by Albert Ingham, the veteran Liberal Agent for the whole of Yorkshire, he calculated that because the Conservatives had never won the seat and there was an historic and continuing Liberal tradition in the community, the right candidate could win it for the Liberals. Wainwright himself later recalled:

> I took to Colne Valley straight away. As a student of history I had always been fascinated by the accounts of a former MP, Philip Snowden, and I was convinced the Liberals could win there.[58]

Wainwright's family recall the careful thought he put into the decision as to whether to seek the nomination, and his successor as Liberal candidate for the Colne Valley, Nigel Priestley, had a similar impression: 'I've never come across a more calculating decision than the one he made: when you talked to him about why he stood in Colne Valley, he'd thought this one really carefully through. He had spotted that obviously it hadn't had a Conservative ever.'[59]

Wainwright had decided that he could succeed where Violet Bonham Carter had so publicly failed.

At a meeting of the Colne Valley Liberal Association Executive in Huddersfield on 1 May 1956, eighteen committee members interviewed Wainwright, who came with Albert Ingham and Joyce. After the formalities, Wainwright was immediately and unanimously invited to be the candidate for Colne Valley;[60] he went away to consider the offer, and within the week a press release announcing his acceptance had been sent to thirteen local papers.[61] He told activists in the constituency: 'I'm not standing anywhere other than Colne Valley.'[62]

Wainwright immediately invested both effort and resources into his candidature. Within a year, he had secured the appointment of Edward Dunford as his full-time agent against some doubters, and set him up in an office in Byram Arcade in Huddersfield.[63] Dunford was to be a vital figure in Wainwright's struggles to win and keep Colne Valley: shrewd, tough and imaginative, he had known Wainwright since the War, and as well as being his Agent at Pudsey, he had served in the same capacity at East Hull in 1951, and became Editor of *The Liberal Agent* magazine in 1954.[64] It was to be the loss of Dunford nearly thirty years later which was to be a major cause of the decline of Liberalism in Colne Valley.

The Colne Valley Liberal Association produced a glossy twenty-six-page Annual Report, supported by advertising bought by seventeen businesses from throughout the constituency, and promoting Wainwright as the successor to a line of Liberal candidates, four of whom had won the seat in living memory. Association Chairman Councillor Holland set the tone in his introduction:

> It was the Liberal stock of Colne Valley that fought for the freedom to worship as they pleased, and who built their chapels on the hilltops when not allowed building space in the valleys. Those Liberals and their descendants have returned Liberal Members of Parliament from Colne Valley on many occasions.[65]

The brochure also reminded readers of the branches of the Association including the Women's Liberal Association and the Liberal Clubs, and of its continuing representation on local councils. It was clear that Wainwright was joining a surviving Liberal network such as did not exist in many seats, but he was determined to inject a more energetic campaigning style into it. In the middle of 1958, two years before the next election was due, Wainwright made seven appearances, including attending the Uppermill Youth Pageant and making a speech to the Slaithwaite Good Companions, within two months. Joyce meanwhile had become the President of the local Women's Liberal Association, and canvassing teams including helpers from the Saddleworth Young Liberals had been distributing contact cards in three of the constituency's five Urban Districts. A new village association had been established at Springhead, and four new branches were in the process of being formed. Two meetings were being arranged in the constituency, and a rally featuring the former Leader Clement Davies was to be held at Huddersfield Town Hall. New subscribers were even being enlisted to *Liberal News*, often the hardest duty of Associations.[66]

The Association was clearly stepping up its activities, and those who witnessed the impact of Wainwright's arrival as candidate such as Lise Newsom were struck by the new dynamism of activities such as Wainwright's regular coffee-morning meetings. He might hold several of these in a day, weekdays and weekends, to hear about local issues.[67] Wainwright himself attributed his election in 1966 to 'an unceasing programme of Liberal house-meetings, local conferences, and Council elections'.[68] When the seat was lost two decades later, he set out to the Association Chairman what had to be done to reverse the loss on the basis of his experience of 'the enormous size of the task of winning the seat of Colne Valley':

> To the actual Liberals, not more than two thousand, some nineteen thousand other voters have to be added, in very keen competition. This means years of ceaseless activity, collecting support by meeting with groups of voters every-where, tackling problems both personal and local, keeping to the front in the media by making news, working closely with all Liberal Councillors, and trying to ensure that the Liberal Party nationally give all possible help to Colne Valley.[69]

Wainwright's personal charm was an important part of this, too. Few descriptions of his manner by those who worked with Wainwright go far before using the terms 'gentleman' and 'integrity', and most then go on to praise his calm, dignified demeanour, his impish sense of humour, his articu-lacy and his thoughtfulness. Saddleworth Councillor Derek Heffernan saw Wainwright disarm the Tory ladies of Greenfield; Councillors Barry Fearnley, Robert Iredale and Gordon Beever were enthused by him as young men at the 1963 by-election.[70] Dorothy Shaw, who first met Wainwright in 1972, sets out his qualities with particular clarity:

> Meeting Richard was for me quite an inspiration. He was what a politician and a human being should be. Richard was a man of stature, not just physically – he held his head high – he was a man of stature in his character, who practised what he preached. He was regarded with the highest respect, but he treated everybody with the highest respect. Young, old, party members, the opposition, the unde-clared. In fact he gained a lot of votes from Labour and Conservatives and the undecided because of his honesty and integrity; he had a very strong personal appeal.[71]

Lord Rennard travelled from Liverpool to help campaign in Colne Valley as a teenager before going on to be the Liberal Democrats' Campaign Director, and recalls the motivational impact of Wainwright's 'assiduous cultivation of people: a warm handshake and a friendly voice. I remember Richard speaking to another candidate who was famously impatient, and who would meet an old lady and hand over two hundred leaflets and say "can you get these done by Thursday?" and rush off. Richard would say, "No, no, no: you've got to stay and ask how her sister is, because she isn't out of hospital yet, and say 'Thank you so much for what you've done, and if you could possibly manage to do these things it would be wonderful if you could have them done by Thursday'".[72]

Colne Valley would not be won by charm alone, however, and Wainwright was capable when occasion required it of using forthright, mischievous, aggressive and even personal tactics to undermine his opponents. His secretary and co-campaigner Joanna Hannam regarded Wainwright's methods as 'tough' without being 'dirty'; he would 'give each part of the constituency what it wanted to hear'.[73] David Clark, who won Colne Valley from Wainwright, suffered this, being accused by Wainwright of becoming less Socialist and more Liberal as he travelled up from Westminster to Yorkshire. Eric Flounders helped Wainwright devise a campaign associating Clark with the far Left: Flounders attended the 1973 Labour Conference to gather ammunition: 'David Clark addressed a meeting which was on the nationalisation of housing stock. He actually spoke against that, but of course we took quite a delight in putting out a leaflet saying that Clark had been to this meeting about the nationalisation of housing, which went down like a lead balloon in Colne Valley.' Wainwright's view was that 'even though we were really being unfair, he thought it was all part of the game'.[74]

Clark himself accuses Wainwright of having given a different impression of Liberal policy to some constituents than to others on matters such as the 1974 miners' strike – depending upon whether he was addressing the remaining pit villages in the east of the constituency or the affluent suburbs of Manchester in the west – but expresses a sneaking admiration: 'he wasn't just this benign, gentle man; he was a very clever, calculating politician who in a sense probably used 'spin' twenty years before anyone else used it. I say it as a compliment'.[75]

The circumstances of Wainwright's contests called for a certain amount of realism: starting in third place, always fighting a marginal seat and with a hugely varied population, shrewd expression and a thick skin would be basic qualifications. Most testing of all would be the intense tactical nature of the battle: Wainwright would have to convince Conservatives that he could win and was worthy of their vote, without losing the loyal, radical Liberals who had deserted Violet Bonham Carter, or weakening his appeal to doubtful Labour supporters. His opponents on both sides, of course, would paint Wainwright as an irrelevance indistinguishable from their 'main' opponents. Tactical voting, Wainwright told a national newspaper at his last election campaign, was 'local sport and recreation' in Colne Valley.[76] The survey of his campaigns below shows that his success rested upon much more than this, however – it needed his supporters, his Party nationally and his own appeal to turn failure into victory.

Notes

1 Such references are often confined to the obligatory subjects of candidate selection and General Election results. Conservative minister Jim Prior mentioned Waveney only twice in *A Balance of Power*; other than to record election victories, his colleague Norman Tebbit gave the same attention to Chingford in *Upwardly Mobile*; Gordon Brown's constituency is referred to five times outside of General Elections by Paul Routledge; and Barbara Castle represented Blackburn for thirty-four years but the town is mentioned only twice for any purpose in her *Fighting All the Way*, and three times by her biographer Lisa Martineau in *Power and Politics*.

2 Hughes, T. (with Fay Godwin), *Remains of Elmet* (London: Faber and Faber 1979), p. 8. The powerful poems and photographs in the book focus on specific locations in the Calder Valley just outside Wainwright's constituency, but Hughes makes this general opening tribute to Elmet, which stretched as far south as Sheffield.

3 Hansard, 14 July 1983. The MP was Spencer Batiste.

4 Defoe, D., *A Tour Through the Whole Island of Great Britain* originally 1724–26 (Ed. Pat Rogers, London: Promotional Reprint 1989), pp. 174–77. Defoe was referring specifically to the eight-mile journey from Blackstone Edge to Halifax, but the activity he describes was evident throughout the West Riding.

5 Perhaps because he thought the image of Colne Valley it projected condescending, Wainwright confided to his secretary (Joanna Hannam, interview, 19 January 2009) that he intensely disliked the TV series.

6 The present author declares an interest here, having been raised in the Pennines twenty miles from the Colne Valley at the time Wainwright was its MP. He nonetheless defies others who have visited Colne Valley to gainsay the claims made here.

7 Joyce Wainwright, interview, 22 February 2008.

8 David Alton, interview, 3 June 2008.

9 Andrew Alexander, interview, 13 March 2009.

10 Nigel Priestley, interview, 30 October 2008.

11 Viscount Snowden, Introduction to Lockwood, E., *Colne Valley Folk*, (London: Heath Cranton 1936), p. 5.

12 Pottle, M. (ed.), *Daring to Hope, The Diaries and Letters of Violet Bonham Carter 1946–69* (London: Weidenfeld & Nicolson 2000), p. 97.

13 *Huddersfield Daily Examiner*, 30 November 1968. Wainwright was speaking at the adoption meeting of Derek Mirfin as Liberal Prospective Parliamentary Candidate for Penistone.

14 *Oldham Evening Chronicle*, 1 March 1974, p. 1.

15 Wainwright, R., *Liberal News*, 1 June 1976. The term, roughly meaning 'arse end first', was used to illustrate the irony of the Layfield Report on local Government being published after the report of the Government's Commission on regional government.

16 Josephs, J., *Inside the Alliance* (London: John Martin 1983), p. 97, where Wainwright's phrase is quoted. Jeremy Josephs had been Steel's assistant since 1981.

17 Hansard, 1 July 1985.

18 Lord Smith, interview, 22 June 2009.

19 Sir Alan Beith, interview, 13 October 2008.

20 Caroline Cawston, interview, 2 June 2008.

21 Chris Greenfield, interview, 1 December 2007.

22 Councillor Robert Iredale, interview, 16 April 2009.

23 Clark, D., *Colne Valley: Radicalism to Socialism* (London: Longman 1981), p. 179.

24 Crewe, I. and Fox, A., *British Parliamentary Constituencies: A Statistical Compendium* (London: Faber and Faber 1984), p. 106. The entry for Colne Valley shows that it was 81st of 650 constituencies for the proportion of its population employed in manufacturing industry, which was 49 per cent.

25 David Whitwam, interview, 15 April 2009.

26 David Ridgway, interview, 31 October 2008.

27 Nigel Priestley, interview, 30 October 2008.

28 Lord Alton, interview, 3 June 2008.

29 Joanna Hannam, interview, 19 January 2009.

30 Tony Greaves, interview, 8 April 2009.

31 Christine Wheeler, interview, 16 April 2009.

32 Lord Smith, interview, 22 June 2009.

33 Lord Wallace, interview, 19 January 2009.

34 *Colne Valley Guardian*, undated, presumed 1963.

35 Gordon Ellis, interview, 15 April 2009.

36 Waller, R., *The Almanac of British Politics* (Beckenham: Croom Helm 1983), p. 187.

37 Clark, *Colne Valley*, p. 178.

38 Colne Valley Labour Party Annual Report, 1951, p. 7.

39 Cited in Pottle, *Daring to Hope*, p. 104.

40 Colne Valley Divisional Liberal Association Executive meeting minutes, 17 September 1952.

41 Colne Valley Divisional Liberal Association Hon. Secretary's Report 1951–52, 29 October 1952.

42 Colne Valley Divisional Liberal Association Executive meeting, 4 March 1953.

43 A.D. Nichols, 'Liberal Assembly – Ilfracombe April 9th–11th 1953', Report to Colne Valley Divisional Liberal Association, p. 2. The Report was presented on 6 May.

44 *Wharfedale and Airedale Observer*, 10 February 1950.

45 Michael Meadowcroft, interview, 17 June 2008.

46 *Yorkshire Post*, November 1984.

47 T.H. Clarke, the Liberal candidate for Pudsey in 1945, had secured 16.4 per cent of the vote, whereas Wainwright, in a constituency with different boundaries, won 17.5 per cent. David and Gareth Butler's *British Political Facts 1900–94* (Basingstoke: Macmillan 1994), p. 216 shows that the average share of the vote for each Liberal candidate fell from 18.6 per cent to 11.8 per cent between these two elections.

48 *Pudsey and Stanningley News*, 26 January 1950.

49 *Wharfedale and Airedale Observer*, 27 January 1950.

50 *Yorkshire Observer*, 18 February 1950.

51 *Wharfedale and Airedale Observer*, 10 February 1950.

52 *Pudsey and Stanningley News*, 16 February 1950.

53 *Wharfedale and Airedale Observer*, 27 January 1950; *Pudsey and Stanningley News*, undated.

54 Lord Shutt, interview, 3 June 2008.

55 *Pudsey and Stanningley News*, 26 January 1950.

56 Ibid., 18 May 1950.

57 Gordon Beever, interview, 31 October 2008. Mr. Beever learned the details of the delegation from some of its members and their families.

58 'Amiable Face of Politics', *Yorkshire Post*, 5 November 1984.

59 Nigel Priestley, interview, 30 October 2008.

60 Colne Valley Divisional Liberal Association Executive minutes, 1 May 1956.

61 Yorkshire Liberal Federation press release, 7 May 1956.

62 Lise Newsome, interview, 17 April 2009.

63 Colne Valley Divisional Liberal Association Executive and Officers' minutes, 27 March 1957 and 17 May 1957 .

64 *The Liberal Agent*, 31 January 1952 p. 5; April 1954, p. 2.

65 A.G. Holland, Colne Valley Divisional Liberal Association Yearbook 1956, Introduction, Wainwright papers file 5/B/5.

66 Colne Valley Divisional Liberal Association Executive minutes, 30 July 1958. These activities had all taken place since the previous meeting on 4 June.

67 Lise Newsome and Robert Iredale, interviews, 17 and 16 April 2009.

68 *Liberal News*, 7 April 1966.

69 RSW to Robert Iredale, 10 July 1987, Wainwright papers file 5/B/16.

70 Cllrs Derek Heffernan, Barry Fearnley, Robert Iredale and Gordon Beever, interviews, 30 March 2009, 30 October 2008, 16 April 2009 and 31 October 2008.

71 Dorothy Shaw, interview, 16 April 2009 .

72 Lord Rennard, interview, 30 July 2009.

73 Joanna Hannam, interview, 19 January 2009.

74 Eric Flounders, interview, 18 May 2009.

75 Lord Clark, interview, 3 June 2008.

76 Smith, I., 'Rivals' Feud Fuels Brutal Fight', *The Times*, 9 June 1983

9 Campaigning

1959

Wainwright's 1959 election campaign took place in a context of a Conservative Government enjoying sustained popularity and a divided Labour Party. An appeal to doubting Conservatives to support Wainwright as the best means of beating a dangerous Labour movement was likely in these circumstances to fall on deaf ears. The Liberal task therefore was to establish a bridgehead and determine the core Liberal vote upon which Wainwright could build, making a positive case for Liberal principles, the effectiveness of the Party nationally and its substance locally. The preliminary nature of the campaign was indicated by Wainwright to his own Association when he told them that he thought they could 'clip a large lump off the Labour vote'.[1]

In this, Wainwright had gained a number of advantages since becoming candidate for Colne Valley: Jo Grimond's leadership since autumn 1956 had raised the profile of the Liberals nationally. The Liberals had enjoyed some impressive performances in by-elections in early 1958, notably the good second place at Rochdale, in which campaign Saddleworth Liberals had taken part and to which result Wainwright drew the Colne Valley Association's attention,[2] and the Liberal victory at Torrington – the Party's first by-election gain for thirty years, which boosted activists' morale as well as winning news coverage; and the growing representation of the Liberals in local government in Colne Valley: in May 1959, five seats were won on Saddleworth, and two in Colne Valley Urban District Councils.

Despite this, Wainwright was fully aware of the challenge ahead of him. Two months before the election was announced, he warned the Colne Valley Liberals of 'the need to start the election campaign with vigour at an early stage' because 'the Liberal Party would not have the benefit of the same Press and Television reporting as their opponents'. In the first week of the dissolution of Parliament, Wainwright addressed his adoption meeting at Slaithwaite on the 'silence barrier' maintained by the two main parties on everything from the H Bomb to strikes, pensions, prices, immigrant labour, the 11–plus and road accidents. His mentor Donald Wade, the MP for Huddersfield West, spoke in his support, predicting that 'the days of the Labour Party and the Socialist Party as a valuable contribution to social progress are nearing an end';[3] but a note of realism was struck, and the long-term nature of the Liberal task in Colne Valley was recognised, in Councillor Ernest Buckley's commitment that 'whatever the result of the General Election we are staying in business.'[4]

As well as Wade's visit, Wainwright recruited a clutch of Liberal notables to inspire supporters and add credibility to his bid for the seat. Recently retired Party Leader Clement Davies had addressed a rally organised by Colne Valley Liberals the previous October, Party President Sir Arthur Comyns Carr attended an 'At Home' at Linthwaite in May, and Lord Rea, Leader of the Liberal Peers, had accepted an invitation to speak at a dinner in September.[5] During the campaign Wainwright was supported at public meetings by familiar Yorkshire names including Philip Rowntree, Lord Airedale, the Editor of the *Huddersfield Daily Examiner* Elliott Dodds, and Councillor James Pickles, later to become a national figure as a controversial Circuit Judge.[6] Wainwright also had the acknowledgement, if not yet the support, of the local press, and the Colne Valley Liberals drew in activists from outside the constituency, from Liberal Associations in Wakefield, Barnsley and Halifax, and even a supporter who travelled from Monmouthshire to campaign in Scisset.

For all of this activity, Wainwright's campaign went largely unnoticed by his opponents. There is no evidence that the Colne Valley Labour Party gave any consideration to the likely impact of a Liberal candidate at their internal meetings, and in his election address the MP Glenvil Hall made no mention of the Liberals. The Conservative candidate satisfied himself with the observation that 'the Liberal Party acknowledge they cannot form a Government.'[7] Colne Valley was assumed by most involved in the election to be a safe Labour seat, and the *Colne Valley Guardian* even commended the candidates on their 'restraint and dignity'.[8]

This was not a mistake the two main parties were to make in future. As at Pudsey, Wainwright delivered a substantial Liberal vote from a position of disadvantage using existing strength on the ground and energetic, confident, persistent and highly organised campaigning. Whilst the vote shares of the parties nationally remained close to those of the previous election, the situation in Colne Valley changed dramatically. Wainwright secured over a quarter of the vote, Labour had one voter in ten less than before, and the Conservatives had lost more. Only in four of over a hundred seats which the Liberals fought in 1959 but not at the previous election was this achieved: one of these was nearby Rochdale, where the broadcaster Ludovic Kennedy who had contested the previous year's by-election stood again; a second was Skipton in West Yorkshire.[9] Wainwright's supporters were not, as they were often to be depicted by his critics, transitory protesting or tactical voters, but people who had chosen a Liberal candidate from scratch.

At the first Liberal meeting after the election, the Association Chairman 'spoke of the wholly admirable way in which Mr Wainwright had worked as the candidate, of Mrs Wainwright's support, the work of the Association officers and the election agent',[10] and the Association Executive immediately invited Wainwright to offer himself again as a candidate. He had no hesitation in accepting: stage one of his campaign plan – the establishment of a sizeable core Liberal vote – had been completed. He now needed an opportunity to prove beyond doubt that the Liberals were the main challengers to Labour in the Colne Valley.

1963

Wainwright's opportunity to overhaul the Tories took the form which propelled many Liberals into Parliament: the death of sitting Member Glenvil Hall caused a by-election in March 1963. During the time Wainwright was standing for Parliament, nearly half of the Liberals in the Commons first arrived there at a by-election: one had been spectacularly won by the Liberals in the previously safe Conservative seat of Orpington a year earlier. Other by-elections at Black-pool, Middlesbrough and Chippenham had seen impressive improvements in the Liberal vote, and there was some expectation that Wainwright might use this fillip to capitalise on his carefully cultivated political base in Colne Valley. The Liberal Party's national level of support was also higher than the last time Wainwright fought the Colne Valley: in the year prior to the 1959 General Election, Gallup polls showed Liberal support never exceeded 12.5 per cent of the public, and at the election itself was less than 6 per cent; in the twelve months to March 1963, the figure never fell below 13 per cent, and was in most polls over 20 per cent.[11]

This expectation was reinforced amongst Liberal leaders by a poll they commissioned in Colne Valley in January 1963. Conducted by NOP, the survey of 500 respondents found Wainwright clearly in second place, with 37 per cent support, whilst Labour retained 44 per cent and the Conservatives languished on 19 per cent. Once again, the poll revealed that the churning of votes in Colne Valley was more complex than the 'tactical' model allowed, concluding that 'the Liberals have gained considerable support from both the other parties, but that Labour has gained some support from former Conservatives and from those that did not vote in 1959.' The key message, however, was clear, as a Liberal press release the following month stressed: 'the Tory is completely out of the fight' and a 4 per cent swing would put Wainwright in.[12] This was, as the main study of the following year's General Election confirmed, 'objective support for their publicised claim that the Conservatives could not win, but that the Liberals could, given Conservative support'.[13] At the opening of the campaign, Wainwright attacked Conservative candidate Andrew Alexander for 'holding the towel' for Labour now that the Tories had no chance in the by-election.[14] The contest was now, as it had been historically in Colne Valley and would be for the next two decades, between Labour and the Liberals.

In private Conservatives already knew this. Their candidate, Andrew Alexander, a genial 27–year-old journalist with the *Yorkshire Post*, knew little of the constituency, and was cautioned by supporters that 'it had never had a Conservative MP, and by implication it was never likely to. I was also told by my colleagues on the *Yorkshire Post*: "This is a very rough constituency full of textile mills, and they'll give you a bad time".'[15] He won the nomination on the strength of his knowledge of Anglo-Japanese textile trade negotiations, about which he had recently written a leading article. In his election literature, no attempt was made to disguise the fact that Alexander was a native of Worthing and a former Chairman of Dorchester Young Conservatives, not the strongest assets of an urgent aspirant to the trust of Colne Valley.

Alexander also represented a tired and divided Government which had since the Liberal victory at Orpington abandoned its 'Pay Pause' policy, endured the 'Night of the Long Knives' in which Macmillan fired a third of his Cabinet, suffered rejection of its application to join the European Economic Community, and was just experiencing the first stirrings of the Profumo scandal. As if to symbolise this distance from public sentiment, the Conservative Party sent Gerald Nabarro to speak at Alexander's eve-of-poll meeting: Nabarro arrived in Yorkshire by train but had one of his four Daimlers with personalised registration plates – this one was NAB 4 – brought north to convey him to the event, at which he so dominated the platform that the local Tory Chairman had to interrupt to remind him 'this is Andrew Alexander's eve-of-poll meeting – not yours!'[16] Colne Valley Liberals sensed the weakness of the Conservative campaign, which they nicknamed 'Alexander's Ragtime Band'.[17]

Victory was not expected of Alexander: instead, he was told by Selwyn Lloyd, 'I really don't mind if you lose; I don't even mind if you lose your deposit, just so long as the Liberals don't win.' The importance of this was reinforced to Alexander on election night:

> When the polling day came and the count was on, I went to dinner with my Chairman who ran the paper mill in Greenfield, and he served me up champagne and a large cigar and various other delights. Then we made our way to the poll, which was already well underway, and I was greeted by the Area Agent, who'd been working in the constituency all the time. He said: 'I've got bad news for you: Wainwright's going to win and you've lost your deposit.' I said 'Oh, well, *c'est la vie*.' He was outraged by this, and reported to Central Office that I had a wholly frivolous attitude towards politics.[18]

The rear-guard nature of the Tory campaign was evident from Alexander's adoption meeting, where he warned that 'a Liberal success here is an even surer guarantee than a Labour success here that Mr Harold Wilson would be returned to No 10 Downing Street' and insisted that 'the Liberal Party now has little in common with the old Party whose name it bears.'[19] On his election address, Alexander drove home the same message, ringing alarm bells in Conservative ranks loud enough for the public to hear:

> There are two ways in which we could get a Socialist Government, either by a straight increase in the Socialist vote, or by a split in the non-Socialist vote by Liberal intervention. If Lady Bonham Carter couldn't win in 1951 with Conservative support, the 1963 brand of Liberalism has no chance at all. There is only one alternative to Socialism, and that is Conservatism.[20]

Wainwright's campaign to displace the ailing Tories was a national affair, drawing in resources from Liberal Headquarters and four hundred canvassers from Associations across the country. He established fifty-seven committee rooms in separate polling districts, addressed twenty-four public meetings in two weeks, and had the benefit of the company of Party Leader Jo Gimond for two days. A 'canvass in depth' visiting all 20,000 households in the constituency was undertaken, though never completed. Supporters came to help from Wakefield, Altrincham and Sale, Middleton and Prestwich, Stretford, Stockton-on-Tees, and further afield. On election night, Conservative candidate Andrew Alexander remembers telling Liberals in the crowd sarcastically that he sympathised with them 'because I know so many of you have come from every corner of the country in the mistaken belief that here was going to be a Liberal triumph over Labour'.[21]

The Labour Party particularly resented this influx of supporters to the campaign, and Barbara Castle refused to answer questions at public meetings until the constituency address of the questioner had been established to her satisfaction.[22] Labour candidate Pat Duffy crowed bitterly on election night that he had won despite Liberals coming in 'from all over the country'.[23] Other senior Labour figures were drafted into the Party's defence, including George Brown and former Liberal MP Megan Lloyd George, who accused her former Party of being Tory stooges, pointing to Donald Wade's pact – by then, in fact, defunct – with the Tories in Huddersfield: 'These are not the radical alternative to the Tory Party. These are Liberals who are working with them and who are receiving their support.'[24] Letters in the local press asked similarly of the Liberal comeback: 'why a "come-back"? Have they been lost, or is it because they conveniently forgot their way and became fellow travellers with the Tories?'[25]

Wainwright and his supporters gave quarter to neither of his opponents. He obtained an early copy of Duffy's election address, and mocked him as outdoing the Tories for 'studied vagueness' when referring to 'new and flexible forms of social ownership' rather than nationalisation, his opposition to which became a theme of Wainwright's campaign.[26] As for the new Labour Leader Harold Wilson, Wainwright observed only that he credited the satirical television show *That Was the Week That Was* with 'having his measure'.[27] The Tories were offended when Jeremy Thorpe suggested that a flag at half mast over Conservative committee rooms to mark a bereavement was portending their fate at the polls, and again when the daughter of a visiting Tory MP found her yellow mini daubed with the slogan 'Vote Liberal' in black paint. At Andrew Alexander's eve-of-poll meeting one critic challenged Gerald Nabarro and anyone else present to bet him a pound that Alexander would lose his deposit.[28] One of Wainwright's canvassers remembers that, on the ground, 'there was a lot of nastiness at the by-election'.[29]

Young Liberals climbed a gasometer and flew a banner bearing the slogan 'Vote, vote, vote for Mr Wainwright' from it. A further injection of colour came to the campaign in the appearances of the Independent candidate Arthur Fox, a Manchester striptease bar owner who used the by-election to publicise his objection to the constraints of entertainment laws, and was accompanied by his performers 'Fraulein von Manuela' and 'Baby Doll' at mill canteen meetings to help make his point. 'Despite the fact that there have been no great issues to get heated about', wrote the *Colne Valley Guardian*, 'the by-election has not been as quiet and gentlemanly as one would have liked.'[30]

This atmosphere lent itself to extravagance, and Liberals began to believe Wainwright's plan was coming to full fruition. Jeremy Thorpe predicted that 'our man is in with a good chance of a win' and Liberal press releases claimed their canvass returns showed Wainwright ahead of Labour.[31] The excitement was more naively reflected in a poem written by Janet Stahelin, the 11–year-old daughter of the Chairman of the Stockton Liberals, called 'Colne Thoughts from Stockton':

> Oh to be in Colne
> Now that Grimond's there,
> And whoever wakes in Colne
> Sees Liberals Everywhere!
> Through lowest dale and highest hill
> Round every house go the canvassers still,
> While speakers shout and banners blow
> For Wainwright now.

Letters reflecting this growing confidence poured into Wainwright's Headquarters from Liberals in Plympton, Smethwick, Bolton, Ilminster, Eastleigh, Kettering, Haltemprice and Beverley, Birkenhead, Chislehurst, Swansea, West Lothian, from the Political Committee of the National Liberal Club and from the National Union of Liberal Clubs. Liberals in Cheshire, Somerset and Norfolk dared to 'hope to see you in the House of Commons before many weeks have passed'; 'that you will be sent to Westminster with a substantial majority'; and urged that 'from what I read it sounds most hopeful'. A friend writing from Birmingham joked that 'now your figure resembles Kruschev's you must have added appeal to the progressive elements of the electorate'. To give the fullest possible temptation to fate, Pratap Chitnis, whom Wainwright had set up at Liberal Party Headquarters, sent a telegram in the last week of the campaign to say he was 'looking forward to Friday's Victory Party'.[32]

There was to be no victory party. Patrick Duffy held the seat for Labour by a margin of over two thousand votes, and told a turbulent crowd of five hundred supporters gathered in driving snow at two o'clock – it was Colne Valley's first night count – outside Slaithwaite Civic Hall, that Labour's vote had remained untouched. Wainwright pointed to the increase in the Liberal share of the vote from 25 per cent to 40 per cent and declared, 'we are advancing at a great speed indeed.' In a scene which reminded Andrew Alexander of the riotous contest depicted by Dickens at Eatanswill, Labour activists sang 'The Red Flag', Liberals chanted 'We won't have a Labour MP for long' and Independent candidate Arthur Fox, still accompanied by his strippers, congratulated Wainwright on winning the protest vote and said that this proved the voters of Colne Valley were 'a thinking people'.[33]

When the furore of election night had died down, the parties reflected upon their fortunes. The losing parties looked to temporary factors to explain their defeat, the Conservatives blaming the Government's unpopularity and organisational weaknesses. The Conservative Agents' journal pointed to their opponents' efficiency in harvesting postal votes, and declared 'this is a warning to all of us for the future.'[34] The two main parties both hoped that Wainwright would be unable to summon as many supporters to his campaign at a General Election, and Andrew Alexander seemed happy he had fulfilled his remit of taming the Liberals. He told a Conservative dinner early in 1964 that they had 'written off the so-called Liberal revival'.[35] National right-wing papers pressed home the same message: *The Times* warned that voting Liberal could prevent the defeat of Labour:

> The Liberals, in an attentively nursed constituency where the old liberalism still has roots, achieved their accustomed increase in their proportion of the poll, but did not quite break through and again failed to make any real dent in Labour's industrial vote.[36]

The *Daily Telegraph* mocked that 'this persisting Tory defection to the Liberals makes nonsense, of course, of the Liberal claim to be a Left-wing alternative to Labour.'[37] The local press too, though admiring, believed that Wainwright's window of opportunity had closed:

> In the case of Mr Wainwright, it was so near and yet so far. No candidate could have made a greater appeal to the unattached voter than Mr Wainwright, none could have rallied more enthusiastic support from his own followers. And yet he could not pull it off. The pundits in London and the national Press have written off Colne Valley as a safe Labour industrial seat, and even in the unlikely event

of the Conservatives standing down to allow a straight fight between Liberal and Labour, it is still doubtful if the Liberals could win.[38]

The Labour Party felt understandably sanguine – even complacent: Party General Secretary Len Williams said, 'The Liberal claim that this would be another Orpington has proved false again.'[39] After winning the Leeds South by-election three months after the Colne Valley contest, future Home Secretary Merlyn Rees observed that the Liberal vote in West Yorkshire had stubbornly remained in a poor third place. 'This is evidence of the "old" Liberalism' Rees reassured Labour activists, 'which has its roots in Leeds as in other parts of the North, which will have nothing to do with the "new Grimond Liberalism".'[40]

Grimond himself could hardly disguise his disappointment in his immediate response, saying only that 'this is a very satisfactory result in a Labour stronghold, which they have held for more than twenty years.'[41] *The Guardian* consoled Liberal sympathisers that 'the Colne Valley by-election result does not fully satisfy anyone's hopes; but it is much better for the Liberals than for anybody else.' Its editorial went on to refute suggestions that Wainwright had unscrupulously aped the Tories, but recognised the key role of his tactical appeal:

> The Liberal revival has been built on solid Liberal principles, not on watered-down Conservatism. Mr. Wainwright himself is the last man to lower his colours in order to conciliate opponents and lure them into his camp. He fought the election on a platform of unadulterated Liberalism, and voters came over to him from the Conservative camp because they had nowhere else to go.[42]

The Liberals saw that Wainwright had simply moved one step closer to victory. Like the Conservatives, they saw room for organisational improvements. Thorpe urged Wainwright to press on with squeezing the Conservative vote, and regretted that one survey had come too late to publicise the strength of the Liberals' position. He advised Wainwright to put up posters thanking voters, to be re-adopted at a mass meeting and to beef up his constituency organisation.[43] The Colne Valley Liberals immediately and unanimously invited Wainwright to seek re-adoption, and he responded by calling on his activists to arrange more public appearances in the constituency for him, and to stress that of every twenty voters at the by-election, nine had voted Labour, eight Liberal and only three Conservative. 'The gap between Labour and Liberal candidates', he asserted, 'was so narrow that it could perfectly well be bridged.'[44]

For most Liberal by-election candidates, the contest is their moment in the sun; even those who win usually lose at the next General Election. The favourable conditions of intense publicity, large numbers of campaigners and readiness of the public to deliver a protest vote to the Government, inflate liberal support in a way which is difficult to repeat. Some Liberals thought this of Wainwright's 1963 campaign, and told BBC reporters that they regarded the defeat at Colne Valley as 'the point at which the Orpington boom began to tail off.'[45] It is testimony to Wainwright's determination that he did not suffer this fate. The by-election was vital, but as a stepping stone rather than as an arrival point: the Conservatives were in third place and vulnerable. Wainwright knew he had to exploit this to the full at the coming General Election.

There was another significance to the by-election, internal to the Liberal Party. Although a national figure within the Party organisation, during the campaign Wainwright consolidated this recognition by the growing membership of the Party outside Yorkshire, and to a number of rising figures in its ranks. As well as good wishes from throughout the country, Wainwright inspired hundreds of visitors to the constituency. Amongst these were Tony, now Lord, Greaves, then an undergraduate from Wakefield, later a Young Liberal leader and founder of the Association of Liberal Councillors; Geoff Tordoff, also now a Peer, who went on to be a candidate in many seats throughout the country and was Party President in 1976, remembers giving a spontaneous public address from a Colne Valley street corner on the benefits of the proposed M62 motorway; and one of Wainwright's polling officers was the young Anthony Batchelor, later Chairman of Worcestershire County Council and candidate for Solihull. Wainwright did the Party the service of encouraging these activists; and he had done his own reputation with them no harm. This relationship was to be an important part of his career.

1964

The General Election of October 1964, being at the last available date, was anticipated by all sides, and relatively little had changed in national politics since the by-election. The Conservatives had a new Prime Minister, Alec Douglas Home, whose arrival in office had served to highlight the divided and anachronistic aspects of the Party's character. Jo Grimond remained popular as Liberal Leader, but the glow of Orpington had dimmed, and the Colne Valley Liberals had confided to themselves that the local election results of April 1964 were 'not encouraging': Liberal candidates came third in two, and second in one, of the constituency's County Council seats.[46] Labour remained ebullient, retaining a single-figure percentage point lead over the Conservatives in national polls all the way into the campaign.

In Colne Valley, however, one central issue of the campaign had been resolved by the by-election: Wainwright was the candidate who could beat Labour. The three parties were fielding the same three candidates as the previous year, and the *Colne Valley Guardian*, previously non-committal but critical of Labour, had noticed a change in the political environment and the response of the parties to it, before the local elections. 'Victory', it predicted, 'will go to the party which has made the best use of the period between the by-election and the general election':

With a Member of Parliament to rally round, Labour have obviously been able to do a valuable amount of digging in, but there is reason to doubt whether their efforts in this field have been any more successful than those of the Liberals – and indeed some would say that in the matter of breaking new ground and consolidating traditional support the Liberals have in many areas left them standing.

Of the Tories the *Colne Valley Guardian* was dismissive: 'Nothing has happened in the last year that suggests they will be in at the finish.' The Editorial concluded that 'the only party that can beat Labour are the Liberals. Labour knows it. The Liberals know it. And in the quiet places of their own hearts the Conservatives know it.'[47] The Liberal pre-election campaign in the summer built upon this: on a well-publicised visit to the Colne Valley in June, Frank Byers, Chairman of the Liberal Election Committee, stressed the Party's hostility to the 'conceited Caesars' of the Labour Party, and warned of the 'horrifying prospect' of 'Harold Wilson, George Brown, James Callaghan and Douglas Jay bringing the woolly-headedness of their amateurism to interfere in industry'.[48] Wainwright himself sought to exploit Tory vulnerability with a letter of appeal to known Conservatives: though insisting that 'I am a Liberal, and do not wish to disguise any differences you may have with Liberal policy', he pointed out that 'if this month's Election result over the whole country turns out to be as close as most people expect, then one less Socialist MP, and one more definitely anti-Socialist, may make a real difference.' Wainwright assured wavering Conservatives that he was 'completely opposed to socialism, and will always vote against any more nationalisation'.[49]

Wainwright's campaign was as energetic as ever: following Thorpe's advice of the previous year, his adoption meeting was attended by 150 followers; in the two days which followed it, 25,000 Liberal propaganda newspapers were delivered round the constituency. In a strategy foreshadowing the introduction of Liberal 'Focus' leaflets a decade later, these took the form of broadsheets for each village – the *Golcar Sun*, the *Denshaw and Delph Sun*, and so on – which drove home the slogans 'Only a thousand need to switch' and 'Labour's proportion of the Colne Valley vote was Labour's lowest for 24 years'. Wainwright also appeared in the Liberals' third television broadcast of the campaign, stressing his favoured theme of the need for 'MPs not tied to groups'.[50] As at the by-election, the Wainwright camp anticipated victory, and even issued souvenir cards with spaces to fill in showing the votes cast with Wainwright's name at the head of the poll. 'By polling day', wrote his Agent, 'we were all very confident that victory was in sight.'[51]

The Labour Party now recognised the threat Wainwright posed, but maintained its contemptuous tone. Pat Duffy, the winner of the by-election, sneered that Grimond's strategy of replacing Labour as the progressive party was in ruins because it was the Tories who were at bay: 'Where does Mr. Wainwright stand now Tory hopes are "shattered"?' he challenged in March. 'Now is the time for all Liberals to join Labour in one final heave to put an end to this fumbling government.'[52] In his Election Address in October Duffy developed this tactical appeal to progressive voters:

> First of all, we must get rid of this Tory Government. We shall not do that by voting Liberal. A Liberal vote is a wasted vote. You can afford to vote Liberal at a by-election, but not at a General Election. Not if you want to change this Tory Government. Not if you want to get Britain on the move again. You can only do that if you vote for LABOUR.[53]

In the end, Duffy clung on by the agonisingly narrow margin of 187 votes. 'It was only as the last bundles of votes came in from the counting tables and were lined up in their thousands that we knew Richard Wainwright had failed', wrote his Agent.[54] Instant analysis from the BBC's election analyst David Butler assumed that tactical squeezing of the Conservative vote had produced this, saying 'Conservatives there must have come to the Liberals compared to the by-election';[55] at the count, Duffy similarly reassured Labour supporters worried by the Liberal challenge that 'it is unlikely that it will be as pointed again. I do not expect we shall see such a low Tory vote at the next election.'[56]

Butler and Duffy were both wrong, because Andrew Alexander had won nearly a thousand more votes, and a larger share of the vote, than at the previous year's by-election. It was – in net terms at least – from Labour that Wainwright had taken his additional 2.1 per cent share of the vote, with Duffy's dropping by 2.3 per cent whilst Labour nationally rose to power. The Conservatives had in fact very effectively resisted Wainwright's attempts to squeeze their vote.

Commentators once again recognised Wainwright's personal appeal, 'probably the most notable' of any non-frontbench candidate according to Butler's study of the election.[57] The Women Liberals of Colne Valley noted that 'we had one of the finest candidates in any party in the country, and the result of the election showed how more and more people recognised his sincerity and worth', and the Colne Valley Liberal Executive immediately recommended the Association to invite Wainwright to be re-adopted as their candidate.[58] 'This is', David Butler acknowledged on the BBC, 'the nearest the Liberals have come to winning a Labour seat' and 'must encourage Liberals elsewhere', and one of his fellow presenters added that 'in some respects this is almost the most encouraging thing that's happened to the Liberals tonight.'[59]

With the Labour Government resting on a Commons majority of only four seats, an early return to the polls seemed inevitable, and Colne Valley Liberals were convinced that their frustration could be ended by one last push. Edward Dunford attributed their greater success to improved organisation, and their narrow failure to occasional 'organisational weaknesses',[60] with Liberal committees established in 'practically every ward'[61] of the constituency, though 'a number of key workers had been unable to function on account of illness and other causes'.[62] The Women's Liberal Association report on the campaign blamed changes in the system of checking canvass returns which left cars unused in the last hour before polls closed, pointed to the need to 'rally round the new voters who have not made up their minds' and believed that 'if we had been able to get around to the people who were out on our first visit and seen them later we could have won.'[63] The hunger of the Colne Valley Liberals for victory seemed only to have been sharpened by its tantalising proximity.

At first Wainwright too seemed ready to renew battle, declaring to the crowd at the count that 'no political observers will now be able to describe the Colne Valley as a Labour area, for Labour is in a minority of seven thousand.'[64] But as the dust of the campaign settled, he suffered an uncharacteristic attack of uncertainty. Even before the Colne Valley Liberal Executive had invited him to be re-adopted, Wainwright had written to their Chairman to express his doubts. The lesson of the 1964 contest, he argued, had been that more activists would be needed just to win, and that winning would make holding the seat more difficult.

> To leave my daily business responsibilities (having no relatives to take them over), in order to sit in Parliament for a brief period, has no attraction to a man in his forties, and still less to his wife and family! If the extra few votes had gone our way last month, a Labour candidate would now be free to work in the constituency night after night, whilst I should be tied up in Parliament quite unable to do the organising and propaganda which I have enjoyed doing with you all during the last eight years, which has been literally almost a daily job in one way or another.

Wainwright dismissed widespread myths that seats once won could more easily be held on a personal vote, pointing to Mark Bonham Carter's loss of Torrington in 1959 and E.L. Mallalieu's loss of Colne Valley in 1931. He argued that those who did cultivate personal votes found their constituencies were lost when they retired. 'By contrast, you will have noticed, as I have done, that the lively and outspoken challenge of MPs like Grimond and Thorpe is largely due to the fact that they are part of a really wide and active Liberal movement in all parts of their constituency.' Wainwright emphasised that if he was to consider standing again 'we need a lot more new people who will be equally active' to the current supporters. 'The question is whether your full Executive has real confidence that in each of twenty-seven places we can quickly widen our active support', cautioned Wainwright: 'it only needs one or two wards to fail, for the whole of the rest of the effort to be lost.'[65]

Wainwright discussed these misgivings about his parliamentary prospects with David Shutt, his Pudsey protégé who had followed him into accountancy in Leeds, at Lady Wade's Dance between Christmas and New Year.[66] Just as Wainwright was on the brink of achieving the goal he had set himself after the War nearly twenty years earlier, he faltered, fearing the challenge of being the sort of MP he wanted to be might be even harder than becoming an MP in the first place.

1966

It was February 1965 before Wainwright made his decision to fight Colne Valley again public. At the Annual General Meeting of the Liberal Association there, he thanked members for their invitation to seek re-adoption before delivering a rousing call-to-arms. The next election, he predicted, would be soon, and should be seen as a national opportunity for the Liberal Party. He launched a fierce attack on both major parties and their record since the General Election:

> The neck-and-neck Party position, aggravated by divisions and contests within the two larger parties, is the enemy of firm government. With the maximum uproar and humbug, the country travels to nowhere over a carpet of soft options. If we now have a government at all, it is either government by gesture or government by Gallup. A new appeal to the country could substantially improve Parliament by installing a force of Liberal MPs large enough to command some Parliamentary time. Policies could then be deployed which were aimed at something more important to the country than the handfuls of marginal voters and party rebels who between them monopolised the concern of the larger parties.[67]

Wainwright's focus on the parliamentary scene conveyed his determination to win, and further encouragement came in March when David Steel won his seat at Roxburgh, Selkirk and Peebles in a by-election. Colne Valley Liberals received with enthusiasm advice from Jo Grimond on how to 'cash in on' the result locally.[68] May saw a District Council seat in Saddleworth retrieved by the Liberals, and another at Slaithwaite was gained for the first time in June.[69] Whilst the Labour Government struggled to survive parliamentary divisions on its paper-thin majority, its Conservative opponents experienced their first open leadership contest and emerged with the lacklustre Edward Heath at their helm.

Conditions were thus favourable for Wainwright as he sought to persuade an extra few hundred Conservatives to help him remove a Labour MP whilst recruiting any former Labour voters unimpressed by the Government. The colossal efforts of his previous three contests would have to be repeated by Wainwright's team, but the additional distance to be travelled now looked by comparison like the electoral equivalent of a golfer's tap-in. Wainwright assured his adoption meeting that victory was within their grasp 'if we get all our supporters out on the day'. In another sweeping analysis of modern British life, he condemned the 'suffocation of individual personality of people and families, underneath a blanket of regulations, fussy administration and Government interference'.

> We are being made into a nation of teachers' pets in which the keynote is obedience and conformity, instead of gumption and initiative. Millions of us carry out imposed routines which we cannot justify to our own intelligence or conscience. In business, words such as 'ethical' are stood on their heads to denote restrictive practices, for which the real word should be 'corrupt'.

In language which was as sincerely Liberal as it was also apt to attract the soft Conservative and the small business owner, he concluded: 'Twenty years of cosiness instead of enterprise, feather-bedding instead of risk-taking, have in some cases destroyed even the memory and the standards of really competitive efficiency.'[70]

The Conservatives themselves in Colne Valley had been demoralised by two bad third places in consecutive years, and by 1966 had become strategically rudderless. Their new candidate David Hall sound simultaneously unrealistic and apologetic, making an ambitious tactical appeal to Liberals to 'leave it to the Tories to fight Socialism',[71] but issuing an Election Address almost disowning his Party:

> Did you vote Liberal last time? I have discussed the reason they did with many people in Colne Valley. They all believed in the broad Conservative principles of private enterprise, freedom and a generous provision for those who meet with bad luck ... but they didn't fully approve of the way the last Conservative Government went about it. I hope you will come and join us now.

'The only alternative', insisted Hall, 'is more Socialism.'[72] Labour's Pat Duffy agreed, but stressed that it was in reality the Labour Party which was the best vehicle for Liberal ideas:

> If you voted Liberal last time, do you not think that the greatest need of this election is to produce a strong government with a clear majority, of whatever complexion? *Why risk another stalemate?* A Liberal vote cannot fulfil the Liberal programme, but a Labour vote can. Just check the last Liberal election address in this constituency. Nine-tenths of it dealt with already by Labour.

Duffy's tone, like Hall's, reflected increasing anxiety, but the Labour candidate's reaction was to lecture rather than beg: 'it is time', he warned voters, 'to put a stop to "make-believe" politics, and start being practical.'[73]

In the context of this intense three-way tactical battle, it is no surprise that when Jo Grimond came to support Wainwright, he chose as the theme for his speech at Uppermill 'A Liberal vote is not a wasted vote'. Two days later Wainwright enjoyed the benefit of giving a party political broadcast on the radio, judged to have been 'a skilful and well-delivered appeal',[74] which returned to his familiar campaign theme of the outsider under the title 'Don't be taken for Granted':[75]

> Every time the bus and rail fares go up, they are taking you for granted. On election day, you can say very firmly to the two political machines which the country has tried in turn that whichever of them forms the Government they're not going to be allowed to take you and your neighbourhood for granted.[76]

Housing was one of the substantial policy issues of the campaign, and Wainwright steered his appeal carefully towards the preponderant home-owners of

Colne Valley, stressing the need for improvements of existing properties rather than the 'regimented removal of families into a New Town' proposed by Duffy at Denby Dale.[77]

The Conservative vote collapsed to Wainwright's net benefit, and Colne Valley became the sole Labour loss of the election. Duffy's vote actually rose by a percentage point, but this could not compensate for the seven-point rise in Wainwright's vote made possible by the halving of the Conservative share of the poll. David Hall became the first Tory candidate to lose his deposit in the Colne Valley. The result came in just as Harold Wilson was being interviewed at the Adelphi Hotel in Liverpool shortly after two o'clock in the morning. The BBC's northern correspondent called it 'the other Liberal cliff-hanger' after news of Michael Winstanley's win at Cheadle came through, and said northern Liberals would be 'cock a hoop' over the two results. David Butler's immediate comment from the studio rightly identified the tactical nature of the change: 'The Conservative loses his deposit, and plainly the Conservatives decide they'd rather have a Liberal than a Labour Member in.'[78]

The outcome shocked Duffy, who had been listed as a 'probable' victor in national elections predictions.[79] His reaction at the count was bitter accusation, painting a picture of conspiracy between Wainwright and the Conservatives, talking of an 'unofficial Lib-Tory pact' and, pointing angrily at Wainwright's ballot papers, he said: 'this vote doesn't represent 22,000 Liberal voters in this constituency, but', pointing to his own ballot papers, 'that vote does represent nineteen-and-a-half-thousand Labour voters.' As Wainwright stepped out of the Town Hall to address the crowd, a young woman ran up and struck him over the head with an umbrella;[80] when he promised to represent all voters in the constituency there were cries from Labour supporters of 'not forgetting the Tories'.[81] Local Tories later added to this, suggesting that Wainwright should wear a green rosette to acknowledge the mixed nature of his support, and characterising him as 'the little canary with a blue tail'.[82]

Duffy told a local Labour Party meeting later that 'it was neither a victory for Liberalism nor liberalism. It was simply the result of a contrived collusion between the Liberals and individual Tory voters at the end of a campaign in which the most illiberal practices had been employed by some Liberal workers.' Labour, he said, was not the only casualty, so was morality. Even the snow which followed the poll was 'a silent rebuke' to Tory deserters. Labour workers 'had campaigned under their own colours' and the Party was stronger for the defeat.[83]

This was a poor case of sour grapes. There was no evidence of 'rolling over' by the Tory candidate, and Duffy's successor David Clark confirms that he saw no evidence of collusion between the Tories and Liberals.[84] The Conservatives nationally and locally had made mistakes which weakened their appeal, but Wainwright could hardly be blamed for this. Wainwright had made candid tactical appeals to Conservative sympathisers, but so had the other two candidates to Wainwright's supporters, and Wainwright could at least say – unlike the Conservatives – that his claims of being able to win the seat were plausible, and – unlike either of his opponents – he had the decency to argue for the abolition of the electoral system which caused such game-playing. Lastly the characterisation of Wainwright as a Tory puppet ignored the fact that in 1959 and 1964 Wainwright had built part of his success on former Labour supporters' votes. The tactical Tory votes were the icing on the electoral cake. Wainwright was to win the seat in the future at polls where the Tory vote grew.

Wainwright himself acknowledged that 'Colne Valley Conservatives do not have the social setting which sparks off Tory effort', but gave an account of his victory which mostly stressed the distinctive features of the constituency and the positive features of his long-term campaign, giving particular priority to the role of Liberal councillors in building up trust:

> The Yorkshire method is to test a case by reference to some detail on which the enquirer is expert. If Liberals make good councillors, and the parliamentary candidate masters some local issue, the inference is drawn that the rest of Liberal policy is likely to be sound. These seem to me the main factors, together with a fine agent and plenty of luck, which made for victory. They are not unique to Colne Valley, or even to the Pennine Country.[85]

This was largely true, and explained most of Wainwright's support. The Tory icing on the cake, however, was an important part of the recipe, and would prove to leave Wainwright unsatisfied when it went missing four years later.

1970

Wainwright's campaign to retain his seat in 1970 followed much the same pattern as his successful one of 1966. On the day before Wainwright's adoption meeting, Party Leader Jeremy Thorpe visited Colne Valley to give his support; the adoption meeting took place at Slaithwaite Civic Hall. The local press at both ends of the constituency stressed the value of independent-minded Liberal Members of Parliament, and Wainwright emphasised his commitment to pensioners, public servants and those on low wages. By the end of the campaign, however, Wainwright's tone already suggested he felt events were slipping away from him:

> Only the Liberals have shown that they care for the ordinary people in the middle, those who are not represented either by big business tycoons or trade union bosses. Liberals fought the sweat shops fifty years ago. Their job now is to take up the cudgels on behalf of those who are rapidly falling behind in the rat race. The election campaign has already descended to vulgarity. Egg-throwing hecklers follow closely on mud-slinging political leaders.[86]

As Wainwright had anticipated, keeping a seat was harder than winning it, and his duties in London and his commitments supporting the adoptions and election campaigns of other Liberals ate into his time in the Colne Valley. Lise Newsome, who had supported Wainwright since his arrival in Colne Valley, remembers that 'he had been busy getting into the ins and outs of it. Some people accused him of having forgotten them.'[87]

Moreover, the Labour Party had made Colne Valley a priority because it was one of the fifty seats most vulnerable to them, but mostly because it had been their only loss at the previous election. Harold Wilson visited Colne Valley High School in January 1970,[88] and gave new Labour candidate David Clark an especially warm message of support at the election as the aspirant to the constituency of the Prime Minister's birth.

Wainwright's problem, however, was not Labour, whose vote dropped by over 3 per cent after six years in office; it was the recovery of the Conservative vote, losing Wainwright the tactical advantage which had won him the seat in 1966. The Tory candidate, Councillor Ken Davy – a descendant of the inventor of the mining lamp – secured over a fifth of the vote and nearly trebled the support secured by his predecessor in 1966. Davy observed pointedly of the result that 'it is significant that neither the Labour nor the Liberal vote has increased, but ours certainly has. There is a tremendous anti-Socialist vote in this constituency.'[89]

The result shocked the Wainwright camp. One Wainwright supporter remembers asking at the time: 'Ten thousand Tories? Where did they get ten thousand Tories from? I drank more than a few beers that night!'[90] Both Liberals and Labour knew the outcome rested upon the short-term circumstances of Edward Heath's success and might easily be reversed, particularly with the Conservatives now in office. The Colne Valley Labour Party recognised in private that 'much remained to be done before we could be satisfied that our organisation was satisfactory', though David Clark reassured them that 'he felt sure that now the seat had been won back we could hold on to it in any future election providing we took full advantage of the present situation to build up and improve our organisation.'[91]

Wainwright was thanked and immediately invited to be re-adopted as candidate by the Colne Valley Liberals.[92] He instigated an immediate programme of public campaigning to restore Liberal support, though he told the local Executive disconsolately that 'he shared the views of Mr Grimond and Mr Steel that the sweat and toil which used to go into party politics was now going into Shelter, the Samaritans and similar organisations.'[93] In an address to the Colne Valley Women Liberals, however, he was more specific about the weaknesses of his position on two key issues: crime and immigration.

Law and order was an issue with a painful resonance in Colne Valley, which included Saddleworth Moor where the Moors Murders had taken place earlier in the decade. The restoration of the death penalty was described in a *Times* profile of the Colne Valley as 'an issue none of the candidates likes very much', though Conservative David Hall argued that abolition had been premature and that some form of corporal punishment should be retained.[94] Wainwright was opposed as a matter of principle to the use of capital punishment, whereas Tory candidates Ken Davy (1970 and 1974) and Graham Riddick (1987–97) specifically called for its return, and Stephen Kaye (1979) argued that 'the liberal do-good brigade has had its say over the past years and has failed, and failed miserably'.[95] Riddick's demand for the return of the death penalty met with an angry riposte from Wainwright, who insisted that he understood the opinions of the Colne Valley public better than Riddick. In the intense atmosphere following the Birmingham pub bombings of 1974, Wainwright acknowledged that 'naturally there is in some quarters a feeling that capital punishment ought to be restored', but added that 'people with longer memories are aware that the IRA dote on martyrs, and one thing we must be very careful not to do is to create cardboard martyrs for the IRA so that they can fan the flames back in Ireland'.[96]

Wainwright told the Colne Valley Women Liberals after the 1970 defeat that crime was growing because 'many police forces are understaffed and this often means that there cannot be a full patrol and adequate reserves for emergencies therefore at present *crime does pay*. The shortage is made worse by the fact that trained police officers spend only 28% of their time solving crimes. The rest is taken up with clerical and traffic duties.'[97]

On immigration, the Liberal Party had held a distinctive and united view opposed to any new controls on entry into the country, and was particularly concerned about the potential for measures such as the Commonwealth Immigrants Act of 1968, hammered through Parliament in three days to curtail the influx of Kenyan Asians, to discriminate racially and to give encouragement to the views being expressed by Enoch Powell and others on the Right. Colne Valley had a far smaller black and Asian population than some other West Yorkshire seats, but race was nonetheless a highly sensitive topic. Again the Conservatives tried to exploit the issue, Davy declaring, 'I deplore the Liberal Party's opposition to any form of immigration control.'[98] Wainwright had been clear in his opposition to the 1968 Act, and once again dismissed the issue after the 1970 defeat as a red herring, saying, 'the three main parties hold the same basic views and at present control is very strict and in 1968/69 more West Indians left here for Canada than came to this country.'[99] He took the immigration issue into his personal life, referring in 1968 to a Kenyan Asian accountant articled in his office at Leeds and in 1972 taking a family of Ugandan Asian refugees, Yusuf and Sara Majothi and their three children, in to stay at The Heath, allowing him to answer constituents who asked how he would like to have Asians living near him that he had them in his home.[100]

Some of Wainwright's most loyal supporters became aware that immigration was an area of vulnerability for him, and were prepared to step in and modify or even contradict his position when hostility on the doorstep became intense. Barry Fearnley remembers that Wainwright came to make active use of this strategy:

> At the time there was a big feeling against immigration, and Richard was all for it. At that time that was creating a few ripples. To be fair, he left us to answer our own questions at the door. It was left to me, as I remember, on immigration. Richard said: 'Pop down there and chat to them and see what you have to say about it', because we didn't always see eye to eye on that, I'm not ashamed of saying it. I'd go and have a chat and say I would usually think Richard's right, but this is my view, and they voted for him.[101]

This was, Fearnley adds, merely proof of 'freedom of speech within the Party'; but it was a freedom Wainwright's supporters did not usually have to avail themselves of, and it now proved vital to maintaining his relationship with certain of his constituents.

Wainwright remembered later that 'I found it indispensable to be able to prepare very actively for the next General Election as soon as each Election was over.'[102] Robert Iredale, then a Young Liberal, remembers: 'Within a couple of days we had a clarion call – lick your wounds, take soundings from the great and the good, learn any lessons you've got to learn and come back fighting.'[103] In organising his campaign, Wainwright was going to rely again on the stamina and the shrewdness of his Party machine. The main cause of Wainwright's defeat, however, had been the national trend of rising Conservative support, and seven Liberal seats – more than half the total – were lost at the 1970 election, with three of the remaining six held by a combined margin of just over 1,500 votes.[104] The Conservatives' fortunes would go into steep decline over the next four years without any assistance from Wainwright; but he had to be ready and able to take advantage of it to retrieve his seat, something no Liberal MP had managed to do since the War.

1974

February 1974 was to be the month of Wainwright's greatest electoral triumph and his deepest personal tragedy. It was the month in which he became the only Liberal MP since the Second World War to retrieve a seat he had lost, and the campaign to achieve this began formally at his adoption meeting at Slaithwaite Civic Hall, on Saturday 9th, where he told sixty-six leading Colne Valley Liberals that the public were 'fed up to the teeth' with the two main parties.[105] Wainwright was unanimously adopted by the meeting with a resolution 'to secure a resounding victory' after which there was a tribute to Wainwright's contribution to Liberalism in the Commons from 1966 to 1970 from

Party President-elect and former MP for Bolton, Arthur Holt.[106] The week which followed, however, began with a harrowing experience which would mark Wainwright for the rest of his life.

Wainwright spent the weekend at The Heath in Leeds, where his son Andrew was staying after attending the adoption meeting. Andrew was twenty-two, a Politics student at Newcastle University, but his last two years had been difficult and disjointed. After Winchester College, he had gone up to Balliol College, Oxford to study Politics, Philosophy and Economics in 1971. Before going to Oxford, Andrew spent six months in Southern Rhodesia supporting farm projects and developing an abiding hostility to the country's racist regime. After a year at Oxford in which he threw himself into campaigning for Third World and Anti-Apartheid causes he transferred to Newcastle, where he continued to campaign 'to the detriment of his academic studies', as friends later acknowledged.[107] Andrew had an idealistic outlook, and deeply held convictions about human rights of which his father must have been proud. He was described by his uncle and Godfather, the Rev. Tim Hollis, as 'a kind of universal brother. Your age didn't count; nor your race; nor your religion. He was a kind of freedom fighter of gentleness and peace against all that divides us from each other.'[108]

In April 1973, however, Andrew suffered depression and underwent treatment. In October of that year he had a mental breakdown and was hospitalised. He seemed to recover, resumed his studies, and on Monday 11 February was due to return to his lodgings in Newcastle, but instead ended his life by setting fire to himself using petrol in the garden at The Heath. It was Wainwright himself who noticed the flames, and on going to investigate discovered the remains. There can be few scenarios which inspire a greater sense of spiralling horror.

When the emergency services had arrived, the inevitable question had to be addressed of what would happen to Wainwright's campaign, and in time for the evening edition of the local papers it had been answered. Edward Dunford made it clear that Wainwright would stand, and that the decision had been made by both of Andrew's parents:

> He was not in two minds about it – his wife has said he must stand. After an interval, which we cannot yet specify, he will continue his campaign. The campaign is going on as planned, except for the next day or two, when Mr. Wainwright will not be here.[109]

Wainwright told another local paper that he 'left the decision as to whether he should withdraw from the election to his wife, Joyce. "She had no hesitation in saying I should carry on" said Mr. Wainwright.'[110] He later wrote to the local press to thank them for their restraint in reporting the tragedy.[111] An ashen-faced Albert Ingham at the Yorkshire Liberal Federation offices learned of the suicide and of Wainwright's determination to continue the campaign that morning in a brief telephone conversation with Wainwright; a scheduled local television debate between Wainwright and his opponent David Clark on the evening of that day was cancelled only because of the broadcasters' misgivings and because Clark withdrew.[112] Wainwright did however deliver a national radio broadcast for the Party later the same week.[113]

From the day of its happening, Wainwright made a valiant attempt to draw a line under Andrew's death: he telephoned his youngest daughter Tessa at school to break the news, even consoling her that he thought, given Andrew's illness, it was 'probably for the best', and asked her to come home to speak to their domestic staff about the tragedy. Local activists were impressed by the discipline with which the Wainwrights resumed the campaign, and colleagues such as Cyril Smith noted that 'he never let it overflow into other people's lives – he never discussed it.'[114] Some like Smith found this stoicism admirable; others, often of a younger generation, were unnerved by it: Wainwright's friend and fellow Joseph Rowntree Trustee Professor Trevor Smith remembers that 'Joyce and Richard were very matter-of-fact about it. They were not outwardly mournful. They just said: "We've planted a rose tree".'[115] The matter was, as Michael Meadowcroft – to whom Wainwright had been an important emotional support when his father died – found, 'a closed book'.[116] A memorial service was held for Andrew, at which Wainwright's mentor Frank McEachran preached and Wainwright himself read from Milton's 'Lycidas'; a book of Andrew's letters was published marking his work in Africa[117] and a charitable trust was established in his memory.

This response to Andrew's death was not without its costs for Wainwright. He became prone to fits of depression, and increasingly dependent upon medication to fend them off. His son Martin was surprised to find on Wainwright's retirement quite how much prescribed medication he was taking.[118] David Alton confirmed that 'Andrew's suicide must have been a deeply traumatic experience', the ongoing effects of which he saw when they shared an office in the Commons five years later:

> There were days when what we used to call the 'black dog' would appear; and there were days when he was haunted by whatever had happened. What was clear was that there were moments when he was very distracted, and there would be days when you would see him physically shake. You could see that something quite deep was really upsetting him.[119]

Wainwright warned Caroline Cawston, his new secretary after the 1974 election, that he might be forgetful because of his reaction to Andrew's death. She took care to steer conversations away from the subject of Andrew, and on one occasion Wainwright became furious at the idea of meeting a visitor to the Commons who proposed to write a play about Andrew. Two years later Cawston also witnessed the fierce protectiveness Wainwright felt towards his other children's safety after Andrew's death when Hilary was involved in a car crash whilst he was at the Liberal Assembly at Llandudno:

> Richard suddenly rang me up first thing in the morning and said: 'Caroline, have you got the cheque book? Have you got the cheque book?' This was the office cheque book: I hadn't brought it with me. I hadn't been asked to. He said 'come and see me, come and see me', and we met in the lobby of the hotel, and he absolutely tore me off a most terrific strip for not having brought the cheque book. I cried when he'd gone. He needed the cheque book in order to get a cab and rush off to wherever it was. So that maybe puts the Andrew thing into context.[120]

Cawston's successor as Wainwright's secretary, Joanna Copsey (later Hannam), also found that 'he became very stressed and my assumption was that it started when Andrew died. He found it very difficult and painful to talk about. He could get very irritable and very stressed, and at that point his hands would shake and he would light up a cigarette. Then he would take his medication and be calm.'[121]

The only person outside his immediate family with whom Wainwright seems to have discussed Andrew openly after February 1974 is fellow MP and Methodist Sir Alan Beith, who had taught Andrew at Newcastle University and who himself lost a son to suicide. Beith remembers Wainwright dwelling not upon Andrew's death, but on his life, 'valuing remembering, and the importance of remembering'.[122]

The exact cause of Andrew's suicide is no more relevant to this study than it is knowable at this distance, but Wainwright's reaction to it is, and he must have suffered agonies of doubt about what might have prevented it. The Inquest into Andrew's death heard evidence from his psychiatrist of his illness, and Hilary revealed that Andrew had suffered from delusions about being poisoned by paramedics, and about being taken by force to Belfast. In fact, he had been at a work camp there.[123] Wainwright may have wondered whether Andrew's optimistic and empathetic disposition had taken to this sort of experience, to life at Oxford, Winchester or the pressures of being an MP's son. Andrew was certainly distraught at aspects of what he had seen in Africa and by the assassination of the leader of the independence movement in Guinea-Bissau, Amilcar Cabral. He wrote to his family at the end of his stay in Rhodesia that 'the whole matter is dismal and so deeply depressing'.[124]

Andrew's House Master at Winchester, Peter Partner, remembered that both he and his father were cheerful, attractive personalities, but that Wainwright was 'a powerful character' who had chosen Winchester as offering the best preparation for entry into competitive academic programmes such as Politics, Philosophy and Economics, being 'more challenging, better on the C.V.' than other public schools. Partner added that 'Andrew was very aware of his father's public figure, and was wary of it.'[125] Wainwright remembered Andrew's life with the honour and pride it rightly inspired; but he could never forget the horror of its end.

Andrew's death and its consequences illustrate significant features of Wainwright's character, notably his faith, which sustained him through the episode, and his extraordinary courage and determination in the face of a challenge which for most people is thankfully unimaginable. The effects of the episode, though less perceptible and more protracted in their emergence, included the increased intensity of Wainwright's commitment to his family and his privacy, and a greater sense of his own vulnerability. For the remaining three weeks of the election campaign, it was to be Wainwright's courage and determination which were at a premium.

The campaign broadly followed the pattern of those at previous elections. Wainwright took part in a 'Radio Report' broadcast for the Liberals on industrial policy;[126] Edward Dunford noted after the result that, despite its impromptu start and brevity, with no Leader's tour, 'the campaign had come up to the standard set in 1966', and that car cavalcades and a 'Good Morning' leaflet had met with a favourable response from voters.[127]

In the context of the miners' strikes, power cuts, the three-day week and division in the Conservatives over Europe and immigration, Wainwright opted to strike the consensual note that he had used at Cambridge, focusing upon the class division and extremism of the two main parties: 'In total contrast to this picture of social class divisions', he argued, 'Liberal support in Colne Valley runs evenly throughout the entire area.' With tactical instinct, Wainwright managed to mention Saddleworth, Emley, Clayton West, Denby Dale and Slaithwaite in a single short appeal, and pointed out to Conservatives that there had been no Tories on Colne Valley Borough Council 'for years'. The Conservatives replied by conflating the policies of Labour and the Liberals as willing to 'pay up' in the miners' dispute; and sitting Labour MP David Clark made familiar coded attacks on Liberal weaknesses, warning that in a neck-and-neck national contest between the main parties, 'there are still those looking for the soft option' and even that 'an indecisive result could mean the beginning of the end of our democracy'.[128]

As in 1964, the Conservative vote proved resistant to tactical appeals, and there was only the tiniest of movements in the parties' shares of the poll. All three candidates won more votes than in 1970 because the turnout had reached an impressive 86 per cent; and David Clark lost twice as large a share of the vote as Ken Davy. The beneficiary of both losses was Wainwright. The belief that Wainwright's victories came only on the back of Tory collapse was again disproved. Liberal Agent Edward Dunford himself was surprised by this, commenting that, 'bearing in mind the Conservative vote held up at 20 per cent, then our majority of 719 over Labour was highly satisfactory'.[129]

At the count at Slaithwaite Civic Hall, frustrated Labour supporters chanting 'We want Clark' were called to order by their own candidate,[130] and the bitterness felt by the West Yorkshire Labour Party was reflected in the assertion by

Huddersfield MP Ken Lomas days later in the Commons that David Clark's defeat was 'one of the tragic losses to this House'.[131] However, when news came through that no Party had an overall majority in the Commons, it was clear that they would have a chance to recover the seat before long, and a fortnight later Clark reassured his activists that he 'felt sure the seat would be won back at the next general election'.[132]

Attempts by Edward Heath to form a coalition government with the Liberals were rejected, as Wainwright later observed to Conservative critics, because their combined forces would not form a parliamentary majority, because Heath would not make serious commitments on electoral reform and lastly because his Government had made itself deeply unpopular, and the Liberals – whose members flooded Party Headquarters with calls urging refusal – did not feel authorised to prop it up.

The expected fresh election therefore followed a brief minority Labour Government in October 1974. It was here – in securing the victory of February – that Wainwright broke the resistance of Conservatives. The Liberals and Labour were clearly in a two-horse race, as the high profile of their campaigns confirmed: Prime Minister Wilson made a speech in the Colne Valley at the start of the month, Jeremy Thorpe held a press conference at Slaithwaite, and Wainwright himself featured in a Liberal television broadcast with fellow MP Alan Beith.

The Conservatives were reduced from 20 per cent to 14 per cent of the Colne Valley vote, and Wainwright's majority doubled. The victory was immediately and angrily dismissed as a tactical trick on Wainwright's part: at the count Ken Davy condemned 'those Conservatives, something like 12,500 in this valley, who have not voted Conservative.[133] I have every respect for every Socialist who votes for his beliefs', he went on: 'That is not a sentiment I can share with those who have not voted Conservative.' David Clark told the crowd that 'I thought some of the Liberal leaflets were well below the level of politics that have normally been conducted in Colne Valley, and if ever I had to resort to such tactics, I'd quit politics.' Davy implicitly concurred, pointedly thanking only Clark for 'a very clean and fair contest'. Wainwright retorted that 'we have won over a vast number of floating voters' and was drowned out by boos and abuse from Labour supporters before being carried aloft from the room by applauding Liberals.[134]

Wainwright had good reason to celebrate: he had in February achieved something no other Liberal would do in the post-war era by winning back a seat he had lost.[135] Just as it was an unwritten rule that Liberal by-election performances were the high water mark of the Party in their own seats, it was assumed that incumbency was vital to Liberal profile and credibility, and if lost, Liberal seats could not be recovered. Wainwright had disproved this, working as earnestly as a beaten MP as he had as a sitting MP or an unelected hopeful, and despite also being Chairman of the Liberal Party for two years and visiting Guinea-Bissau for the Joseph Rowntree Trust in the interim. It was to his recovery of Colne Valley that Lord Steel referred in attesting to one of Wainwright's greatest strengths as 'dogged determination. That showed in his battles for the Colne Valley constituency.'[136] Wainwright himself never lost faith: he continued to handle constituency cases in his four years out of office, and even kept his personalised House of Commons writing paper for use upon his return.[137]

Professor David Butler again focused upon the role of the Conservatives in Wainwright's victory, arguing that he was probably 'saved by this tactical switch'.[138] However, Wainwright had already won the Colne Valley in February without crushing the Tory vote, and he would do so again at the next election with a rising Conservative vote and a falling Labour one. Tactical Conservative votes were an important, sometimes vital, element in Wainwright's support, but it was an unsophisticated and often partisan view which ignored the other, preponderant and positive parts of it. These were to be essential to his next win.

1979

Some Liberal activists came away from the 1979 election feeling that 'I never want to fight an election like that again';[139] others thought it was 'the election that defined Wainwright'.[140] Both responses are understandable, for Wainwright's victory in 1979 was unique: it was won after the Thorpe affair and against the rising Conservative tide in opposition to an ailing Labour Government. In normal circumstances this would have given heart to the third-placed Conservative, and – in the expectation of those who saw Wainwright's campaigns as chiefly tactical appeals to the Tories – undermine the Liberal vote. Yet he held Colne Valley with a majority half as big again as he had achieved in 1974, despite the near-doubling of the Conservative share of the vote.

Wainwright was aware of the advancing threat of the Conservatives, whose candidate Stephen Kaye emphasised that the Lib-Lab Pact was a betrayal of Conservatives who had voted for Wainwright. Kaye pointed out that the Conservatives had taken 19,541 votes in Colne Valley at the last County Council elections, compared with 10,035 for the Liberals and 9,918 for Labour, and had won six District Council seats at the last elections to the Liberals' one. Wainwright told a BBC interviewer on the night of the fall of the Labour Government that he expected the Conservatives to win an overall majority of thirty seats.[141]

A number of factors explain the outcome of the General Election. First of all, Wainwright's diligent attention to constituency work paid off, and on his eighth campaign, of which three of the last four had been successful, he was becoming the assumed Member of Parliament amongst an increasing number of non-attached voters. In the mid-1980s, Conservative candidate Graham Riddick was to discover that this assumption was so ingrained that even households in Holmfirth with five Conservative voters displayed Liberal posters because 'they always put that in there'.[142]

Secondly, Wainwright had a new campaigning weapon in the form of Joanna Copsey (later Hannam), his new secretary, who brought to Colne Valley some of the hard-hitting techniques of electioneering she had learned as a councillor in Liverpool, including targeted leaflet drops and enhanced polling-day propaganda. David Wheeler, a Saddleworth Liberal who campaigned alongside her, described her as a political streetfighter whose approach was 'handbags at dawn' and who 'galvanised the campaign'.[143] Wainwright blended her approach with the more measured and experienced head of Edward Dunford. It was a potent combination.

Thirdly, Wainwright collected a larger share of the Labour vote than before. Of course, although the Labour share of the vote fell, it is not possible to be certain which of the other parties collected it; however, Labour candidate Peter Hildrew believed he knew: 'Most people in the Labour Party', he argued after the election, 'are still not taking the Liberals seriously, and there is a danger that the outcome of the general election will encourage that complacency.' He described the trend he had seen in Colne Valley of 'one-time Labour voters switching to the Liberals':

> The Lib-Lab Pact appears, if anything, to have encouraged this, and in the more fluid electoral atmosphere now developing there is a danger of Labour losing votes wherever the Liberal is in with a serious chance … We had hoped to regain this seat, since the Tories were polling strongly and Richard Wainwright had only won in the past when Tories switched to Liberal to keep Labour out. This time the pattern broke. The Tories did even better than expected, but Labour lost more votes than the Liberals, leaving Wainwright still in command.

Hildrew also complained that the Liberals in Colne Valley had benefited from more modern printing facilities and 'sheer persistence and hard work' in tending to local concerns.[144]

One event which Hildrew acknowledged had strengthened Wainwright's case in a Labour seat had been the victory of David Alton – whose constituency party had been twinned with Colne Valley's for campaigning for over a year – at the Liverpool Edge Hill by-election only weeks earlier. Alton spoke at Wainwright's 1979 adoption meeting stressing the appeal of northern Liberalism, and activists took heart that whatever the fortunes of the Party nationally, as a challenge to Labour it remained strong.[145] The significance of the result was not lost on them, and Wainwright reminded his supporters in a post-election letter that 'nobody can say, now, that our success in Colne Valley depends on a freak Conservative vote.'[146]

Much of the campaign had been unremarkable: Wainwright took part in a televised debate with his former opposite number in the Lib-Lab Pact Eric Varley and future Chancellor Kenneth Clarke at Bentinck Colliery Miners' Welfare Club in Kirkby-in Ashfield;[147] he issued his usual reminder to Colne Valley Conservatives that 'in all its 103 years, Colne Valley has *always* had either Labour or Liberal Members of Parliament. The General Elections of the last 15 years have all been close-run between Liberal and Labour' and warned that 'the Tories are trailing a very poor third.'[148] The officers of the Yorkshire Liberal Federation sent their usual note to Edward Dunford 'congratulating him on getting Richard Wainwright re-elected.'[149] However, the outcome of the election showed a far more balanced three-way contest than had characterised Colne Valley recently. The portents of the result were different, too.

1983

Three major changes took place after 1979 which significantly affected Liberal fortunes in the Colne Valley. Firstly, the slump in Labour support accelerated as the Party swerved Left, giving trade unions the largest say in who would become Labour leader, and proposing tax rises and nationalisation unwelcome to many moderate Labour voters in Colne Valley. Secondly, and partly as a result of the first change, a new political party had emerged – the Social Democrats – with whom the Liberals were in an electoral alliance, and the national poll rating of this combined third force had reached 50 per cent at its peak in 1981. This left Wainwright's traditional bogeyman, the Labour Left, at bay, and the local implications of the formation of the Alliance were at best uncertain. More ominous was the third change: the dismemberment of the existing Colne Valley in a redrawing of constituency boundaries.

The preliminary recommendations of the Boundary Commission in 1981 proposed that Wainwright's constituency be shortened and widened. In the west it would lose Saddleworth with its 7,000 Liberal voters, and in the east the chiefly Labour Denby Dale area would be taken out of the constituency. The numbers would be made up by adding Huddersfield suburbs: Lindley, which was strongly Conservative, and further south Crosland Moor, where Labour won. The overall effect was to leave a constituency which based on the 1979 figures would have been 38.2 per cent Labour, 33.8 per cent Conservative and only 27.8 per cent Liberal. *The Guardian* commented drily that 'only the more sanguine party workers dared to predict the results in the Colne Valley constituency of West Yorkshire before the Boundary Commission amputated its outstretched arms';[150] under the new circumstances, Robert Waller warned that 'Wainwright faces a tough fight to hold the seat', although he noted that voting patterns within the changed boundaries at the 1982 local elections were 35 per cent for the Alliance, 33 per cent for Labour and 32 per cent for the Conservatives.[151]

A futile rearguard action was fought to save the boundaries, but the only concession granted by the Boundary Commission was that instead of the proposed new name Huddersfield West, the seat would retain its old name. This, according to Wainwright's successor as candidate, 'was at one level a tremendous victory, because he was "Mr Colne Valley";[152] but it was a sign of his limited hopes of any movement that Wainwright had already declared he would fight the seat under the new name.[153] In Saddleworth, there was great sadness at losing Wainwright as what the Leader of Oldham District Council later called 'the epitome of a good MP'.[154] A formal dinner with 170 guests from all parties was held at Uppermill Civic Hall by the Parish Council to mark his departure, and in Springhead a road was named after him. Wainwright felt the loss of Saddleworth badly, retained contact with activists in the new seat of Oldham East, and later came to argue that the boundary change was the main reason for the loss of the Colne Valley in 1987:

> The massive change in the electorate when the Boundary Commission took away an entire (and very Liberal) Urban District and replaced it with 30,000 'new' voters from the suburbs of Huddersfield – introducing suburbia into the constituency for the first time. It was pressure from us which led to the Colne Valley being retained because it suited us at the time. But in hard fact the electorate should not be titled Colne Valley.[155]

Gordon Beever, who worked with Wainwright on their appeal to the Boundary Commission, agrees that its decision was 'the beginning of the end'.[156] Saddleworth's psychological importance to Liberal success was reflected in 1966, when Jeremy Thorpe taunted Pat Duffy that he would lose the seat because 'we've got Saddleworth!'[157] There was an historic Liberal tradition in the western districts of Huddersfield, where Wainwright's mentor Donald Wade had been the MP until 1964, and Martin Wainwright remembers meeting some of Wade's old voters who felt 'like released prisoners' because their Liberal vote now counted again.[158] But the plain facts were as Wainwright feared, if less dramatically so than he suggested. He was beginning the 1983 campaign from a seriously weakened position.

The Conservative candidate, John Holt, was in buoyant mood, and headed his election literature 'The New MP for the New Constituency'. As well as being a native of Lindley, he represented it on the County Council, and had drafted in five hundred canvassers to contest the seat. He took encouragement from the Conservatives' recent capture of two Liberal council seats in the Holme Valley, and was rated the evens favourite by local bookmakers. Holt, who later left the Conservative Party under controversial circumstances, was an idiosyncratic and determined opponent. Selected as the Liberal candidate for Dewsbury in 1963, he had left the Party before the election to become a Powellite Conservative, and was accused of racism by Liberals in Huddersfield, where he had stood for the Conservatives in 1970. His campaign against Wainwright also caused controversy for its alleged personal attacks; Wainwright was so incensed by the tone of the Conservative campaign that he refused to debate with Holt publicly.

Labour, on the other hand, was struggling both nationally and locally. Their candidate acknowledged he was the outsider – the bookies had him at 2–1 against – and he faced humiliation when a constituency tour by Michael Foot was surrounded by protesting packs of hunting dogs at Holmfirth.[159]

On the day, Wainwright won by more than he had ever enjoyed by way of a majority. He dismissed the national campaign as having offered the poorest support he had ever had from Headquarters,[160] but the national profile of the Alliance, which secured a quarter of the vote across the country, may have helped to reinforce credibility in some of the areas Wainwright had not represented before, and his personal vote was once more an enormous asset. In addition, he had also benefited from the transitional nature of the relationship between his opponents, which meant that only Wainwright could present himself as being a clear contender, whilst Holt and Williams jostled for the challenger's mantle. A new political landscape was emerging, but it had not quite become clear yet. When it did on election day, with the Conservatives in a clear second place, it presented Colne Valley Liberals with a new tactical scenario, and new dilemmas about how to approach it.

1987: The failed succession

It is part of the standard template of the school history essay that monarchs are judged last on how they secure their succession. It would be kind and fair to Wainwright to apply different criteria to him, for the end of his parliamentary career marked the start of a period of dramatic electoral decline for the Colne Valley Liberals. Wainwright must have been hurt by this, because it represented the undoing of his life's work in the seat, and because his role in the episode reflected his increasingly limited control over events.

Wainwright had always intended to retire by seventy, and the timing of the 1983 General Election made its end a natural departure point. In the summer after the election Wainwright discussed this with Joyce, and confirmed his decision not to fight the next General Election. The Liberal nomination for a seat held by him at five of the preceding six contests was thus available; but Wainwright was to see his legacy pass to an unexpected candidate who would lose the seat. The result would send the Colne Valley Liberal Association spiralling into bitter division and repeated defeat, leaving it in its worst position at parliamentary elections since the 1950s.

The first problem was of delay in the nomination process, provoking a 'phoney war' between aspirants. Wainwright's broad intentions about his retirement had always been known to close colleagues, and he confirmed this in writing to leading members of the Association within two months of his last victory, urging a prompt process of selection to allow 'the new PPC [Prospective Parliamentary Candidate;] for Colne Valley' as long as possible to nurse the constituency.[161] Yet Wainwright was reluctant to push the process forward: ten months later the Colne Valley Liberal Association reported on progress in selecting a candidate to the Yorkshire Liberal Federation, saying 'MP already selected.'[162] The same confusion marked Wainwright's reaction to a lunch party to mark the twenty-fifth anniversary of his first contest as Liberal candidate for Colne Valley. In front of 209 guests at a hotel near Huddersfield in November 1984, tributes were paid to Wainwright by former Liberal Leader Jo Grimond, Wainwright's ally since childhood Donald (now Lord) Wade, and – in the form of a portrait of Wainwright in oils – by Yorkshire artist Trevor Stubley. Celebrating with them were local stalwarts Ernest and Ira Gilpin, James Crossley who had begun work for Wainwright as an Oxford student in 1959, Edward Dunford and a party of Free Democrats from the Colne Valley's German 'twin' town of Unna. The Colne Valley Women's Council marked Joyce's decades of energy and success with gifts of an embroidered bell-pull and a hand-stitched tablecloth.

It was a fittingly splendid event marking a unique career which was the result of a personal mission. Wainwright told the organisers that he and Joyce 'enjoyed every minute' of the event and – his modesty notwithstanding – mounted his portrait and Joyce's bell-pull permanently at home. There had inevitably been a tone of valediction to the event, and the question of Wainwright's future hung in the air: Wainwright expressed to the organisers his relief that – although he stressed there was no question of changing his decision – there had been 'no "requiem" note at any point'.[163] When the local press asked whether he would contest Colne Valley again, Wainwright even teased them 'with a Mona Lisa-like smile' that 'on that my lips are sealed.'[164]

Awareness of the impending vacancy was spreading beyond the constituency boundaries: David Steel's speechwriter William Wallace wrote to Dunford and Association Chairman Nigel Priestley the following month to seek guidance on the likely selection schedule, and urge progress for the sake of the Association in nearby Shipley, where he was then the candidate.

Approval of the proposed selection process was given by Liberal Party Headquarters in March 1985, and it was not until 3 April that the Association Executive was formally told of Wainwright's decision to retire. On 10 June – two years and a day after the previous General Election – the Executive approved the shortlist for a selection meeting a month later. During the preceding year, tensions had been building up in the Association which produced a selection process, a Liberal candidate and a General Election result contrary to Wainwright's wishes.

Controversy dogged the selection process from the outset: one leading local activist, Gordon Beever, had joined the Liberals during Wainwright's 1963 by-election campaign, and had represented Colne Valley on Kirklees District Council since the early 1970s, but was ruled out by the shortlisting committee, perhaps to strengthen the hand of another local figure, Association Chairman Nigel Priestley. Beever believed he had a good chance of winning a selection meeting, and was resentful at being 'dumped' in favour of Priestley, who in his assessment had 'come from literally nowhere'.[165]

Priestley's rise had certainly been swift: after returning to Huddersfield from training as a lawyer in 1978 he emerged as a rising star of the Colne Valley Party. Based in Meltham, he first represented the Liberals as a school governor, and in 1982 scored successes as a local election agent gaining two seats from Labour. The following year he became a town councillor in Meltham, and supported Wainwright's General Election campaign as a Sub-agent. Wainwright was struck by Priestley's contribution: by August 1983 he was canvassing support for Priestley as a possible Chairman of the Association:

> I am greatly impressed with his vast amount of expert effort which he devotes to immigrant clients of his firm, who cannot possibly be profitable, because of all the intricate work he does in connection with immigration. He is a practising Lay Preacher of the Church of England, and I have found that he is very highly thought of in the Wakefield Diocese.[166]

In February 1984 Priestley took over as Chairman, and prepared what Wainwright commended as 'an admirable plan for constituency strategy', leading to discussion between the two on a programme of political education meetings across Colne Valley. Reporting gossip he had heard about embezzlement of funds in two other Liberal MPs' Associations, Wainwright added assuredly 'we have things for which to be soberly thankful!'[16] It was Priestley who in November organised the 'superbly planned ... heroic undertaking' of the twenty-fifth anniversary celebration for which Wainwright and Joyce declared themselves 'immensely grateful'.[168]

Nobody doubted the determination and energy with which Priestley worked in the Association. Many new members of the Association were recruited by him, and by his wife Sue to the Women's Council, particularly in Meltham and the Holme Valley: membership of the Liberal Association rose by 10 per cent in the year to June 1984. Significantly, as Priestley rose in the ranks of the Association, Wainwright observed that the membership of the Executive 'has been substantially renewed during this year and it has become, in my opinion, an admirable body'.[169] For some, however, this activity had a thinly disguised ulterior motive for a man who, because of Wainwright's reluctance to acknowledge his retirement officially, was in an ideal position to use the extended waiting period to build up support for his candidature in the Association, and as Chairman to monitor and control the selection process. Wainwright deferred to Priestley about the date of the announcement: 'that must await a decision from you and the Executive on the best timing.'[170] Priestley inevitably developed a very close working relationship with Edward Dunford. Meanwhile, amongst the Colne Valley membership, 'Nigel was', according to Wainwright's secretary at the time, 'very assiduous in building networks within the Holme Valley and with the Liberal office in Huddersfield and courting supporters.'[171] William Wallace, who as Priestley's main rival for the nomination had met with him early in the process, concluded early on that 'he was very determined to be the candidate.'[172]

Though four candidates for the nomination were chosen by the short-listing committee, Wallace was Priestley's competition. Although by origins an outsider, Wallace was in most senses the favourite. His national profile was as distinguished as a Liberal parliamentary aspirant's could be: from being a chorister at Queen Elizabeth's coronation, to joining the Liberals at Cambridge a decade later, to becoming a speechwriter and advisor to both Jo Grimond and David Steel, writing two Party manifestos whilst building a career as a Professor of International Relations, Wallace had been at the heart of events – as Priestley put it, 'an all-round good guy.'[173] Moreover he had fought five parliamentary contests in the neighbouring constituencies of Huddersfield, Manchester Moss Side and Shipley, where he had a home, and his marriage to the daughter of Yorkshire Liberal notable Edward Rushworth, Liberal candidate for Bradford in 1950 and 1951, consolidated his Northern Liberal credentials.

Wainwright had been an associate of Wallace's since the 1960s when Wallace had awarded Wainwright's daughter Hilary the prize for the best speech at the Young Liberal Conference of 1966 and Wainwright had supported Wallace's adoption as Liberal candidate for Huddersfield before the 1970 election. Helen Rushworth had campaigned for Wainwright at the 1963 Colne Valley by-election, and Wainwright had worked for her father's campaigns in the 1950s. Everyone in Colne Valley assumed at the beginning of the selection process that Wallace was Wainwright's preferred successor. That assumption is still shared by both Priestley and Wallace, and is confirmed explicitly by Joyce, who says Wainwright 'was interested in William and thought he'd be very good. He liked Nigel very much, but didn't think he was a strong enough candidate. He'd have much preferred William.'[174]

Just as the 'phoney war' for the nomination developed, Wainwright lost key members of his staff. Edward Dunford, his election Agent since before his arrival in Colne Valley, died unexpectedly in January 1985. Like the death of Harry Senior three years earlier, this deprived Wainwright of not only a trusted friend, but a vastly experienced political ally who was his eyes and ears in the constituency.[175] Also lost during this period was another giant of post-war Yorkshire Liberalism, Agent for the county, Albert Ingham. Secondly, Wainwright already knew, his secretary Joanna Hannam would take maternity leave just as the process of inviting applications for the nomination got underway in mid-May. Copsey was a veteran of internal constituency politics as well as electoral campaigning in Liverpool. Together with Dunford, she might have managed the tensions in the Colne Valley Association better and kept Wainwright in touch with events; in their absence, Wainwright drifted further away. Copsey herself recalls that this was not characteristic of Wainwright's approach: 'it is clear to me Richard's decision to announce his retirement knowing he had no full time agent in place posed a risk to any serious plans for succession management. It was not his usual sure-footed thinking.'[176]

The selection process reached its climax at a meeting of the Colne Valley Liberal Association in the Golcar Central Liberal Club on Saturday, 6 July 1985. As well as 230 Colne Valley Liberals including the Wainwrights, there were the four candidates, local Social Democrats who were invited as observers, and former Liberal MP David Austick, in attendance as President of the Electoral Reform Society to confirm the probity of the result. The atmosphere was tense at the outset, and grew worse. Priestley's followers had stressed during the campaign the local credentials of their candidate and Wallace remembers 'his supporters portrayed me as an outsider – went to a lot of lengths';[177] Joyce Wainwright said 'they thought he might not spend enough time in the constituency because his wife was a Professor at Sussex University and they had a house in London';[178] and Priestley himself believes 'I got it because I was the man on site … I was in the right place, and I was probably more in touch with the membership.'[179]

If Wallace's camp believed that some of these accusations about him in the run-up to the selection meeting had tested the boundaries of decency, the meeting itself was in Wallace's characteristically understated words 'really quite difficult',[180] particularly when questions came from the floor. 'Nigel had people planted there' said Gordon Beever: 'they put planted local questions which were bound to favour an insider rather than an outsider. You can make someone look ordinary if they don't know the answers to questions.'[181] One of these hostile questions – 'the killer question' in the phrase of one activist close to the person who asked it – concerned press coverage which Wallace had gained, unwittingly breaking selection rules. Challenged over it, Wallace lost his assurance and composure, and was left looking vulnerable and unreliable. Wallace regards the description used by some other Colne Valley activists of the meeting – a 'stitch-up' – as fitting.[182] Joyce told Joanna Hannam of her shock at events, and blamed some 'little-minded' members of the Women's Council for the anti-Wallace intrigue: 'who were very nasty to William and Helen … People can be very bitchy if they've been on a committee for a long time; they feel that they like to call the shots.'[183]

The selection meeting remains a sensitive matter with some of those present: the Councillor who had the unenviable task of chairing it still refuses to discuss it.[184] The vote was painfully close – it was not publicised in Association reports, but Wallace remembers it was 102 to 105 in Priestley's favour.[185] One member who was persuaded by Priestley's 'eloquent and convincing' speech to switch from Wallace on the day said, 'Wallace was the hot favourite. When the vote was announced, the look on his face was hard to believe.'[186]

Wainwright had watched this divisive struggle unfold without saying a word. 'Richard very studiously stood back' said Gordon Beever, 'but one can read the body language.'[187] The body language, however, was not visible enough to most Colne Valley Liberals to prevent factionalism. 'He was', Hannam stresses, 'undoubtedly rightfully wary or concerned not to be seen to try and overtly persuade or influence people of the decision.'[188] At no stage in the process had Wainwright expressed to anyone outside his family any opinion about the succession, and this in itself was admirably restrained, being intended to avoid resentment at a result perceived to be imposed. Moreover, it can be argued that the closeness of the contest had been produced in part by the restrained nature of Wallace's campaign: he had hardly visited the constituency, though encouraged to do so by Edward Dunford, and was inhibited by his commitments to work in London and his young family. 'I should have made sure I went to one or two occasions in Colne Valley in '84. It was a complete surprise to me', says Wallace; 'it wasn't yet the style if one wanted to become a candidate to go round and see everyone in advance. This is what one would do now.' Moreover, Priestley's emphasis upon his local knowledge was in Wallace's words 'the obvious tactic'[189] and played upon what Joanna Hannam called 'a genuine sense among some that it would be good to have someone who lived and worked in the area.'[190] It was not improper for Priestley to point out his local credentials, nor for him to encourage others to do so; he was guilty only of organisation and ambition.

However, Wainwright allowed the nomination process to be put back, and during the delay a damagingly divisive contest developed of which he was either not close enough to events in the constituency to be aware, or else he was not confident enough to step in and contain Priestley's supporters or warn Wallace. Whichever is the explanation, his inertia makes him partly responsible for the outcome, and perhaps for the loss of the seat. Two months before the selection meeting, and following a bitter 'fiasco' of a selection process in Saddleworth, part of the old Colne Valley seat, the Liberal Area Agent for Yorkshire had prepared a report warning of the need for 'more guidelines (or more widely known guidelines) in constituencies likely to have a hard-fought selection campaign – Colne Valley for example.'[191] Wainwright knew of events in Saddleworth because he had publicly endorsed Chris Davies, the successful candidate who later became the MP, and of the Area Agent's concerns for Colne Valley; but he remained distant from the process in Colne Valley.

Wallace believes Wainwright was out of the Colne Valley loop and did not know how much was being done by Priestley to discredit Wallace's candidature; but that even knowing, Wainwright would have been reluctant to intervene: 'would he have told me had he known, Richard being the sort of person he was? I guess he would have found some indirect way of getting somebody else to tell me.'[192] One former Association Chairman feels that Wainwright may even have begun to change his mind and accept the need for a local candidate, but lacked the conviction to say so, and another believes that Wainwright had decided to let the chips fall where they may as a matter of principle.[193] These explanations are disproved by Wainwright's reaction to the result, for he became 'very cross' on learning that leading Liberals outside the constituency, and some of his own staff, had actively supported Priestley: some of these he even refused to speak to for weeks afterwards.[194] Nonetheless, Wainwright defended Priestley's candidature against attempts to reopen the selection following defeats at the 1987 and 1992 elections.[195] The two main contenders each reflected elements of the combination of talents Wainwright had relied upon to win Colne Valley: one the energetic provincial professional, an efficient organiser, Lay Preacher and Yorkshireman; the other a public school- and Cambridge-educated intellectual linked to the national Liberal leadership since the days of Jo Grimond. Wainwright could easily have felt identity with either. But he had wanted Wallace to win and expected it to happen; he had not read the mood in his own constituency accurately.

The effects of this indecision did not go unnoticed in the Association. Bill Oldham, a former Chairman, regretted the timing of the nomination contest:

> One of the things that shouldn't have happened in my opinion is that he retired halfway through a term. That really wasn't a good thing. I think instead of retiring then, he should have fought the seat, and he would have probably won it. Then if he'd wanted to retire he could have done that later on.[196]

In fact events indicated that, if anything, Wainwright's retirement should have been made public earlier rather than later. Wainwright had already stretched his parliamentary career beyond normal retirement age, and a further contest – if successful – would only put off the evil day of announcing retirement. The process Oldham suggests might well have saved the seat for the Liberals – but it should have taken place in 1983, not 1987.

The bad blood within the Association left by the nomination process is reflected in the euphemism and litotes of branch records. At the Executive meeting following the selection, Stuart Webb was singled out for congratulation on his chairing of the meeting, and Webb responded by emphasising that 'it was now necessary to rally behind the new PPC'.[197] Webb took over as Association Chairman when Priestley stood down, and wrote insistently in his first Annual Report that 'the selection process was carried out in strict accordance with the Liberal Party Constitution', reminding members that in 'what had proved to be a very positive and exciting election contest, Councillor Nigel Priestly was democratically elected.' Webb intoned hopefully that 'the adoption of Mr Priestley as our PPC marks a new turning point for the Colne Valley Constituency.'[198]

It is a danger of choosing a local candidate that they can provoke different reactions from different wards, especially in a constituency as diverse as Colne Valley.[199] Graham Riddick, selected as Priestley's Conservative opponent the next year, heard that there had been 'some high-profile outsider' involved in the selection, and quickly realised that loyalties in the Liberal Association were divided. This was confirmed to him by Liberal activists after he had beaten Priestley:

> I was aware that there seemed to be two factions. Some of the Liberals them-selves told me they couldn't stand Nigel Priestley. I think some of the Colne Valley Liberals didn't care for him. There was obviously a number of people who didn't really like Nigel and hadn't supported him.[200]

At an Executive meeting barely a year after Webb's optimistic remarks, 'concern was expressed at the lack of some wards to pay a substantial portion of their quota' and at 'the situation in Marsden in general', where members of Colne Valley West said that they were doing all in their power to revitalise Liberal interest. Priestley warned Executive officers that the General Election was likely to be held that year and that 'if he was to be successful, he would need the help of every member in the constituency.'[201]

When the 1987 General Election came six months later, Priestley was not successful. For the first time in seventeen years, Colne Valley was lost by the Liberal Party, and by the frustratingly narrow margin of 1,677 votes. For the first time in history, the seat was won by the Conservatives. The reasons for this, and for the more general failure of the Alliance, are explored below. In Colne Valley, no-one could claim that disloyalty on Wainwright's part for Priestley played any role in the outcome: he gave his successor as candidate unambiguous support. But Wainwright must have suspected that, uncharac-teristically, he had missed an opportunity to secure a different nomination, or at least to preserve unity in the Colne Valley Association as the selection was made, so as to bring about a win. The episode had been an object lesson in the fragility of constituency politics and the dangers of taking their smooth running for granted. Lord Rennard, who became Campaigns Director of the Liberal Democrats shortly after the 1987 election and had first-hand knowledge of events in Colne Valley, was keen to ensure that handovers of candidature in Liberal-held seats were more carefully managed under the new Party.

If Wainwright had been a monarch (admittedly the last position he would ever have wanted to occupy), the story of his succession would have seen his kingdom divided and left open to invaders: he was not principally to blame, but unlike a departing monarch he had to suffer the experience of watching the downfall and its aftermath, and he must have wondered whether it was inevitable.

Notes

1 Colne Valley Divisional Liberal Association Executive minutes, 30 July 1958.
2 Ibid., 13 February 1958.
3 Ibid., 16 July 1959.
4 *Colne Valley Guardian*, 25 September 1959.
5 Colne Valley Divisional Liberal Association Executive minutes, 16 July 1959.
6 Ibid., 10 November 1959. Pickles, whose father had been Liberal Mayor of Halifax, had only just defected to the Party from Labour. See Pickles, J., *Judge for Yourself* (London: Coronet 1993), pp. 49–51.
7 Christopher Barr, election address 1959; the Labour address, 'Will Hall Writes to You', and the Labour Party Colne Valley Labour Party minutes for 1959, contain no reference to the Liberal Party.
8 *Colne Valley Guardian*, 2 October 1959.
9 Butler, D. and Rose, R., *The British General Election of 1959* (London: Macmillan 1960), p. 233. The fourth seat was Greenock.
10 Colne Valley Divisional Liberal Association Executive minutes, 10 November 1959.
11 King, A. (ed.), *British Political Opinion 1937–2000* (London: Politico's 2001), pp. 5–7.
12 Wainwright papers file 6/7.
13 Butler, D., *The British General Election of 1964* (London: Macmillan 1964), p. 207.
14 *Colne Valley Guardian*, 8 March 1963.
15 Andrew Alexander, interview, 13 March 2009.
16 Ibid.
17 David Whitwam and Gordon Ellis, interviews, 15 April 2009.
18 Andrew Alexander, interview, 13 March 2009.
19 *Colne Valley Guardian*, 8 March 1963.
20 A copy of Alexander's election address is in file CV3, Huddersfield Labour Party archives, University of Huddersfield.
21 Andrew Alexander, interview, 13 March 2009.
22 David Whitwam and Gordon Ellis, interviews, 15 April 2009.
23 *Colne Valley Guardian*, 29 March 1963.
24 *Huddersfield Daily Examiner*, 20 March 1963.
25 'The Liberal Come-back', Letters, *Colne Valley Guardian*, 15 March 1963. Signed 'F.F.'.
26 *Colne Valley Guardian*, 15 March 1963.
27 Ibid., 8 March 1963. The show had first aired in November 1962.
28 'Bad Feelings to the Last', ibid., 22 March 1963.
29 David Whitwam, interview, 15 April 2009.
30 'The Last Lap', *Colne Valley Guardian*, 15 March 1963.
31 *The Times*, 20 March 1963.
32 All the above correspondence is in the Wainwright papers, file 6/7.
33 *Colne Valley Guardian*, 29 March 1963.
34 *The Conservative Agent's Journal*, No. 494, April 1963, p. 4.
35 'The Next Election', *Colne Valley Guardian*, 20 March 1964.
36 *The Times*, 23 March 1963, Leading article, p. 9.
37 'Still in the Valley', Editorial, *Daily Telegraph*, 23 March 1963, p. 8.
38 'The Election and After', *Colne Valley Guardian*, 29 March 1963.

39 *Daily Telegraph*, 22 March 1963.

40 Rees, M., 'Recent By-elections: Leeds South', *Labour Organiser*, August 1963, p. 152. In that election, on 20 June, the Liberal vote rose from 10 per cent to 14 per cent. There was no report of the Colne Valley contest.

41 *Daily Telegraph*, 22 March 1963.

42 'Colne Valley', *The Guardian*, 23 March 1963, p. 6.

43 Jeremy Thorpe to RSW, 25 March 1963, Wainwright papers file 6/7.

44 Colne Valley Divisional Liberal Association Executive minutes, 5 September 1963.

45 BBC election coverage, 16 October 1964.

46 Colne Valley Divisional Liberal Association Executive minutes, 16 April 1964.

47 'The Next Election', *Colne Valley Guardian*, 20 March 1964.

48 *Huddersfield Daily Examiner*, 22 June 1964; *Yorkshire Post*, 22 June 1964; *Colne Valley Guardian*, 26 June 1964.

49 RSW campaign letter, 12 October 1964, Wainwright papers file 6/8.

50 Butler, *The British General Election of 1964*, pp. 178–79.

51 Dunford, E., 'How Richard Wainwright Almost Won Colne Valley', *New Outlook*, No. 37, November 1964, p. 35.

52 *Colne Valley Guardian*, 26 March 1964.

53 'Vote Labour and Return Duffy', 1964.

54 Dunford, 'How Richard Wainwright Almost Won', p. 35.

55 David Butler, BBC election night coverage 1964.

56 *Colne Valley Guardian*, 16 October 1964.

57 Butler, *The British General Election of 1964*, p. 353.

58 Colne Valley Women's Liberal Association General Election Report, 15 October 1964; Colne Valley Divisional Liberal Association Executive minutes, 10 November 1964.

59 BBC election coverage, 16 October 1964.

60 Colne Valley Divisional Liberal Association Executive minutes, 10 November 1964.

61 Dunford, 'How Richard Wainwright Almost Won', p. 34.

62 Cllr A. Holland, Chairman, Colne Valley Divisional Liberal Association Executive minutes, 10 November 1964.

63 Colne Valley Divisional Women's Liberal Council Election Report, 15 October 1964.

64 *Colne Valley Guardian*, 16 October 1964.

65 RSW to Cllr A. Holland, 6 November 1964, Wainwright papers file 6/8.

66 Lord Shutt, interview, 3 June 2008.

67 Colne Valley Divisional Liberal Association AGM, 6 February 1965.

68 Colne Valley Divisional Liberal Association Executive minutes, 31 March 1965.

69 Colne Valley Divisional Liberal Association AGM, 29 January 1966.

70 *Oldham Evening Chronicle*, 14 March 1966.

71 Ibid.

72 'David Hall', election address 1966.

73 'A.E.P. Duffy', election address 1966.

74 Martin Harrison in Butler, D., (ed.), *The British General Election of 1966* (London: Macmillan 1966), p. 142.

75 Derek Moon's Campaign Notebook, *Oldham Evening Chronicle*, 21 March 1966.

76 *The Times*, 22 March 1966.

77 'Clash on Workers' Houses', *The Times*, 31 March 1966 p. 8.
78 BBC Election coverage, 1 April 1966.
79 Roth, A., *General Election Forecast 1966* (London: Parliamentary Profile Services 1966), p. 103.
80 'Profile: Richard Wainwright', *The House Magazine*, 6 March 1987.
81 *Oldham Evening Chronicle*, 1 April 1966.
82 *Holmfirth Express* letters page, April 1966. These comments were made by a member of Holmfirth Conservative Club and a Mr. Clifford Mellor.
83 *Colne Valley Guardian*, 29 April 1966.
84 Lord Clark, interview, 3 June 2008.
85 *Liberal News*, 7 April 1966.
86 *Oldham Evening Chronicle*, 9 June 1970.
87 Lise Newsome, interview, April 2009.
88 Adamson C. et al., *Adventure On: Celebrating 50 Years of Colne Valley High School* (Huddersfield: Colne Valley High School 2006) confirms details of visits by both Wilson and, at other times, Wainwright.
89 *Colne Valley Guardian*, 26 June 1970.
90 Councillor Robert Iredale, interview, 16 April 2009.
91 Colne Valley Constituency Labour Party Executive minutes, 5 July 1970.
92 Colne Valley Divisional Liberal Association Executive minutes, 30 July 1970.
93 Ibid., 3 September 1970.
94 *The Times*, 31 March 1966, p. 8.
95 Stephen Kaye, Election Address 1979, University of Bristol Special Collection.
96 'Meet Your MP', Radio Leeds broadcast, 26 November 1974.
97 Colne Valley Divisional Women's Liberal Council AGM, 14 July 1970.
98 Ken Davy, Election Address October 1964, University of Bristol Special Collection.
99 Colne Valley Divisional Women's Liberal Council AGM, 14 July 1970.
100 Joyce Wainwright, interview, 22 February 2008. The Majothis, who built up a restaurant business in York, remained lifelong family friends.
101 Barry Fearnley, interview, 31 October 2008.
102 RSW to Robert Iredale, 10 July 1987, Wainwright papers file 5/B/16.
103 Councillor Robert Iredale, interview, 16 April 2009.
104 David Steel held Roxburgh by 550 votes, John Pardoe's majority in North Cornwall was 630, and Party Leader Jeremy Thorpe came within 369 votes of defeat at Devon North. The Liberals had thirteen MPs by the time the 1970 General Election was called following Wallace Lawler's victory at the Birmingham Ladywood by-election of 1969. This was reversed the following year.
105 *Colne Valley Guardian*, 15 February 1974.
106 Colne Valley Divisional Liberal Association minutes, AGM, 9 February 1974.
107 Introduction to Wainwright, A., *Letters from Zimbabwe* (Leeds: Andrew Wainwright Students' Fund 1971), p. 69.
108 Cited in ibid., p. 70. This was Hollis's tribute at Andrew's memorial service.
109 *Oldham Evening Chronicle*, 11 February 1974.
110 *Colne Valley Guardian*, 15 February 1974.
111 RSW to the Editor, *Oldham Evening Chronicle*, 4 March 1974, Wainwright papers file 6/17.

112 Michael Meadowcroft, interview, 17 June 2008.

113 *The Times*, 16 February 1974.

114 Sir Cyril Smith, interview, 29 May 2008.

115 Lord Trevor Smith, interview, 22 June 2009.

116 Michael Meadowcroft, interview, 17 June 2008.

117 Wainwright, *Letters from Zimbabwe*.

118 Martin Wainwright, interview, 22 February 2008.

119 Lord Alton, interview, 3 June 2008.

120 Caroline Cawston, interview, 2 June 2008.

121 Joanna Hannam (nee Copsee), interview, 19 January 2009.

122 Alan Beith, interview, 13 October 2008.

123 *The Times*, 8 March 1974.

124 AW to family, 28 August 1971; Wainwright, *Letters from Zimbabwe*, p. 41.

125 Dr Peter Partner, interview, 20 November 2008.

126 Butler, D., *The British General Election of February 1974* (London: Macmillan 1974), p. 167.

127 Colne Valley Divisional Liberal Association Executive minutes, 21 March 1974.

128 'Last Words', candidates' final appeals in the *Oldham Evening Chronicle*, 26 February 1974.

129 Colne Valley Divisional Liberal Association Executive minutes, 21 March 1974.

130 *Colne Valley Guardian*, 8 March 1974.

131 Ken Lomas, Hansard, 12 March 1974.

132 Colne Valley Constituency Labour Party Executive Committee minutes, 10 March 1974.

133 *Colne Valley Guardian*, 11 October 1974.

134 *Oldham Evening Chronicle*, 11 October 1974.

135 The Liberal MP for Cheadle, Michael Winstanley, returned to the Commons briefly in 1974 after defeat in 1970 – but this was for the different if neighbouring seat of Hazel Grove.

136 Lord Steel, correspondence with the present author, 22 June 2008.

137 'John Gaunt's Northern Scrapbook', *Oldham Evening Chronicle*, 8 March 1974. RSW's new Assistant at Adel, Kathleen Dick, who began work in 1973, confirms that he had no doubt he would return to Parliament; interview, 12 December 2009.

138 Butler, D., *The British General Election of October 1974* (London: Macmillan 1975), p. 339.

139 Bill Oldham, interview, 29 October 2008.

140 David Wheeler, interview, 26 July 2009.

141 BBC Radio Manchester, 22 March 1979. The present author is grateful to David Wheeler for supplying this recording.

142 Graham Riddick, interview, 16 March 2009.

143 David Wheeler, interview, 26 July 2009.

144 *Labour Weekly*, 18 May 1979.

145 RSW press release, 11 April 1979, Wainwright papers file 6/18.

146 RSW to Colne Valley Liberals workers (undated), Wainwright papers file 6/18.

147 Butler, D., *The British General Election of 1979* (London: Macmillan 1979), p. 217.

The broadcast went out on 27 April.

148 'Wainwright' election address 1979, and *Oldham Evening Chronicle*, 2 May 1979.

149 Yorkshire Liberal Federation Officers' meeting, 5 May 1979.

150 Parkin, M., 'New Taste to the Summer Wine', *The Guardian*, 23 May 1983.

151 Waller, R., *The Almanac of British Politics* (London: Croom Helm 1983), p. 199.

152 Nigel Priestley, interview, 30 October 2008.

153 *Liberal News*, 16 July 1981.

154 Knowles, R., *Oldham Chronicle*, 17 January 2003.

155 RSW to Nick Harvey, Liberal Democrat Joint States Candidates' Committee, 2 January 1993, Wainwright papers file 5/B/33.

156 Gordon Beever, interview, 31 October 2008.

157 Cited in Keane C., *Colne Valley Labour Party Souvenir Centary History 1891–1991* (Colne Valley: Colne Valley Labour Party 1991), p. 49.

158 Martin Wainwright, interview, 22 February 2008.

159 Information in the preceding two paragraphs is from Parkin, 'New Taste' and Smith, I., 'Rivals' Feud Fuels Brutal Fight', *The Times* 9 June 1983.

160 Owen, D., *Time to Declare* (London: Penguin 1992), p. 592.

161 RSW to Gordon Beever, copied to Heather Swift and Edward Dunford, 5 August 1983, Wainwright papers file 5/B/23.

162 Return to Yorkshire Liberal Federation, Colne Valley Liberal Association, June 1984.

163 RSW to Nigel Priestley, 5 November 1984, Colne Valley Divisional Liberal Association papers.

164 *Yorkshire Post*, week beginning 5 November 1984. It is a reflection of the mixed signals being sent at the time, however, that Wainwright's son Martin remembers the event as having been 'definitely and openly Dad's farewell do' (correspondence with present author, 2 November 2009).

165 Gordon Beever, interview, 31 October 2008.

166 RSW to Heather Swift, 1 August 1983, Wainwright papers file 5/B/23.

167 RSW to Nigel Priestley, 26 June 1984, Colne Valley Divisional Liberal Association papers.

168 RSW to Nigel Priestley, 5 November 1984, Colne Valley Divisional Liberal Association papers.

169 RSW to James Crossley, 7 September 1983, Wainwright papers file 5/B/23.

170 RSW to Nigel Priestley, 5 November 1984, Colne Valley Divisional Liberal Association papers.

171 Joanna Copsey (later Hannam), interview, 19 January 2009.

172 Lord Wallace, interview, 19 January 2009.

173 Nigel Priestley, interview, 30 October 2008.

174 Joyce Wainwright, interview, 17 June 2008.

175 Dunford died aged fifty-nine on 26 January 1985; Senior's funeral service was held at Linthwaite Methodist Church on 7 May 1982.

176 Joanna Copsey (later Hannam), correspondence with author, 21 January 2009.

177 Lord Wallace, interview, 19 January 2009.

178 Joyce Wainwright, interview, 17 June 2008.

179 Nigel Priestley, interview, 30 October 2008.

180 William Wallace, interview, 19 January 2009.

181 Gordon Beever, interview, 31 October 2008.

182 William Wallace, interview, 19 January 2009.

183 Joyce Wainwright, interview, 17 June 2008.

184 Stuart Webb, 14 March 2009. Webb declined to comment on this or any other aspect of his work with Wainwright.

185 Lord Wallace, interview, 19 January 2009.

186 Gordon Ellis, interview, 15 April 2009.

187 Gordon Beever, interview, 31 October 2008.

188 Joanna Hannam, interview, 19 January 2009.

189 William Wallace, interview, 19 January 2009.

190 Joanna Hannam, interview, 19 January 2009.

191 Jane Merritt, Area Agent's Report, 7 May 198, Yorkshire Liberal Federation Records, University of Bristol Special Collections.

192 William Wallace, interview, 19 January 200.

193 David Ridgway, interview, 21 October 2008 and Robert Iredale, interview, 16 April 2009.

194 Lord Rennard, interview, 29 June 2009.

195 RSW to Robert Iredale, 10 July 1987, Wainwright papers file 5/B/16; RSW to Chris Rennard, 10 February 1992, Wainwright papers file 5/B/33.

196 Bill Oldham, interview, 29 October 2008.

197 Executive meeting minutes, 17 July 1985.

198 Colne Valley Liberal Association Annual Report, 1985.

199 Barry Fearnley, interview, 31 October 2008.

200 Graham Riddick, interview, 16 March 2009.

201 Colne Valley Divisional Liberal Association Executive meeting minutes, 8 January 1987.

PART THREE: IN PARLIAMENT

10 The Parliamentary Liberal Party

The Parliamentary Liberal Party as it existed from the end of the Second World War until the Liberal Party's merger with the Social Democrats forty-three years later was a distinctive political body whose type is unlikely to be recreated, and Wainwright was an excellent example of the way it operated. It was said, with varying degrees of accuracy, to be distinctive in three ways: its size, its composition and its behaviour.[1]

The limited size of the Parliamentary Liberal Party is beyond dispute. Though twelve MPs were elected as Liberals in 1945, they were, in the words of one of their own number, 'a *very* mixed bag',[2] most of whom subsequently defected to another Party – two of them leaving before the next election in 1950, the first at which Wainwright stood for Parliament. Only half of them survived that election, to be joined by three others, and this number fell again to six the following year, where it remained for over a decade.

At the General Election of 1966, the number of Liberal MPs grew to a dozen at the point where Wainwright joined the group. After a setback in 1970, when Wainwright lost Colne Valley, there were fourteen Liberal MPs elected in the first General Election of 1974 when he returned, and only one less for most of the 1970s. Even the electoral boost provided by the SDP-Liberal Alliance in 1983 could not raise the size of the Parliamentary group, of which Wainwright was one to more than seventeen. Throughout this period, the Liberal MPs could comfortably hold their weekly meetings around a large dining-table. Cyril Smith, who attended these meetings with Wainwright, described the atmosphere as that of 'a pleasant, often amusing "think-tank" session where future plans and policy were discussed to a background of gentle banter'.[3]

The restricted number of Liberal MPs imposed a harsh burden upon those who were elected, in terms both of portfolio responsibilities – they were often called upon to shadow several ministers or track unfamiliar Bills in the Commons – and of media appearances and touring other constituencies to drum up support. Jo Grimond acknowledged in 1960 that his MPs 'have been acting like an overworked and rather ragged repertory company insisting on putting up a spokesman in every major debate. One day it is *East Lynne*, the next *Hamlet* or *Waiting for Godot*.[4] Wainwright managed these demands better than some MPs, sticking with economic portfolios and avoiding media exposure except by prior arrangement, usually as part of an election campaign. Nonetheless, he gave generously of his time to campaign for other Liberal candidates, and this was a contributory factor in his defeat in 1970.[5]

The make-up of the group of MPs was different from that of other parties, or of the Liberal Democrats today. This difference was centred around the cause of their election, but it had implications for their behaviour in Parliament. Most Liberal MPs owed their election to their individual profiles and personalities much more than their Labour or Conservative counterparts. They had often been exposed to extensive media attention, and had strong local credentials which they needed to cultivate in order to secure re-election. Journalist David Walter, who joined the Party in 1962, remembers Liberal MPs at the time as a 'group of outsize local personalities who frequently diverged on policy issues',[6] and Michael Steed, a former President of the Party, described the Liberals as 'a league of independents' who 'never found a natural role' in Parliament.[7]

Of the thirteen Liberal MPs elected alongside Wainwright in 1974, for example, apart from the Leader and his predecessor, five had won their seats at by-elections, two continued careers as television presenters, and two others successfully piloted Private Members' Bills onto the statute book.[8] The paragon of personalities was Cyril Smith: former Labour Mayor of Rochdale and stalwart of its Chamber of Commerce, he lived in his childhood home. He scoffed at Michael Steed's prediction that no Liberal could win Rochdale, but did so in his own words 'largely on personality grounds'.[9] Wainwright was not a high-profile figure nationally, but it was evident that both his personal appeal, and Colne Valley's Liberal traditions and organisation – which were themselves distinctive in flavour – were essential to his victory.

This background gave Liberal MPs a strong sense of their individual importance, and inhibited efforts to coax MPs into a common position. More than one Liberal Whip from these years has used the phrase '*prima donnas*' to describe such figures – 'individuals who were there only because they were individuals'[10] – and the challenge their self-confidence raised to co-ordination. Alan Beith even identified 'a Darwinian process of natural selection of Liberal MPs' which filtered out all but the strongest personalities.[11]

Another constraint which might have qualified Liberal MPs' sense of their own independent authority was also ineffective, because – partly because of their rarity and vulnerability – they were rarely disciplined or even given direction by their constituency parties. At national level, historically the Parliamentary Party had come into existence before the Party in the country; constitutionally it was separate from it, and its Leaders had insisted upon this several times during the post-war period. The annual Joint Liberal Assembly was the occasion at which representatives of the branches and recognised units of the Party gathered to assert their views. The problem of the Assembly was that it had neither legal authority nor political power in the Party. Studies pointed to the 'powerlessness' of the Assembly compared with the Council and the Standing Committee, which Wainwright chaired,[12] or dismissed it as 'a largely self-selecting group of grandees, candidates and principal activists. Its composition was also heavily dependent upon where it met.'[13] Jo Grimond streamlined Assembly business considerably and even toyed with the idea of abandoning it altogether.

Even those constituency branches with Liberal MPs were timid in their attempts to influence policy. Some would go for more than a year after an election without meeting. Wilfrid Roberts was Liberal MP for North Cumberland until 1950: after a contentious discussion with his local Party Executive about Liberal Parliamentary strategy, the minutes recording that he 'accepted the views of the committee' were diplomatically altered to state that he merely 'heard' them.[14]

Wainwright had a similarly Burkean[15] relationship with the Colne Valley Liberal Association: they expressed their views, he listened, but he did not consider himself obliged to obey. On a number of sensitive issues, including the Lib-Lab Pact and the formation of the Alliance, Wainwright either persuaded or contradicted most of his members. Before winning Colne Valley he wrote to his Association Chairman contemptuously about the kind of MP who retained his seat only 'if he appeases everybody and miserably avoids every challenge which might make him unpopular'.[16] Wainwright's Parliamentary secretary in the 1970s, Caroline Cawston, describes Wainwright's idea of the relationship between opinion in Colne Valley and events at Westminster:

> It was an entirely different thing. The people in Colne Valley were good, solid folk, and they were interested in the basics of life, and how they went about getting the basics of life they left to Westminster. So as long as he did the right thing by them, that was okay by them, I think would have been his view.[17]

The Chairman of the Association in the 1980s, David Ridgway, had the same impression as Cawston of the relationship from the other side:

> Richard did *not* like to be crossed, particularly by his own Party members; but at the same time, he would also subsequently consider what had happened. Time would demonstrate an opportunity where the divisions between two people could be brought together again.

David Ridgway himself offended Wainwright merely by challenging him for bringing a member of his staff to an Executive meeting. 'He called me "Derek" for the next two years', remembers Ridgway.[18]

Lastly, Liberal MPs could not be brought into line by the patronage possessed by the Whips of the two main parties. There was no prospect of ministerial office with which to deter the rebellious Member, and so Liberal

MPs could speak their mind with impunity. In fact, the Liberal Party chose to make a virtue of this particular necessity, celebrating the division amongst MPs it sometimes produced as a reflection of free thinking and expression. Party propaganda cartoons sneered that the only place Labour and the Conservatives had adapted to the challenge of automation was in the handling of their back-benchers, whose Liberal counterparts were hailed as 'the only people in Parliament who were given the privilege of freedom of conscience to vote as they considered best' and 'the only men in the House of Commons not compelled by three-line whips to vote against their conscience.' The 1953 Liberal Assembly deplored the regular use of the three-line whip by the main parties.[19] The very idea of a Liberal Whip sometimes seemed like a contradiction in terms: Cyril Smith regarded his appointment as Whip as 'the ultimate irony of my career' because of 'my deeply held and often expressed animosity towards the whipping system itself, trampling, as it so often does, on Parliamentary freedom.'[20]

Wainwright joined in this cry for the greater exercise of independent judgement by MPs, and the claim that the Liberals put the principle into practice. He told the electors of Pudsey that 'I believe you would prefer to have a Member free to speak your mind, and his mind, in Parliament',[21] and Martin Wainwright remembers his father letting him take hold of the loudspeaker at the age of four in the 1955 General Election campaign in Pudsey to call out the slogan 'Do not vote for the party stooges! Do not vote for the slave machines!'[22] Wainwright told a meeting at Skelmanthorpe that 'I am proud to be one of the only twelve people in Parliament who can genuinely behave independently, consult his own conscience and vote according to the situation'[23] and the Holmfirth Rotary Club that 'Parliament is at its best when the whips of the two main Parties are off.'[24] Both of Wainwright's 1974 Election Addresses called for 'a strong group of Liberal MPs, not the slaves of a Party Machine', and later that year he complained that 'Parliament today is so strangled by the party system that MPs in the two main parties are forced to put party loyalty before conscience and constituents' welfare.'[25] Lord Rennard remembers this as the keynote of his speech at the opening rally of David Alton's successful 1979 Edge Hill by-election campaign:

> Richard spoke very well, talking about the difference between a Liberal MP and an MP from any other Party, because a Liberal MP stood up for their conscience, they did what they thought was right, and wasn't subject to party control of the whips in the same way as people in the Labour and Conservative Parties were.[26]

At the opening of another successful by-election campaign in Littleborough and Saddleworth in 1995, some sixteen years later, Wainwright made the same speech. Wainwright's own literature at the 1979 General Election stressed that 'I continue to be directly responsible to you, the Colne Valley voters – not to Party Headquarters, not to whips and not to political bosses behind the scenes.' In his last Parliament, Wainwright coached his long-term protégé and new parliamentary colleague Michael Meadowcroft in dealing with Whips that 'if you want a "free vote", take one', though he cautioned that 'there are free votes and free votes.'[27] This attitude of determined but charming, measured and utterly rational dissent could disconcert even the most sympathetic of Liberal Whips trying to co-ordinate their colleagues: Cyril Smith advised Alan Beith on handing over the Whip's duties to him in 1977 that 'he's a funny bugger, you know, is Richard.'[28] That this was said entirely affectionately is confirmed by Smith's own admiring testimony of Wainwright years later that 'he was a little rebel.'[29]

Wainwright was subjected to one of the more common attacks made by opponents upon Liberal MPs, namely that they did not attend Westminster often enough. The year after he entered Parliament, Wainwright was criticised in the local press by Huddersfield MP Kenneth Lomas for missing a debate on defence.[30] It was true that Liberal MPs did attend less often than those of other parties, but the causes of this were not simply laziness. Liberal MPs had since 1950 never matched the average attendance at parliamentary divisions of about three-quarters, and had only once been at more than six in ten divisions in the space of a year. In at least three parliamentary sessions in the 1950s and early 1960s, Liberal MPs had been absent more often than present. During Wainwright's first Parliament Liberal MPs were at between 59 and 46 per cent of divisions. Wainwright himself exceeded this average in each session, and voted in 59 per cent of divisions across all three sessions, whereas the figure for all Liberal MPs was 55 per cent. The exact figures below demonstrate that in his first Parliament, Wainwright may have been at Westminster less than the average MP, but he had a better attendance record than the average Liberal.

	Liberal MPs' attendance	Wainwright's attendance
1966–67	59%	64%
1967–68	57%	60%
1968–69	46%	50%
1966–69	55%	59%

Wainwright's attendance in the 1970s edged towards the lower end of the range – he took part in 51 and 52 per cent of divisions during 1975–76 and 1976–77 – perhaps because he was even more immediately aware of the danger of losing his seat and the need to be seen to tend to its problems first hand.[31] The reasons for individual Liberal MPs' absenteeism were varied, but the general cause was common: some had other jobs – Roderic Bowen, the MP for Cardigan-shire, spent most of his time on his legal practice, for example – to which they reasonably feared they might at any election need to return; others were elderly and ill, or invested much of their time in projects outside Parliament, such as Russell Johnston's work in the European Parliament. All, however, needed to tend their seats.

Labour opponents in the Colne Valley regarded Wainwright's professional and business activities as something of an Achilles' heel, and throughout the 1970s presented them as a distraction from his parliamentary duties. In 1970, 1974 and 1979, Labour candidates David Clark and Peter Hildrew used the slogan 'Colne Valley needs a full-time MP' or promised 'a proper full-time service as your MP'. Hildrew went further and added a Declaration of Interests to his Election Address, saying 'neither I nor my wife holds any company shares, directorships or public relations consultancies. We will neither acquire nor accept any if I am elected to Parliament.'[32] Letters in the local press criticised Wainwright for acquiring shares in Yorkshire Television,[33] and David Clark claimed that he had been obliged to be an 'unpaid MP' during the short 1974 Parliament taking up local issues which he alleged Wainwright had neglected.[34] He stressed his own record of constituency work when he had been the Colne Valley MP, and that he 'was full-time as an MP, with no outside directorships'.[35] Into the 1980s, Wainwright's name was called out in the Commons by angry Labour Left-wingers as an example of a Liberal MP with directorships.[36]

These criticisms angered Wainwright, and he responded robustly. His interest in Yorkshire Television was 'purely an investment',[37] and he dismissed attacks on his directorships and his partnership at Peat Marwick Mitchell accountants indignantly:

> It is a very foolish and short-sighted policy to choose an MP who has no other job to fall back on ... A constituency is wise to choose somebody who is in a position to be independent, and particularly to be independent in the interests of his constituency ... Democracy has been killed in some parts of Europe by being run by full-time politicians with no other skills at their command.[38]

In his February 1974 Election Address Wainwright asserted that 'I was glad to do a 60 hour week as Colne Valley's MP, and I am wholly at your service.'[39] Wainwright sharply rebutted Clark's claims to have taken up neglected issues: 'when Mr Clark has lived in Skelmanthorpe for a longer time, he will realise that in these valleys there are literally thousands of people who assist others by taking up cases ... There is a great tradition of voluntary help in this area, and most of the people who do it, do it quietly.'[40]

What interfered more seriously with Wainwright's attendance was his insistence upon keeping what Sir Menzies Campbell called 'Methodist hours': he resolutely refused to attend any debate in the chamber of the Commons after Midnight, and was notorious for gathering up his gabardine and marching out of Parliament ostentatiously as the clock struck. He would even agree to return at 5.30 a.m. at the end of an all-night sitting to relieve more flexible colleagues rather than break this rule.[41]

Most fundamentally, the criticism of Liberal MPs for not taking part in parliamentary divisions fails to recognise that the purpose of being a Liberal MP was different from that of Labour or Conservative backbenchers, and that the pressures coming to bear upon them were different. Most Liberal MPs had remote, sizeable constituencies with small majorities which required careful tending if the Member was to retain the right to attend the House at all. This was certainly true of Wainwright. Secondly, the Commons was an unwelcoming and unrewarding place for twelve Liberals amongst 650 MPs: they had few opportunities to speak or to question ministers, and no influence over the legislative programme. They had no route by which to contact the Government or the prospective government, and earned little media attention for their work in the House. The howling which until the recent formation of the coalition Government habitually greeted the Liberal Democrat Leader on all sides at Prime Minister's Questions is only an echo of the exclusion Wainwright and his colleagues must have felt. In most cases they also – and this was undoubtedly true of Wainwright – had little affection for the capital, and according to Lord Greaves, 'hated going to London'.[42] Under these circumstances, it is unsurprising that Liberal MPs like Wainwright placed limits on the time they devoted to parliamentary processes. Their approach had nothing to do with neglecting their constituents, and everything to do with objecting to the way Parliament ran.

This disdain for the hollow rituals of Parliament was shared by Wainwright even before his entry into the Commons. 'To sit in Parliament', he put it to veteran Colne Valley Councillor A.G. Holland in considering whether to stand again after the 1964 election, 'must surely be one of the most deadly jobs'.[43] Around the same time, he wrote to Liberal Headquarters complaining about the ineffectiveness of the Liberal MPs.[44] At his 1964 Adoption meeting, Wainwright anticipated his role as an outsider in the Commons, saying that 'a lot of people today needed somebody to stand up for them and Parliament should be made to do so'.[45] At the end of his first Parliament, Wainwright expressed exasperation that 'we have the almost nightly experience as to whose company we should keep in the lobby and from time to time it causes us revulsion'.[46] A decade later he told a Yorkshire Liberal Federation meeting in Huddersfield that 'Liberal MPs are prepared to join their fellow Liberals throughout the country rather than waste their time on the type of pre-determined politics which is taking place in the House of Commons at present'.[47] Even as he retired, Wainwright complained that 'the barracking and raucous laughter which dominates broadcasts from the House of Commons shows the feeble character of many people who get into Parliament, and the unhappy lack of real characters in the Commons'.[48] He reflected privately that 'to me, coming to terms with no-more-Westminster was instant and full of delight'.[49]

Critics noticed Wainwright's unease in the Chamber. Andrew Alexander, who had been his Conservative opponent in 1963 and 1964, later turned to parliamentary sketch-writing for the *Daily Telegraph*, and – though admiring of Wainwright's constituency profile – hardly noticed him in the Commons. 'He was just a sort of straight up-and-down Liberal MP. He didn't sparkle particularly in the House of Commons.'[50] David Clark, who defeated Wainwright in 1970 and after losing Colne Valley twice in 1974 was elected for South Shields in 1979, looked in vain for his old adversary during Wainwright's last two Parliaments:

> If you'd asked me the question: 'What's my memory of him in Parliament?', I haven't got one. I sat here with him for certainly eight years, and I've got no memory at all of him. He's a man whom, obviously, I looked out for, because I'd beaten him and he'd beaten me twice, so it's a person who I was looking for. I'm just conscious that he made the responses at Budget time – but none of them made an impression.[51]

Though hardly sympathetic observers, these reflect a pattern which makes sense for Wainwright as a personality and as a Liberal MP. Wainwright was not a spontaneous orator; he rehearsed after-dinner speeches for Huddersfield Town Hall verbatim in the bathroom mirror, and twitched his hand nervously even when speaking to constituency activists. He spoke well, clearly, coherently and with serious preparation; but the theatrical, adversarial atmosphere of the Commons Chamber did not play to his strengths. One set-piece performance which Wainwright gave responding to the Queen's Speech suffered the additional indignity of being interrupted by a power cut plunging the Chamber into darkness.[52]

Wainwright preferred to place his faith in enquiry based upon evidence rather than prejudice, and debate driven by reflection rather than playing to the gallery. Add to this the fact that Liberals had pitifully little opportunity to take part in what they regarded as the Punch-and-Judy show of the Commons, let alone to change it, and it is no surprise that Wainwright sometimes steered clear of the floor of the House. In the 1974 Parliament, for example, he asked only two or three oral questions to ministers per year, but submitted hundreds in writing.[53] Joanna Copsey (later Hannam)'s job was to draft such questions, and she quickly understood their purpose for Wainwright:

> What he saw as important was keeping his name in the press locally and therefore part of my job was to scan the horizon for what was happening in the constituency, and to think of Parliamentary Questions that we could table that would make news for us. Questions about apprenticeships or job losses, skills training or anything that we could look at, get interesting results from, that would help inform Richard's work in the Colne Valley, or his profile in the Colne Valley.[54]

This does not mean that Wainwright took no pride in his work at Westminster or that he was cynical about it – in fact, he made over 1,200 interventions in debates in the Chamber of the Commons. However, he focused his efforts on activities which were more likely to be productive than general debates. Foremost amongst these were Select Committees: Wainwright was on the Expenditure Committee from 1974–79 and then, as a member of the Treasury Select Committee, one of only two Liberal MPs given seats on the new Departmental Select Committees. Committee work allowed him to use his detailed analytical skills and financial expertise to the full in a less partisan and more deliberative atmosphere. Sir Cyril Smith, who became familiar with the difficulties faced by Liberal MPs over a parliamentary career of twenty years, gives a balanced judgement on Wainwright:

> He was more of a questioner than a speaker. He could make speeches, and did make speeches, I don't want to underestimate him, but he was a prober, and a man willing to expose things that needed exposing. He'd no fear. He was never one that wondered what the consequences would be, and he wasn't afraid to criticise opponent ... The really effective ones are those that can – and Richard was capable of that – of asking a question that stung, and then sit down. The best ones are where he makes his speech, the minister, or he's answering a question, and you stand up with a Supplementary Question and say: 'Why?' and sit down.[55]

Wainwright, then, had particular uses for his place in the Commons, and a distaste for certain aspects of its procedures. His effectiveness did not go unrecognised: Labour MP Jack Diamond credited Wainwright with being 'persuasive in his brevity'. After a Budget debate, Diamond noted that 'in his typical fashion, he took a swipe with his left at the Government and followed it up with a tremendous right at the Opposition';[56] within a year of Wainwright taking his seat, future Prime Minister James Callaghan noticed that the Member for Colne Valley 'although he has not intervened very much, has always been cogent in what he said'.[57] Harold Lever was particularly effusive in his praise of Wainwright's maiden speech, 'delivered with great charm and which exhibited all the characteristics of combativeness and good nature which I should have thought are the qualities which most commend speeches to Honourable Members'.[58] He introduced a proposed amendment based on his 'Own as You Earn' principles of share ownership[59] and an Anti-Dumping Bill to protect the textiles industry;[60] he represented the Liberal Party at the Committee stage of the 1968 Finance Bill, and at the 1970 election *The Sunday Times* identified him as one of the 'Liberals whom Parliament can manifestly not afford to lose'.[61] *The Guardian* gave Wainwright as an illustration of the fact that Liberal MPs 'on their own topics, speak with an authority unusual amongst backbenchers'.[62]

Responding to one of Wainwright's last contributions in the Chamber assessing the 1987 Budget, veteran Conservative MP and journalist George Gardiner described him as 'a senior and respected Member of this House'.[63] After Parliament reassembled, his Conservative successor in Colne Valley called Wainwright 'a respected Member of the House and a good constituency

Member who was always on hand to help constituents with their problems, however small'; Labour Member Alan Williams, who had been made a Privy Councillor on the same day, said 'I have always felt friendship and affection for him', and fellow trustee of the Parliamentary Pension Fund, Geoffrey Ginsberg, described him as 'a very distinguished and very hardworking Member who looked after the interests of all Honourable Members.'[64]

Unsurprisingly, the relationships within the over-burdened, small group of distinctive and strong personalities within the Liberal Parliamentary Party were often intense, and Wainwright was not a clubbable colleague. In 1966 he became one of a group shoe-horned into a single room high up in St Stephen's Tower, to which Rochdale's Labour MP Jack McCann had shown him. They had claimed the right to use it, with a touch of historical poetic justice which amused Wainwright, because its former occupant, the Chief Whip of the National Liberals (who had split away from the official Party in 1931) had died, and the 'absurd group', as Wainwright called it, had been subsumed into the Conservative Party. 'Notwithstanding Sir Herbert Butcher being dead, the Vote was delivered daily to this room, and the huge piles of unopened pages did not deter daily delivery addressed to the deceased. With glee, I emptied my suitcases into one of the desks, and invited four other homeless Liberal MPs to use the room as well.'[65]

Wainwright liked the company of David Penhaligon and Geraint Howells, and was pleased to see protégés David Alton and Michael Meadowcroft enter the Commons in 1979 and 1983, though he came to differ with both on particular issues. He admired three other northern Liberal MPs – Alan Beith, the MP for Berwick; Rochdale's Cyril Smith, whose life story he described as 'a tale of positive democracy'[66] though he could be disconcerted by Smith's spontaneous style; and Michael Winstanley, who won Cheadle at the same election that Wainwright entered the Commons, and to whom he was happy to surrender some of his economic portfolio for his understanding of industrial issues.[67] It must have been a particular source of Yorkshire pride to Wainwright just before the 1987 General Election to host the Yorkshire Liberal Federation Assembly at Holmfirth, and take part in a 'Question Time' panel with Meadowcroft and the winner of the recent Ryedale by-election, Elizabeth Shields. He respected the intellectual prowess of John Pardoe, the Liberal Treasury spokesman, with whom he worked closely and whom he supported in the leadership contest of 1976, though he took a different view of the outgoing Leader, Jeremy Thorpe, from Pardoe.

Wainwright was especially impressed with the MP who was Party Leader when he entered the Commons, Jo Grimond. Wainwright provided invaluable support for Grimond's organisation, and supplied financial and intellectual substance for the Party's policy and campaigning operations under Grimond, but he regarded Grimond's unique contribution as being to articulate these ideas, motivate activists and inspire voters, and so to restore the Liberal Party's fortunes. Wainwright's role was to complement this profile with his own organisational abilities and his empathy with Liberal activists.

'Richard saw it as his job to pump Jo up to do something', remembers Lord Trevor Smith, who worked with both of them from the 1950s onwards.[68] Michael Meadowcroft, who helped organise Grimond's speaking tours in the 1960s, agrees that 'we had terrible trouble getting on the road before eleven o'clock';[69] and Luise Nandy remembers that her father, Frank Byers, had a similar relationship with Grimond, starting earlier, in which 'Jo could be the philosopher and talk to governments, and that seemed to work very well.'[70] Vince Cable, then a student, noticed the common faith of Wainwright and Grimond in economic liberalism.[71] Lord Tordoff, who went on to be Party President, noted that 'Jo was never a Party man, whereas Richard was.'[72] Wainwright's admiration for Grimond was reflected in the care with which the Leader's visits to Colne Valley were managed: as one present remembers, 'Jo Grimond's visits were like royalty coming – more important.'[73]

Grimond and Wainwright both wanted the Liberal Party to achieve greater national standing, and brought distinctive talents to the task. They both saw the need to spread its base beyond the 'Celtic Fringe' seats which had sustained its parliamentary existence in its darkest days, and to win urban voters over. Yet Wainwright was aware that positioning the Liberal Party on the Left made his job in Colne Valley more difficult, and it is testimony to his loyalty that he saw the need for this in the Party's national interests; he was also to be disappointed by Grimond twice over Grimond's support for Jeremy Thorpe's leadership, an experience which showed that Wainwright was, for all his talent and experience, always an 'outsider'.

Wainwright's relationships with other colleagues could be frosty. Like other Liberals, he was uneasy about the populism, especially on race, of Wallace Lawler, who won Birmingham Ladywood at a by-election in 1969 only to lose it the following year. He regarded Peter Bessell, the MP for Bodmin who was a close associate of Jeremy Thorpe, as 'a bit of a joke.'[74] He was unimpressed by the intellectual rigour and political achievements of Russell Johnston, who had represented Inverness since before Wainwright came into the Commons, and stayed there after he had gone. 'Russell feeds our philosophical enemies', he wrote to Michael Meadowcroft: 'I think that is why the world ignores him. Perhaps it also accounts for his remarkable lack of clout, and the small harvest of his European activities.'[75]

Wainwright also came to disapprove of the conduct of Jeremy Thorpe and David Steel as Leaders, the very different reasons for which are explored below. Otherwise, the chief challenge to his patience in the Liberal Parliamentary Party was Clement Freud. Restaurateur, television presenter and night-club owner, Freud had become a Liberal MP in 1973 with the encouragement of

Jeremy Thorpe, whom he repaid by supporting him through his resignation, even cooking dinner for him each night during the former Leader's trial. Stories abound of Freud's womanising in the office he shared with Wainwright and spending days placing large bets on the office telephone – on horses and on by-election results. Sir Menzies Campbell, who took over Freud's desk, found the drawers still contained Freud's notepaper marked with racing tips. When Freud's sophisticated sense of smell was offended by the perfume worn by Wainwright's secretary, he angrily ordered her not to use it, only to find the next day that Wainwright brought her a huge and heavily scented bouquet of gardenias, which he placed between her desk and Freud's. Freud, in turn, was amused at having used his national newspaper column to compliment Joyce Wainwright as the creator of a highly alcoholic cake he had bought at a Liberal Assembly. Mistakenly believing the Wainwrights to be teetotallers and that Joyce had not known what she had put in the cake, he thought he had embarrassed them.

Freud himself said that he could not recall a single conversation with Wainwright, 'though I always felt he rather disapproved of me'.[76] Freud's flamboyant, self-assured style – he would ostentatiously dictate correspondence in French, German and Latin in their shared office – certainly got under Wainwright's skin very quickly, but there were more substantial reasons for their mutual suspicion: Freud not only supported Thorpe after the resignation which Wainwright had triggered but also backed David Steel as his successor, when Wainwright supported John Pardoe, during which period Wainwright's secretary remembers, 'it was really quite bitter'.[77] Worst of all, Wainwright came to suspect Freud of being involved in the disappearance from his cluttered desk of sensitive files regarding the Thorpe case and his investigations into the activities of the South African Secret Service, details of which found their way into the *Daily Express*, for which Freud wrote a column. All of this made Wainwright understandably wary of Freud, in contrast to his relationship with other Liberal MPs, as Eric Flounders, who worked in their shared office, remembers:

> It was quite tense … At that time we were in a little office up a spiral staircase off the central lobby, and there was Cyril [Smith], Richard, me, Freud and Freud's assistant. Next door was [John] Pardoe and his secretary. We were all squashed in, and of course you've got to get on under those circumstances. Cyril and Richard got on very well; Pardoe got on well with everybody; but as soon as Freud came into the room there was a definite cooling of conversation.[78]

Election to Parliament had been Wainwright's goal for twenty years, but arrival there confirmed some of his reservations about the way it ran. Like all institutions with which he was involved, however, Wainwright decided to put it to what he considered its best use – and to urge others including his Leaders to do the same.

Notes

1 A more detailed account of the nature of the Parliamentary Liberal Party can be found in Norton, P., 'The Liberal Party in Parliament', in Bogdanor, V. (ed.), *Liberal Party Politics* (Oxford: Oxford University Press 1983), pp. 143–72. For comparison across the whole of the period from 1945 to the present day, see Cole, M., 'Growing Without Pains?: Explaining Liberal Democrat MPs' Behaviour', *British Journal of Politics and International Relations*, Vol. 11 No. 2, pp. 259–79.

2 E. Roderic Bowen (MP, Cardiganshire, 1945–66), interview, 8 August 2000.

3 Cyril Smith, *Big Cyril: The Autobiography of Cyril Smith* (London: W.H. Allen 1977), p. 195.

4 *Daily Mail*, 8 December 1960.

5 Gordon Beever, interview, 31 October 2008. Beever was a member of Wainwright's campaign team at the 1970 election.

6 Walter, D., 'A Golden Dawn', *The Guardian*, 24 September 2003.

7 Steed, M., 'The Liberal Party', in Drucker, H.M. (ed.), *Multi-Party Britain* (London: Macmillan 1979), p. 79.

8 Alan Beith, Cyril Smith, Clement Freud, David Steel and Emlyn Hooson were elected at by-elections; Freud was a national television personality and Michael Winstanley was a broadcaster on North-West television; and Steel had piloted through the Abortion Act 1967, whilst Stephen Ross was to promote the Homeless Persons Act of 1977.

9 Cyril Smith, interview, 8 January 2000.

10 David Steel (Liberal Whip 1970–75), interview, 28 February 2007.

11 Alan Beith, interview, 9 August 1999.

12 Lees, J.D. and Kimber, R., *Political Parties in Modern Britain* (London: Routledge 1972).

13 Ingham, R., 'Battle of Ideas or Absence of Leadership', *Journal of Liberal History* No.47, Summer 2005, p. 38. There are some more favourable accounts of the Assembly, e.g. Burton 1983, unpublished PhD thesis, Reading, but these tend to confuse the perception of representativeness with the reality of influence.

14 Cumbria Liberal Association General Purposes Committee minutes, 2 February 1946, Cumbria RO DSO/117/4.

15 Whig MP Edmund Burke famously said in his speech to the electors of Bristol in 1774 that it was 'his duty to sacrifice his repose, his pleasures, his satisfactions, to theirs; and above all, ever, and in all cases, to prefer their interest to his own. But his unbiased opinion, his mature judgment, his enlightened conscience, he ought not to sacrifice to you, to any man, or to any set of men living.'

16 RSW to Cllr Alex Holland, JP, 6 November 1964, Wainwright papers file 6/8.

17 Caroline Cawston, interview, 2 June 2008.

18 David Ridgway, interview, 31 Oct 2008. Wainwright apparently enjoyed causing amusement or annoyance by deliberately mistaking or adapting others' names: during the 1979 General Election campaign, he referred in private to his Labour opponent, *Guardian* journalist Peter Hildrew, as 'Mr. Mildew' (Joanna Hannam, interview, 19 January 2009).

19 A.J.F. Macdonald (Ross and Cromarty 1950–51), 'Activities of the Liberal Party in

Parliament', Scottish Liberal Federation General Council minutes', 7 October 1950, Scottish Liberal Party papers Acc. 11765; John Arlott, 'This is a Party of Free Men', *News Chronicle*, 10 March 1956.

20 Smith, *Big Cyril*, p. 177.

21 'A Letter to You from Richard Wainwright', Pudsey election address, 1955.

22 Wainwright, M., 'Reliving the Liberal Party of the 1950s', http://www.guardian.co.uk/politics/blog/2008/jun/13/tomorrowsat14junetheres (accessed 15 September 2008).

23 Cited by K. Lomas in 'Independence in Parliament', letters, *Huddersfield Daily Examiner*, 3 August 1967.

24 Press release, 7 June 1972.

25 Wainwright, R., 'Toeing the party line can be agonising', *Oldham Evening Chronicle*, 30 November 1974.

26 Lord Rennard, interview, 30 July 2009.

27 Michael Meadowcroft, interview, 17 June 2008.

28 Alan Beith, interview, 13 October 2008.

29 Cyril Smith, interview, 29 May 2008.

30 Lomas, K., 'Independence in Parliament', letters, *Huddersfield Daily Examiner*, 3 August 1967.

31 *Oldham Evening Chronicle*, 28 May and 24 December 1977.

32 Peter Hildrew, Election Address to the voters of Colne Valley 1979, Bristol University Special Collections.

33 Undated cutting in Colne Valley Labour Party papers, University of Huddersfield Archives file CV3. Presumed *Huddersfield Daily Examiner* 1970.

34 *Colne Valley Guardian*, 27 September 1974.

35 *Oldham Evening Chronicle*, 4 October 1974.

36 Denis Skinner, interrupting Paddy Ashdown, Hansard, 17 May 1984.

37 Undated cutting in Colne Valley Labour Party papers, University of Huddersfield Archives file CV3.

38 *Colne Valley Guardian*, 5 June 1970, p. 1.

39 RSW Election Address February 1974, University of Bristol Special Collection.

40 *Colne Valley Guardian*, 27 September 1974.

41 Beith, A., *A View from the North* (Newcastle: Northumbria University Press 2008), p. 96.

42 Lord Greaves, interview, 8 April 2009.

43 RSW to Cllr Alex Holland, JP, 6 November 1964, Wainwright papers file 6/8.

44 Tim Beaumont to Richard Wainwright, 13 November 1964, Wainwright papers file 9/5.

45 Colne Valley Divisional Liberal Association Special General Meeting minutes, 22 September 1964.

46 Wainwright, R., Hansard, 17 December 1969.

47 Yorkshire Liberal Federation meeting minutes, 12 January 1980, University of Bristol Special Collections.

48 RSW press release, 1 June 1987.

49 RSW to Joanna Hannam, 21 July 1987, Wainwright papers file 5/B/25.

50 Andrew Alexander, interview, 13 March 2009.

51 Lord Clark, interview, 3 June 2008.
52 *Oldham Evening Chronicle*, 4 November 1977.
53 *The Political Companion* shows that Wainwright asked three oral, and 332 written question, from 1975–76, and 2 oral and 247 written questions the following year.
54 Joanna Hannam, interview, 19 January 2009.
55 Sir Cyril Smith, interview, 29 May 2008.
56 Hansard, 22 June 1966 and 7 June 1967.
57 Ibid., 30 June 1967.
58 Ibid., 5 May 1966.
59 Ibid., 14 June 1967.
60 This was a proposed amendment to the Customs Duties (Dumping and Subsidies) Act 1969. See Wainwright papers file 4/14.
61 'Where Votes for Men Matter', *The Sunday Times*, 14 June 1970.
62 *The Guardian*, 29 May 1970.
63 Hansard, 19 May 1987.
64 All of the above, Hansard, 13 July 1987.
65 'Members Only', *The House Magazine* 27 March 1987.
66 RSW's review of *Big Cyril*, *Yorkshire Post*, 19 September 1977.
67 RSW to Jeremy Thorpe, 7 November 1968, Wianwright papers file 8/19.
68 Lord Trevor Smith, interview, 22 June 2009.
69 Michael Meadowcroft, interview, 17 June 2008.
70 Luise Nandy, interview, 18 January 2009.
71 Cable, V., *Free Radical: a Memoir* (Atlantic Books, 2009), p. 42.
72 Lord Tordoff, interview, 27 July 2009.
73 Caroline Cawston, interview, 2 June 2008.
74 Joyce Wainwright, interview, 17 June 2008.
75 RSW to Michael Meadowcroft, 10 February 1988, Wainwright papers file 11/5.
76 Clement Freud, correspondence with the present author, 3 July 2008.
77 Caroline Cawston, interview, 2 June 2008.
78 Eric Flounders, interview, 18 May 2009.

11 Wainwright and Jeremy Thorpe

In 1976 the Liberal Leader Jeremy Thorpe resigned office amid allegations that he had had an affair with a male model, Norman Scott, that he had paid Scott to keep the affair from the public, and later that Thorpe and several associates had arranged to have Scott murdered. The alleged attempted killing was bungled, and Scott survived to see Thorpe and his co-accused stand trial for Conspiracy to Murder at the Old Bailey. Thorpe and his co-accused were all acquitted in 1979, but the trial was the subject of fierce controversy and the episode opened up a view of Thorpe's private life which even some of his supporters found disconcerting. At yet another point of jeopardy for the Liberal Party, Wainwright was at the centre of events, and his conduct threw into its sharpest relief his willingness to take risks with his own interests to do what he thought was right for Liberalism.[1]

Wainwright and Thorpe had been on the Party Executive together since the early 1950s. Thorpe campaigned in the Colne Valley by-election of 1963, by which time he had already been in the Commons for four years. The relationship between Thorpe and Wainwright was never especially warm, and it was not natural that it should be; events only served to bring simmering mutual suspicion to the boil.

Whereas Wainwright was a no-nonsense radical Methodist preacher, a Yorkshire patriot and a highly principled figure who valued consistency above popularity, Thorpe was a flamboyant, volatile performer: a brilliant raconteur and mimic, he partied with celebrities from Noel Coward to Jimi Hendrix, and relished the metropolitan high life – his lavish wedding reception, for example, was held at the Royal Academy. Thorpe was a London barrister, the son of a judge who was also a Tory MP; Wainwright was a Leeds accountant born of another Leeds accountant. Wainwright had endured six parliamentary contests over sixteen years to get into the Commons at the age of forty-eight; Thorpe had sailed in as a thirty-year-old at the second attempt after only four years. Both had attended public school, but where Thorpe's was Eton, Wainwright's was the less prestigious Shrewsbury. They were at best an odd couple.

Some commentators on Thorpe's downfall have attributed Wainwright's opposition to Thorpe to homophobia, but this should be discounted. Even some close colleagues of Wainwright's are prepared to acknowledge that disapproval of homosexuality is at least plausible as an element in his motivation, and that he probably regarded it as sinful.[2] The main local paper in his constituency – which in its own words 'has always had a high regard for Mr Wainwright's judgement of affairs' – challenged Thorpe's critics to 'say what it is they are most concerned about', and asked 'Is it whether Mr Thorpe has been lying? Is it whether he once had a homosexual affair with Norman Scott?'[3]

Whilst it would have been unsurprising to find a middle-aged man with a pre-war upbringing uncomfortable with male homosexuality, there is no clear evidence that this was true of Wainwright. In fact, there is evidence to the contrary: unlike one Liberal MP, he voted for the Sexual Offences Act of 1967 which decriminalised most male homosexual relations[4] and, more significantly, he employed an openly homosexual man amongst his parliamentary staff and even helped to finance his first house purchase.[5] There were explicitly reactionary elements in the Liberal Party on this issue – as the hostility to the National Executive's 1976 'internal education' campaign to support its advanced position on gay liberation showed – but Wainwright did not support them.[6] If Wainwright was hostile to homosexuality, it did not emerge explicitly in public or in any testimony now publicly available, and it was in any case not his motivation in the Thorpe affair. What made him suspicious of Thorpe's leadership was nothing to do with the Party Leader's alleged sexuality – it was something to do with personal style, partly about policy-making, but crucially about trustworthiness.

It is worth remembering that Thorpe's leadership had been opposed from the outset by others in the Party, too. This opposition centred around differences of style in policy-making. In this, Wainwright was reminiscent of the great Liberal Prime Minister and fellow West Yorkshireman, Asquith: cerebral, understated and cautious in public commitments. Thorpe's style by contrast was closer to that of Asquith's rival Lloyd George: outspoken, unpredictable and with a mercurial – supporters might say 'heroic' – approach to policy. Michael Meadowcroft, who had joined the Liberal Headquarters under Wainwright's patronage as Local Government Officer in 1962, said Thorpe 'had no depth, no rigour and no passion. I did not like his style as Treasurer. He was autocratic and tried to sack people, which was unheard of.' Meadowcroft added: 'He never forgave any of us for opposing him.'[7] Jo Grimond's speech-writer William Wallace felt similarly frozen out: 'Jeremy worked with a closed coterie of friends and associates and none of the rest of us knew what was going on, and [we] got increasingly suspicious of what was going on as the years went by.'[8] Wainwright shared these anxieties about Thorpe's lack of strategic sense, accusing him of turning the Party into 'an up-stage circus',[9] his parliamentary staff reporting that Wainwright 'was quite scathing about Thorpe not knowing where he was leading the Party, not having an idea in his head.[10] Thorpe's public suggestion that Rhodesia be bombed to cripple its rail network was one of the spontaneous policy departures which Wainwright found particularly ill-considered.

The tension between Wainwright and Thorpe did not escape the notice of their fellow Liberal MPs. 'The contrast couldn't have been greater between them', David Alton acknowledged: 'I don't think there could be any great rapport at a personal level. I think Richard was always deeply suspicious of Jeremy's motives and I think he just assumed he was motivated by his own personal ambitions. That was not something you would ever say about Richard Wainwright.'[11] Another more outspoken parliamentary colleague, Cyril Smith, said that Wainwright 'believed Thorpe was a crook, to put it bluntly – and in the Parliamentary Party he made it clear exactly what his view of Thorpe was'. Smith went on:

> He thought he was more of an act than a reality. He was a first class speaker, you see, was Thorpe, he was a very good orator, and Richard used to say: 'Yes, but you want to examine *what* he's saying, Cyril, not *how* he's saying it.' He never waged a campaign against Thorpe, but he just made his views known, and Thorpe was under no illusions about Wainwright.

Smith speculates that whereas Wainwright envied Thorpe's gifts of communication, Thorpe resented Wainwright's financial security. Certainly, he argued, their mutual dislike was long-standing and, given the chance, 'Richard would've gone for him earlier.'[12] David Steel also noted that Wainwright was 'never a fan of Jeremy's'.[13] For his own part, Thorpe remembers Wainwright as 'puritan'; a principled man misled by religious zeal, 'he was intolerant of those who did not match his intellectual and self-imposed moral standards.'[14]

In Parliament, they were almost immediately at odds: shortly after the 1966 election, Wainwright heard from Peter Bessell, the MP for North Cornwall and a close ally of Thorpe's, of rumours that Thorpe had had homosexual relationships. Soon afterwards Wainwright was asked to sign in a guest of Thorpe's who was visiting the public gallery when Thorpe was not available. Wainwright was later asked by Palace of Westminster staff to leave the dining room to deal with the guest, who was evidently drunk, and had begun shouting allegations about his relationship with Thorpe from the public gallery in the hearing of Members, visitors and the press. Wainwright ushered the visitor out of the main lobby and returned to his dinner. This was, as he later confided to his secretary, foolishly innocent, for minutes later the same visitor was haranguing members of the public queuing for the Commons, and Wainwright was obliged this time to put the troublemaker into a taxi. In fact, he took the precaution of getting into the taxi to see that it reached its destination, and during the journey the distressed young man explained in full his grievances against Thorpe. The visitor, Wainwright told his secretary some years later, was Norman Scott.

Thorpe apologised to Wainwright with characteristic charm for associating him with the incident, and dismissed the noisy visitor as 'a complete fantasist'.[15] Though annoyed, Wainwright was inclined to believe that an extravert such as Thorpe might attract weak personalities, and gave him the benefit of the doubt. However, he immediately told two parliamentary colleagues the story, which angered Thorpe, and according to one account, 'Wainwright was left with a feeling of uneasiness about the friends Thorpe seemed to have.'[16]

The Party leadership fell vacant in January 1967 when Jo Grimond announced his resignation, allowing only twenty-four hours before Liberal MPs had to choose a replacement. On the basis of his experiences to date, and of warnings he had received from Richard Rowntree at the 1965 Liberal Party Assembly in Scarborough about the dangers represented by a Thorpe leadership, Wainwright opposed Thorpe's bid to succeed Grimond. The circumstances of the election left little opportunity for anyone to challenge Grimond's preferred heir, however: the outgoing Leader had ensured a minimal run-in, and the election would be held amongst only the twelve Liberal MPs, amongst whom Thorpe ran a well-prepared and aggressive campaign in the hours available.[17] In those hours over the night of 17 and 18 January 1967, Wainwright received telegrams and telephone messages from dozens of Party officers, candidates and activists, particularly in the north, urging him to stand for the leadership; some met hastily to gather support for a Wainwright campaign, and the whole of the North West, Manchester and Cheshire Liberal Federation Executive gave its endorsement. Lord Tordoff, then candidate for Knutsford, remembers one such meeting taking place at the home of Barry Downs, recently candidate for Stockport North: 'there was a whole string of candidates there desperate to get Richard to stand – not that I suspect he would have made a great Leader of the Party, but he was the man of integrity, which we all felt Thorpe wasn't.'[18]

However, this was a futile endeavour. Not only did Thorpe enjoy the support of the outgoing Leader, but his public profile, his talents of communication and his parliamentary service – only Grimond had been in the Commons longer – made Thorpe the runaway favourite with the Party in the country. Michael Meadowcroft was working in Liberal Headquarters at the time, and was given the task of sounding out opinion amongst activists by telephoning each of the hundreds of Liberal council group Leaders. Though he wanted Wainwright to stand, and tried surreptitiously to gauge support for him, he found that Thorpe was almost universally preferred:

Even if he'd been keen, it wasn't possible. What we said to each [group] leader was: 'the three candidates are Thorpe, Hooson and Lubbock – who would you vote for?' and they were all saying Thorpe. I would freelance, and say 'And if Mr Wainwright were to stand?': no, no, no it was Thorpe.[19]

Wainwright was in any case not keen: he had less than a year's parliamentary experience, a marginal seat, and a strong antipathy to high-intensity fast-moving media attention and to the metropolis. 'To lead from day to day here under the eye of the whole Press and TV, mostly hostile and all critical', wrote Wainwright to his supporters, 'requires more than six months of parliamentary sittings and of general political life in the capital.'[20]

Wainwright and Cheadle MP Michael Winstanley voted for Eric Lubbock, the MP for Orpington, in the leadership contest. Wainwright, however, did seek assurances from Thorpe's backers about skeletons in the heir apparent's cupboard. When Wainwright reminded Grimond of the picture that Bessell had painted of Thorpe, the outgoing Leader dismissed it as 'irrelevant'.[21] Immediately before the vote amongst the MPs – the quaintly arcane nature of which was reflected in the use of a champagne cooler as a ballot box – Wainwright marched Peter Bessell out of the Whip's rooms, past waiting news reporters, to a separate room, just before the vote. He reminded Bessell of the confidences he had shared with him about Thorpe, and asked him directly: 'is there any risk of that matter – or anything else – becoming public?' Under 'calm but urgent' repeated questioning, Bessell insisted that it was 'all in the past'. Bessell confessed years later that 'I had lied to Wainwright and through him to an unknown number of Liberal MPs.'[22] To colleagues, Wainwright took Bessell at his word, but privately he remained uncertain.

In the vote, Lubbock and Emlyn Hooson had three supporters each, which meant that six MPs backed Thorpe, and his opponents withdrew. Wainwright accepted Thorpe's victory and told supporters afterwards that 'all of us here are lined up with him', but he also reassured them that Thorpe's victory was muted by recognition of the opposition to it: 'I know Jeremy positively wants a team effort (from all parts of the country) and will not consider wearing the mantle which Jo Grimond wore so well, of being an answer to almost all Liberal problems.'[23] It was only at the time of Thorpe's trial in 1979 that Wainwright acknowledged with characteristic reserve that, even in 1967, 'I felt he was not fitted to be leader.'[24]

Within little more than a year, Thorpe's leadership faced a public challenge from the radical Young Liberals, culminating in a vote of confidence at the Party Executive meeting on 28 June 1968. Thorpe's leadership was endorsed overwhelmingly – by forty-eight votes to two. However, Thorpe's awareness of a threat to his position was reflected by his acceptance of a resolution calling for an element of 'collective leadership' to influence policy decisions. Wainwright, though no part of this challenge, was associated with the YL leadership, particularly through his daughter Hilary, already drifting out of the Party to the Left, and the following year a small group of YLs, including William Wallace, Richard Holme and Michael Meadowcroft, visited Wainwright at The Heath in a failed attempt to persuade him to run against Thorpe for the leadership. 'We walked around this wonderful garden' remembers Wallace, 'and Richard, as was characteristic, *just* avoided saying why he wouldn't stand against Jeremy.'[25] Though circumspect about his suspicions of Thorpe, Wainwright at least reiterated why he did not wish to be Leader himself, as Michael Meadowcroft remembers:

> He said: 'stop this trying to promote me as a way of getting rid of Thorpe. I am not a leader; it's not me. I'll tell you why' he said: 'because leaders are first thinkers and I'm a second thinker. Leaders are people who have the intellectual confidence to do an analysis of something straight off: the media gets in touch, and here's the situation, straight away. That's not me. I'm the person who puts it together once that analysis has been made. That's why I'm not a leader.'[26]

At the 1970 General Election, Thorpe again visited Yorkshire to support Wainwright at the start of his campaign,[27] but the tensions were never far away. Allegations about Thorpe's relationship with Norman Scott became wider knowledge amongst Liberal MPs after the 1970 election. A constituent of Emlyn Hooson, Liberal MP for Montgomeryshire, wrote on Scott's behalf to alert Thorpe's colleagues to his behaviour. Hooson instituted an Inquiry into the allegations, conducted by himself, David Steel and Leader of the Liberal Lords and former Chief Whip, Frank Byers. The Inquiry sat on 9 June 1971, but found no conclusive evidence that Scott's allegations were true. The chief outcome was a commitment on Thorpe's part that if the matter became a source of public controversy in the future, he would step down as Leader. Thorpe escaped further action partly because Byers resented Scott's demands for money: 'this was an absolute red rag to a bull to Dad' said Byers's daughter, Luise Nandy, 'because he had seen blackmail so often in the armed forces.' She remembers David Steel describing her father reacting to five minutes of Scott's testimony by saying 'you're nothing but a bloody blackmailer – I'm not having anything to do with you!' before walking out. 'That absolutely rings true for me' says Nandy: 'he had a very short fuse, and he would have hated him from the start. If somebody had come and said: "I've got the evidence; I don't want anything out of this" – it would have been a totally different ball game as far as he was concerned.'[28] According to Hooson, Scott collapsed under Byers's questioning and wept 'like a jilted girl'.[29]

Thorpe's anxiety about his fellow Liberals was sharpened: he wrote to Home Secretary Reginald Maudling (who had been informed confidentially of the whole process) that 'the first lesson in politics is that no one can be as disloyal as one's own colleagues.'[30] Hooson remained sceptical about Thorpe's denials, and though the Inquiry was kept secret from the rest of the Liberal Party, Hooson told Wainwright – now Party Chairman, and out of Parliament – about his doubts two weeks later. Ostensibly, Wainwright accepted the outcome of the 1971 Inquiry and the commitment made by Thorpe to resign if the matter arose again. In practice, however, he found it difficult to keep his doubts to himself.

Wainwright asked Cyril Smith casually on a car journey to Oxford in 1974: 'Did you know there was an inquiry about Jeremy in 1971?' Smith said he did not, and Wainwright explained that 'some fellow came to the House of Commons and claimed he once had a homosexual affair with Jeremy. We had a meeting with Jeremy and decided there was nothing to it.'[31] Before the matter came out in court in 1976, Wainwright had more than once raised the matter over lunch with Liberal Chief Whip Alan Beith, insisting repeatedly: 'this can't go on.' Like Cyril Smith, Beith already felt that Wainwright's challenge to Thorpe 'was going to come at some time.'[32]

His continual raising of the issue with colleagues indicates the proportions the potential crisis was already assuming in Wainwright's mind. After all these events, Wainwright's secretary has said, 'he didn't know quite what to think: and as he said to me, this is nothing to do with the man's personal life; but if he lies about that, what else does he lie about? And then it became clear that he was lying about the money, and that was vital.'[33]

The controversy about Thorpe's handling of money surrounded his period as Party Treasurer between 1965 and 1967, and as Leader thereafter. During this period, incoming and outgoing resources grew substantially, partly due to Thorpe's energetic activity and that of his Deputy Treasurer (and contemporary at Oxford, and best man) David Holmes. It was ultimately alleged that Thorpe had used some of the funds he had recruited to pay those who were making damaging allegations about him. For Wainwright, this was the final straw: the charge was now not merely dishonesty, and potentially politically damaging dishonesty; it was dishonesty with other people's money – and other Liberals' money at that. David Alton remembers:

> Although he was a very private man, just occasionally there would be glimpses, for me, of just how deep the hurt went over the way that Jeremy Thorpe had behaved towards the Party. The Party, remember, was an extension of Richard's family in many ways ... Richard felt that, specifically on the issue of where money had been used, Party funds which were very precious, and these were funds which had been given by volunteers, often not very wealthy people, just to keep the Party going; the thought that some of that might have been used, as was alleged at the time, in an attempt to silence people during the allegations over conspiracy to murder, was something that I think he found unbearable.[34]

Hooson claims that now Wainwright was giving him the gossip about Thorpe: 'He was absolutely convinced that Thorpe should not be the Leader because of some financial problem – he discovered some impropriety by Thorpe when he was Party Treasurer. He took me on one side and said: "Some trouble about Thorpe; some money he's borrowed to keep someone quiet".'[35]

When in February 1976 the allegations surfaced in the national press following an unrelated court appearance by Scott, Wainwright got in touch with Peter Bessell, by this time living in the USA, to hear the full story of his role and that of Thorpe in the affair, ringing Bessell first from the offices of Richard Rowntree, a former business partner of Bessell's, in York. He taped the calls, and kept the tapes in Rowntree's safe because a file he prepared on the Scott affair had mysteriously disappeared from his office in the Commons. Wainwright lobbied other Liberal MPs to remove Thorpe, and by March had convinced half of them; in April, Wainwright, Bessell, Rowntree and Pratap Chitnis, whom Thorpe had fired from his position as Head of the Liberal Party Organisation, corresponded and spoke by telephone to discuss the growing revelations about Thorpe in the press. Wainwright told Bessell that 'I think all of us except Frank Byers – whose role is a little odd – feel it's now just a matter of time before a fairly unsavoury story about Jeremy is proved.'[36]

Wainwright approached Thorpe twice to demand that he refute Scott's claims: Thorpe expressed his intention to issue law suits 'against somebody', but did not; Wainwright appealed to Grimond to put pressure on Thorpe to sue or resign, but was deeply disappointed to find that – as in 1967 – Grimond backed his Etonian protégé. As Thorpe prepared to publish letters he had sent to Bessell to answer claims that they demonstrated the intimate nature of their relationship, David Holmes complained to Peter Bessell that 'Wainwright is being particularly poisonous … asking difficult questions, and spreading rumour and discontent.'[37] Other supporters of Thorpe, including Young Liberal Leader Steve Atack, were warning colleagues against listening to Wainwright.[38]

The letters appeared in the *Sunday Times* on 9 May 1976, but their revelations were foreshadowed in public speculation some days earlier. The day before, Saturday 8 May, Wainwright went to give a previously arranged interview, on Radio Leeds which was ostensibly about the local election results, but which in one Liberal MP's assessment came to be seen as 'delivering the fatal blow' to Thorpe. Alan Beith, Liberal Chief Whip at the time, said 'this finally tipped the scales for Jeremy.'[39] In formal language which betrayed nervousness, and in David Steel's phrase 'brimming with Methodist outrage',[40] Wainwright set Thorpe an ultimatum:

> Why has not Mr Thorpe sued for libel, which is the proper way in England for clearing one's name? Why does he not sue for libel Mr Scott and others who have made these allegations outside the court, in public? I must emphasise that this is not tittle-tattle. It is a serious matter, and the truth – I do not know what the truth is – but the truth has got to be brought out.

Wainwright insisted Thorpe answer the questions raised by the Scott affair. 'The answers must come quickly; they must come this week' and if Thorpe were to continue as Leader he must 'answer these questions properly.' Asked if he thought Thorpe a liar, Wainwright replied: 'No. But I am simply saying he has not done anything to convince the British public that he has been telling the truth, and the public are entitled to have the answers.'[41]

Wainwright seems to have consulted nobody before dropping this bomb-shell: neither fellow MPs, nor staff, nor family members – even Joyce – was taken into his confidence prior to the interview. Tony Greaves sees this as typical of Wainwright:

> Richard had this central core of what some people would call moral righteous-ness. He understood what in his terms were right and wrong, and he would never countenance what was wrong. He would have thought about that and thought about it, and probably prayed about it. He will have come to the view that it had to be done, and there was nobody else there prepared to do it. And he would not have enjoyed doing it.[42]

Another Young Liberal recruit to whom Wainwright expressed his anxiety about Thorpe, future Labour minister Peter Hain, confirms that Wainwright's approach was 'almost a moralistic one'; that Wainwright thought Thorpe had 'no moral compass' and that 'I think he had formed the opinion that Scott was probably telling the truth.'[43]

The Radio Leeds interview sparked outrage amongst Thorpe loyalists. Thorpe himself told friends he found it particularly hurtful – more so than attacks by the press. He still believes Wainwright's intervention to have been 'unnecessary and disloyal – it saddened me'.[44] Thorpe had supported Wain-wright in the Colne Valley more than once, offering encouragement and detailed campaigning advice during and after the 1963 by-election, and even his mother had helped Joyce's Women Liberals in the constituency, opening their Autumn Fair shortly after Thorpe became Leader.[45] The Liberal MPs had recently given Thorpe a unanimous vote of confidence, and agreed the previous week not to comment on the allegations for the time being. Some Liberal MPs rallied to Thorpe's aid, Russell Johnston describing the pressure being put on the Party Leader as 'intolerable'; Wainwright's old comrade Lord Byers called his intervention 'quite inexcusable'.[46]

The strength of this indignation reflected Thorpe's vulnerability. On Monday 10 May Thorpe resigned the Party leadership, pointing bitterly to the fact that 'a parliamentary colleague has now taken to the air publicly to challenge my credibility' and saying that no man could effectively lead a party if he had to devote most of his time to countering continuing plots and intrigue.

Bernard Levin condemned the ousting in *The Times* and rounded on Thor-pe's critics 'who have been prancing round him like Apaches working them-selves up for a scalping' and 'have behaved, these past few months, like a bunch of hysterical and vindictive ninnies'. He argued for David Steel's succession after an interim return by Grimond, but suggested that this would be unac-ceptable to Thorpe's critics, in particular sarcastically referring to Wainwright's image of innocent simplicity, predicting that 'Mr. Richard Wainwright would be saying that there were many things he did not understand.'[47] The Speaker of the House of Commons at the time, George Thomas, attributed the resignation specifically to Wainwright's broadcast and shared Levin's view that 'Jeremy Thorpe was destroyed by his parliamentary colleagues' and that 'the Liberal MPs behaved very badly ... He had a right to expect far greater loyalty from those around him than he received.'[48]

Alan Beith sought to calm the atmosphere by revealing that 'most Liberal MPs knew my opinion that it would not be helpful to make further statements on this subject, but I was not in touch with Mr Wainwright last Thursday, therefore he was not party to any such agreement'; and Wainwright stressed that 'it follows that suggestions ... that I broke an agreement are entirely without foundation.'[49] He also reminded his detractors of Thorpe's promise five years earlier to resign if Scott became an embarrassment to the Party. This damage limitation, however, could not protect Wainwright from what was to be a bruising reaction, from both the Party he loved and the media he feared. Beith has acknowledged that Wainwright understood the agreement amongst the MPs, but Beith knew Wainwright was deeply unhappy:

> I can't have been all that surprised, really. I knew that Richard was a potential problem in this respect, a problem to what the Parliamentary Party had agreed essentially, which was that since we don't agree to throw him out of the leadership, we have to hold the line for the moment. Richard was dissatisfied with that. I suppose I could have been no more than disappointed that it had happened.[50]

Michael Meadowcroft says that the Radio Leeds interview, was at once Wainwright's most uncharacteristic and his most characteristic action: characteristic in its pursuit of integrity; but unusual because it cut him off from so many former friends and supporters in the Liberal Party and exposed him to media scrutiny.[51] It was not only amongst Liberal MPs that Wainwright found former allies unable to understand his actions: Councillors in the Colne Valley Liberal Association condemned him and letters berating Wainwright were reportedly sent to him personally as well as to *Liberal News*, although the latter had the discretion to publish only those making general reference to 'the backstabbing behaviour of certain Liberal MPs' and saying 'with friends like these who needs enemies?'[52]

Wainwright's distaste for the media, especially television news, was brought to the fore as he was called upon to debate the matter with fellow Liberals on *News at Ten*, and, when he and Joyce stayed at a pub in the Lake District to avoid attention, Wainwright was pursued throughout the north by three *Daily Mail* reporters, who were misdirected at every turn by Wainwright loyalists in the Liberal Party. When Wainwright was unavoidably located at a public meeting in York, he and Joyce reached home undetected only by crawling through the grass at the back of The Heath's extensive gardens. To his amusement, Wainwright was touted in the national press as a possible successor to Thorpe, and David Alton's Liberal Association in Edge Hill encouraged him to stand. To too many Liberals, however, he was at the time seen as having over-reacted to a press witch-hunt against Thorpe. Thorpe was given an ovation at the Special Liberal Assembly to make arrangements for the election of his successor;[53] Wainwright was not listed as a supporter by the candidate he endorsed in that contest, John Pardoe, in his public appeals. Today Pardoe still declines the opportunity to comment on his relationship with Wainwright. Even the Colne Valley Liberal Association ignored Wainwright's advice and voted for David Steel.[54] Had he wanted it, which he did not, the man who was seen to have wielded the knife was never likely to be given the crown.

Hostility to Wainwright for his undermining of Thorpe was vividly demonstrated at the 1978 Liberal Assembly in Southport. The man who was then General Secretary of the Party, Sir Hugh Jones, sets the scene in his memoirs:

> The Assembly began with the usual Party business session, held in private. This time, no business of any consequence was achieved. It was devoted entirely to an intense and at times bitter debate on the Parliamentary Party's alleged failure to stand behind Jeremy Thorpe. Gruff Evans chaired it with the difficult task of standing loyal to the Leader's and Parliamentary Party's stance while giving the passionate objectors their say and somehow drawing the sting of the debate. He did remarkably well, aided particularly by Alan Beith, the Chief Whip. In all my years of working with Evans, this was the only occasion I ever saw him tremor with nerves.[55]

The Thorpe controversy was thrown into sharp relief because of the former Leader's declared intention to attend the conference the next day, in anticipation of which the Assembly was under siege by dozens of tabloid press photographers and journalists. Thorpe was travelling up to the Assembly from the West Country, in Hugh Jones's view, 'to hijack it'. David Steel had understood he would not attend, and Wainwright, Michael Meadowcroft and Geoff Tordoff had made it clear they thought he should stay away. Tordoff remembers the reaction to their stance, and the distinctive role of Wainwright's Radio Leeds interview, in this controversy:

> Gruff [Evans], Michael Meadowcroft and I all were being excoriated for suggesting that Thorpe should not come to the Southport conference. I made what I consider to be one of the best speeches of my life. It was a closed session, and there was a hell of a row. I said: 'Do you people here realise that if it had not been for the courage of Richard Wainwright, Thorpe would have been here today as your Leader?' and there was a sudden silence – and that was the point I think it got through to them. It took a lot of courage for him to do that.[56]

Alan Beith, who helped Chair the session, recalls that Wainwright, Emlyn Hooson and other critics of Thorpe were subjected to lengthy, personal attacks as 'assassins' with 'a personal vendetta against Jeremy' by what he terms 'The Bring Back Jeremy people'.[57] These included some of Wainwright's erstwhile Yorkshire Liberal associates such as Claire Brooks, the energetic candidate for Skipton, who remained loyal to Thorpe throughout the episode. Michael

Meadowcroft had to arrange two security staff to protect Wainwright as he spoke from the rostrum, because a death threat against him had been received from a young Thorpe loyalist. Following the session, Wainwright had to be ushered out of the conference hall under guard from his secretary and research assistant.[58]

Wainwright was at the centre of the drama again the next day when Thorpe arrived at the Assembly. Conference organisers managed to limit sensational media coverage by ushering Thorpe into the building without using the front entrance, but the press pack who were waiting there surged into the hall sweeping aside delegates as Thorpe was shown his seat on the platform by Clement Freud. Some delegates cheered Thorpe; others cold-shouldered him. Wainwright, according to the *Daily Mail*, 'swept up his papers and walked bitterly off the stage as a snub to Thorpe', followed by Lord Wigoder.[59] The *Daily Express* and *Daily Mirror* also gave the incident extravagant coverage, and *The Sun*'s front-page headline was 'Libs in Turmoil'. Wainwright was widely quoted for his reminder to activists in a radio interview, that 'Jeremy has deceived and betrayed us on several occasions.'[60]

Wainwright was fully aware of the level of support Thorpe still enjoyed in the Liberal Party and tried to keep his finger on the pulse of opinion. He asked the House of Commons library to try to find any previous examples of Party leaders on trial. He carefully monitored press coverage of the political and legal proceedings in which Thorpe was involved in everything from the *London Evening Standard* to *The Sun* to *Private Eye*, and kept copies in files he headed 'What the Papers Say'. He highlighted references to Thorpe's refusal to sue his accusers and to his neglect of his Party's interests. He also kept notes of what he believed reaction amongst activists was like, under the heading 'What the Papers Will Say': these included the beliefs that 'it's all a Tory plot', that 'the press are always hounding him' and that Liberals should 'look at what Jeremy's *done* for the Party'. The idea that the attack on Thorpe was in reality a right-wing press witch-hunt with an undercurrent of homophobia was perhaps tempting to conspiracy theorists, and attracted some leading politicians beyond the Liberal Party such as Labour Minister Joan Lestor and Lord Soper. In Wainwright's papers is a defence prepared in Joyce's hand refuting the accusations that Wainwright was 'holier than thou' and stressing the danger to the Party which Thorpe represented. Apparently the text of an intended speech or article, its opening strikes a highly rhetorical, somewhat defensive, tone:

> People are very fond of saying that politics is a dirty business – that politicians are all the same. Now how do the 'public', or the articulate public, react when a politician is consistent? As in the Thorpe affair with RSW? Thorpe himself talks about one MP who 'spoke out against him' and so caused his downfall – *the facts*.

The defence argues that by the time of Thorpe's resignation, Liberal MPs 'were well aware that public statements by JT did not tally with known facts.

The situation for the Party in the country and Liberal MPs became more and more impossible.' It is a sign of the tension between Wainwright's fierce hostility to Thorpe and his desire to be strictly accurate and to court Liberals who remained disbelieving of the accusations against the former Leader that the phrase 'web of deceit' is entered in, but then deleted from, this account of Thorpe's conduct.[61]

Most of the Parliamentary Party were pleased to see the Thorpe issue drop from public view, and gave muted congratulation to Thorpe on his acquittal, which David Steel announced 'has come as a great relief to a large number of his friends and colleagues within Parliament and outside it'.[62] Wainwright, however, had been ready to give the media his reaction to a conviction, and had called for Thorpe to be prevented from standing at the 1979 General Election whilst on trial. For good measure he set out his criticisms of Thorpe again in *New Outlook* four months after the election, at which Thorpe lost his seat.[63] Nearly ten years later he still expressed his suspicions of Thorpe in conversation about the Party with Sir Menzies Campbell when they met on holiday.[64]

There was a genuine, if strictly limited, basis of mutual respect between Thorpe and Wainwright. Wainwright had always admired Thorpe's inspirational abilities on the platform and the campaign trail; Thorpe still recognises the vital work done by Wainwright in stabilising the Party's finances. Thorpe remembers sharing jokes with Wainwright about being able to foresee the impending demise of Tory MPs and the by-election opportunities that would follow;[65] he appointed Wainwright to investigate Party funding and organisation in 1975, and has recently confirmed that Wainwright was 'a good organiser [who] could handle money'.[66] For his part, Wainwright paid tribute at a meeting twelve years into his retirement to the effectiveness of Thorpe's 'special seats' targeting strategy at the February 1974 General Election, which was 'monitored by Jeremy himself to the most rigorous standards'. Thorpe, by this time frail and ill, was present to hear these remarks, which Joyce regards as signalling something of a rapprochement. However, it is a poignant sign of the continuing sensitivity of the relationships involved a generation later that when Thorpe sought to ask a question after the speeches had finished, the Chair refused to call him.[67]

It was inevitable if the Liberal Party was to prosper that Thorpe should resign the leadership, and it was Wainwright's actions that determined the timing of that departure. Wainwright's actions prevented the Party from descending into a slump from which it might have taken many more years to recover than it actually did. Though it took some time to heal internal Party splits, and to improve performance in the polls and at by-elections, surely no Liberal could have supposed that a man on trial at the Old Bailey for Conspiracy to Murder could remain Party Leader, and the sooner he left the better. David Steel, who had been Thorpe's unofficial campaign manager in the leadership contest nine years earlier, had sat on the inquiry which dismissed Scott's allegations five years before, and who as Acting Whip received Thorpe's resignation 'with great sadness', appreciated later that Wainwright 'took to the airwaves because all private pressure, including mine, had failed to persuade Jeremy to go'.[68]

Nine of Thorpe's twelve colleagues had already told the Chief Whip they thought he should go 'because of the considerable damage the process was doing to the Party', but most would not insist on it.[69] The author of *Parliamentary Profiles*, Andrew Roth, published a bulletin at the time of the Thorpe resignation which reported on the political background to the affair. Roth argued that other Liberal MPs including Cyril Smith were criticising Thorpe privately, but that Wainwright had the distinctive ability to express in public what others recognised but would not or could not say. Thorpe's attack on Wainwright in his resignation letter 'made Richard Wainwright's radio interview, on Saturday ... seem some sort of *lèse-majesté* ... In his letter of resignation, Mr Thorpe only had harsh words for Mr Wainwright, not for Cyril Smith. Was it that the upright Mr Wainwright could really pull the rug of his remaining credibility from under him?'[70] Michael Meadowcroft agrees that 'It had to be him; there was no-one else who had the respect', and Tony Greaves put the criticism from some of those at close quarters to Wainwright into context:

> It would've been amongst the Westminster people, the Thorpe people. I'm sure there was a huge amount of resentment from people in the South West; but events showed he was right ... A lot of other people just breathed a great sigh of relief that somebody had said it.[71]

Like the boy who observed that the Emperor had no clothes, Wainwright was saying what most knew to be true; but the court and many loyal subjects did not thank him for it.

Though the testimony of partisans on both sides of the argument is vitiated by their experience and outlook, and at its worst it descends into caricature, no stereotype of either figure is required to show that their personalities, values and histories made it unlikely that Wainwright would overlook what he saw as Thorpe's self-seeking deception. 'It was perhaps more important to Richard than to some people not to be lied to', says his secretary at the time, Caroline Cawston: 'particularly, as he would see it, close political colleagues with whom you work. So his disillusionment was great.'[72] The relationship threw into the sharpest possible relief Wainwright's integrity and, where the two collided, of loyalty to the Party rather than its leadership. For the Liberal Party, it was the most important of many occasions on which Richard Wainwright put his principles before his popularity.

Notes

1 The fullest accounts of the Thorpe trial are: Chester, M., Linklater, M. and May, D., *Jeremy Thorpe: A Secret Life* (London: Fontana 1979) and Freeman, S. with Penrose, B., *Rinkagate: The Rise and Fall of Jeremy Thorpe* (London: Bloomsbury 1996). Thorpe's own account of his life is *In My Own Time: Reminiscences of a Liberal Leader* (London: Politico's 1999) but discusses his leadership of the Party only briefly, mentioning 'the so-called Norman Scott Affair' just once (pp. 134–7).

2 Lords Smith and Tordoff both agreed that Wainwright may have been hostile to male homosexuality, and the Free Methodists argued that it was contrary to Christian teaching, and even a 'perversion'; interviews, 22 June 2009 and 27 July 2009.

3 'The End of Many Roads?', *Huddersfield Daily Examiner*, 10 May 1976, p. 4.

4 McKie, D. and Cook, C., *Election '70* (London: Panther Books 1970), p. 122 Alasdair Mackenzie, the Liberal MP for Ross and Cromarty, missed both main votes on the Act. It should be noted, however, that voting for the Act does not in itself demonstrate indifference towards homosexuality, since the Methodists, who thought homosexuality immoral, nonetheless welcomed both the 1967 Act and the Wolfenden Report which foreshadowed it ten years earlier, on the grounds that the law should not be used for purely moral questions.

5 Eric Flounders, interview, 18 May 2009. Flounders, who worked in Wainwright's parliamentary office between 1972 and 1976, confirmed that Wainwright knew he was gay, but 'was never bothered about it'. Wainwright lent him the deposit on his first home in East London.

6 See Editorial, *Liberal News*, 27 April 1976, which defended the proposed campaign against highly critical letters published in the same edition. The campaign was eventually postponed by a year because of the Thorpe controversy.

7 Cited in Freeman, *Rinkagate*, p. 116.

8 William Wallace, interview, 19 January 2009.

9 Cited in Roth, A., *Parliamentary Profiles* (London: Parliamentary Profiles 1984), p. 853.

10 Chris Greenfield, interview, 1 December 2007.

11 David Alton, interview, 3 June 2008.

12 Sir Cyril Smith, interview, 29 May 2008.

13 Steel, D., *Against Goliath: David Steel's Story* (London: Weidenfeld & Nicolson 1989) p. 102.

14 Jeremy Thorpe, interview, 9 June 2008.

15 Caroline Cawston, interview, 2 June 2008. Cawston was the secretary to whom Wainwright made the revelation about Scott's visit to the Commons.

16 Chester et.al., *Jeremy Thorpe*, p.76.

17 This is detailed in Bartram, P., *David Steel: His Life and Politics* (London: Star Books 1982) pp. 68–71, where the development of a 'Stop Jeremy' campaign in northern constituencies is also confirmed.

18 Lord Tordoff, interview, 27 July 2009.

19 Michael Meadowcroft, interview, 17 June 2008.

20 RSW to Bernard Dann, 26 January 1967. This was a stock reply letter sent to supporters at the time.

21 Notes in Association of Liberal Trade Unionists Diary 1976, Wainwright papers file 10.
22 Bessell, P., *Cover-Up: The Jeremy Thorpe Affair* (privately published, USA, 1980), p. 117.
23 RSW to Bernard Dann, 26 January 1967, Wainwright papers file 8/19.
24 RSW interview, with Barrie Penrose, 1979, cited in Freeman, *Rinkagate*, p. 116.
25 William Wallace, interview, 19 January 2009 .
26 Michael Meadowcroft, interview, 17 June 2008.
27 *Colne Valley Guardian*, 22 May 1970.
28 Luise Nandy, interview, 18 January 2009 .
29 Cited in Doig, A., *Westminster Babylon* (London: Allison & Busby 1990), p. 227.
30 Thorpe to Maudling, 13 July 1971, cited in Chester et al., *A Secret Life*, p. 148.
31 Smith, C., *Big Cyril: The Autobiography of Cyril Smith* (London: W.H. Allen 1977), pp. 184–5.
32 Alan Beith, interview, 13 October 2008 .
33 Caroline Cawston, interview, 2 June 2008.
34 David Alton, interview, 3 June 2008.
35 Emlyn Hooson, interview, 3 June 2008.
36 Bessell, *Cover-Up*, p. 348.
37 Chester, *A Secret Life*, pp. 320–1.
38 Chris Davies, interview, 24 July 2009. Davies, now an MEP for the North West, had come to know Wainwright as an activist in Liverpool, but was also a leading Young Liberal.
39 Beith, A., *A View from the North* (Newcastle: Northumbria University Press 2008), p. 94.
40 Steel, *Against Goliath*, p.102.
41 *The Times*, 10 May 1976.
42 Lord Greaves, interview, 8 April 2009. Lord Greaves, Lord Shutt, Sir Alan Beith, Sir Cyril Smith, Lord Wallace, Wainwright's secretary Caroline Cawston, his Research Assistant Eric Flounders and Joyce all confirmed specifically that Wainwright had not discussed the interview with them before giving it. Wallace remarked that 'he would commune with himself and his delphiniums', to which Greaves added: 'his delphiniums and his God'.
43 Peter Hain, interview, 30 January 2009.
44 Jeremy Thorpe, interview, 9 June 2008.
45 Colne Valley Women's Liberal Association minute book 1964–79, 28 October 1967.
46 *The Times*, 11 May 1976.
47 Levin, B., 'The One Man, the One Way, for the Liberals', *The Times*, 11 May 1976, p. 14.
48 Thomas, George, *Mr Speaker* (London: Arrow Books 1986), pp. 146–7.
49 *The Times*, 12 May 1976.
50 Alan Beith, interview, 13 October 2008.
51 Michael Meadowcroft, interview, 17 June 2008.
52 Letters, *Liberal News*, 13 July (Ken Friswell) and 25 May (D.J. Bunce) 1976. Eric Flounders, interview, 18 May 2009, suggested that other, more specific letters had been sent to Wainwright and to *Liberal News*.
53 *Liberal News*, 22 June 1976.

54 *Liberal News*, 27 July 1976. The CVLA cast its votes in the electoral college which chose the Leader 27–37 in Steel's favour.

55 Jones, Sir H., *Campaigning Face to Face*, (Brighton: Book Guild 2007), p. 41.

56 Lord Tordoff, interview, 27 July 2009.

57 Alan Beith, interview, 13 October 2008.

58 Michael Meadowcroft, interview, 17 June 2008; Caroline Cawston, interview, 2 June 2008.

59 'How Could Thorpe Do This To Us?' *Daily Mail*, 15 September 1978, p. 1. It should be noted that *The Times* report of the same events said no MP was seen to leave the platform.

60 *The Sun*, the *Daily Express* and the *Daily Mirror*, 15 September 1978. Wainwright's radio interview was quoted on p. 7 of *The Sun* as well as elsewhere.

61 This diary is in file 10 of the Wainwright papers at the London School of Economics.

62 'Jeremy, we Rejoice for You', *Liberal News*, 26 June 1979, p. 1.

63 *New Outlook*, September 1979. This article is cited in Andrew Roth's *Parliamentary Profiles* 1984.

64 Sir Menzies Campbell, interview, 23 July 2009.

65 Stratton, A., 'Jeremy Thorpe: I remember the Lot', *The Guardian*, 28 January 2008.

66 Jeremy Thorpe, interview, 9 June 2008.

67 '1974 Remembered', Liberal Democrat History Group fringe meeting at Harrogate Liberal Democrat Conference, 19 September 1999. Reported in *Journal of Liberal Democrat History*, No. 26 (Spring 2000), pp. 19–21.

68 Steel, *Against Goliath*, p. 102.

69 Beith, *A View from the North*, p. 94.

70 Roth, A., 'The passing of the Liberal Caesar', *Westminster Confidential*, 13 May 1976.

71 Michael Meadowcroft, interview, 17 June 2008; Lord Greaves, interview, 8 April 2009.

72 Caroline Cawston, interview, 2 June 2008

12 The Lib-Lab Pact

Shortly after the immediate repercussions of Jeremy Thorpe's resignation were over, with David Steel in place as Leader, a new political dilemma confronted the Liberals. James Callaghan's Labour Government lost its wafer-thin majority[1] and in March 1977 faced a Commons motion of 'No confidence' tabled by Leader of the Opposition, Margaret Thatcher. Callaghan needed a formal agreement to secure his position, and the obvious partners for this agreement were the thirteen Liberal MPs.

Steel had always believed in the potential benefits of co-operation between the Liberals and other parties. His arguments for an arrangement to support the Labour Government were both general and particular; partisan and national; negative and positive. In general, he argued, party co-operation was the logical corollary of the Liberals' belief in proportional representation (PR), and they had to be seen to engage in it; in particular this arrangement offered the Liberals the prospect of influence over all areas of Government policy, and of the introduction of PR for devolved Scottish and Welsh bodies, and for direct elections to the European Assembly. Most importantly, the Liberals could legitimately present this as a stabilising measure bringing the Party into the periphery of government and avoiding a third General Election in four years. Though Steel denied this, the Liberals in particular might suffer most from such an election, being at a low ebb in the polls and least able of the three main parties to fund another campaign. Steel argued at the time that the Pact was 'stopping Socialism', and subsequently defended the agreement because 'it achieved its main short-term objective of controlling inflation ... it demonstrated that bi-partisan government meant the extreme dogmas of the larger party were under control' and 'it presented the country with the first taste of a distinctive Liberal policy.'[2] He also acknowledged that an aim was 'to get the Liberals thinking about sharing power.'[3]

As Roy Douglas observes, 'peacetime arrangements with other parties have usually been decried by large sections of the Liberal Party,'[4] and there were from the outset sceptics who doubted the Labour Government's readiness to make concessions and stressed the danger of propping up an unpopular

Government, particularly in those seats like Wainwright's where Labour were the Liberals' main opponents. Why would either disillusioned Labour or tactical Tory voters support a Liberal Party which was challenging Labour at the polls but supporting it in office? Unsurprisingly, therefore, some of the earliest critics of the arrangement like Cyril Smith[5] and elements of the Association of Liberal Councillors – who within six months were complaining that the Party was 'bleeding to death'[6] – had long experience of fighting Labour; others doubted Steel's ability to bargain effectively with Callaghan or were more generally concerned for the impact of the agreement on Liberal independence. Liberal Treasury spokesman John Pardoe complained afterwards that 'David was determined to do a deal at all costs.'[7]

Much national commentary on the Pact at the time was, alternately and sometimes even at once, critical of the Liberals for holding the Government to ransom and disdainful of their significance in the deal.[8] A more balanced division of opinion, similar to that within the Liberal Party itself, marked analyses of the Pact amongst political journalists and historians writing in its aftermath. One argued that the Lib-Lab Pact 'saw the final abandonment of any attempts at radical reform by the Callaghan administration' and claimed there had been 'a number of minor, though significant, policy victories for the Liberals, for example in the increased attention paid by the government to encouraging small businesses and industrial democracy', the measures for which Wainwright was particularly responsible.[9] Jo Grimond, who was generally apprehensive about the Pact, also acknowledged Wainwright's effectiveness in promoting the interests of small businesses, and Alan Beith, Chief Whip at the time, took some pride in these achievements.[10] Others, like Philip Whitehead, scoffed that 'the "terms" were heard with some incredulity by the Cabinet' and that 'the [Labour] Party had simply undertaken to do what it had anyway intended to do and desist from what it could not do.'[11]

From a purely Liberal point of view, if there were policy achievements during the Pact – and if so, then Wainwright had one of the stronger claims to have made them – they were mostly in giving greater urgency to measures to which the Labour Government had no objection (such as Stephen Ross's Homeless Persons Bill); or putting more controversial issues such as electoral reform and industrial democracy on the political agenda where they had previously been mostly associated with academic speculation and the dreams of cranks in the political wilderness. Getting these issues discussed was an advance, but was not the same as implementation, which – to Steel's chagrin and the sceptics' vindication – the Labour Government was not prepared to give. The main benefit from the Liberals' perspective was that a small Party with a new Leader, few resources and a damaged reputation was able to turn the threat of an election into an association with power. This was a wasting asset, bought at a higher price for those Liberal MPs fighting Labour than for those fighting the Tories;

that, and the tension between loyalty to immediate Party decisions and long-term Party independence, were dilemmas with which Wainwright and other Liberals struggled throughout the Pact.

Wainwright was attracted by the 'national interest' element of the case for the agreement – he conveyed to his secretary his distaste for the scenario in which a minority Government keeps itself in office by whipping the sick through the division lobbies – but he also found certain practical aspects of the Pact to be rewarding. He enjoyed having the opportunity at last to engage with the real policy-making process, to argue his case with the Government with the reasonable expectation that he would have a hearing. His family and his staff noticed the purpose with which he approached his role, negotiating with public sector trade unions and dealing with the National Enterprise Board.[12] The early meetings of the Shadow Administration, as the Liberal team came to call itself, show Wainwright pressing for greater clarity in the setting of government economic targets and joking wryly about contradictions within proposed government legislation that a precedent had been set for this by Gladstone's Home Rule Bill.[13]

As Liberal Trade and Industry spokesman he was involved in discussions over the Post Office Bill, where an attempt was made at introducing Wainwright's long-cherished goal of industrial democracy and consumer representation, and on economic policy more generally, where the relationship between Chancellor Denis Healey and his Liberal opposite number John Pardoe was particularly tense. Both were able personalities unburdened by self-doubt or any disinclination for public attention: Healey later described Pardoe as 'simply Denis Healey with no redeeming features' and complained that 'in the literal sense he was totally irresponsible';[14] during the Pact Pardoe called Healey 'the Second worst Chancellor since the War' in a radio broadcast,[15] and went into print to say that Healey 'loves to play the bully. He talks through people. He mistakes the sledgehammer for the rapier.'[16] Unsurprisingly, Healey recalls they 'sent the crockery flying' more than once.[17]

Wainwright's relationship with his Labour counterparts was a complete contrast to Pardoe's with Healey, and to some extent compensated for it. He worked first with Secretary of State for Trade and Industry Eric Varley, who testified to more than one of Wainwright's colleagues that their relationship had been 'one of the most productive aspects' of the Pact.[18] Varley's Junior Minister was Sir Gerald Kaufman, who agrees that 'such contacts as we had were pleasant and constructive, and in Wainwright, our Department was luckier than several others with Liberal MPs allocated.' Kaufman later wrote of the Post Office legislation that the Liberals had 'insisted that the independent members of the board should include spokesmen for the Post Office users, and after a certain amount of haggling this was agreed'.[19] Roy Hattersley also responded positively, promising to 'sharpen up' government policy on monopolies after Wainwright, in a two-day Commons debate in June 1977, urged that powers to regulate prices and monopolies should be under a single powerful body to monitor symptoms of restrictive practices.[20]

Wainwright's closest partnership during the Lib-Lab Pact, however, was with Joel (now Lord) Barnett, the Chief Secretary to the Treasury, who found Wainwright 'a nice, decent, honourable man' who was prepared to be realistic about painful public expenditure cuts and who understood public finances. It was fortuitous that Barnett's constituency was Heywood and Royton near Rochdale, which shared a great deal with Colne Valley; he had ten years earlier drawn comparison between their constituencies as 'so-called grey areas' of unemployment.[21] He was also a Mancunian accountant, and spoke the same professional and regional language as Wainwright. After the former Chief Secretary went to the Lords, Wainwright referred to 'the lamentable absence of Joel Barnett.'[22] According to Wainwright's secretary it was Barnett's intellect which made the brief of working with him such a pleasure,[23] and Barnett reciprocates the compliment:

> I worked very well with him, enjoyed working with him, and he seemed to enjoy it. He wanted to do something practical. He was knowledgeable financially; I could have serious discussions without difficulty. Had he been in another party, he would have been Cabinet material.[24]

It is the price he paid for his loyalty to the Liberal cause that Wainwright was denied the opportunity to fulfil the promise Barnett confirms in him; and that the country was denied the gifts of such a talented public servant at the highest level when economic insight was most needed. While the shadow of that opportunity was there, however, Wainwright tried to make use of it. He was, moreover, encouraged by his local newspapers, which supported Liberal participation in the Pact and highlighted Wainwright's achievements. The *Huddersfield Daily Examiner* urged Callaghan and Steel to 'Carry on Talking'[25] in the run-up to the agreement, asked 'One Night Only?'[26] after the Liberals saved Labour in the March confidence vote, and in February 1978 praised Wainwright and his fellow economic spokesmen on 'a striking coup by using the Lib-Lab Pact to persuade the Government to publish a consultative document on profit-sharing ... Even if the proposals do not become law in the immediate future the Liberals will at least be able to congratulate themselves on having secured, for the first time, a national platform for ideas which too many vested interests have for too long wanted to keep out of the public arena.'[27]

At the other end of the Colne Valley, the *Oldham Evening Chronicle*, though more equivocal, looked back on the Pact at the end of the Parliament to assert that 'in retrospect ... there was much to be gained by co-operation ... The Liberals may have been damaged by their 18–month affair with the Labour Party, but if the result of tomorrow's poll is a tiny Tory majority, it may well become clear before long what they are trying to achieve.'[28]

These factors led Wainwright to support the Lib-Lab Pact at the outset, and to back it until the summer of 1977, when he told a two-day meeting of Liberal MPs at St Ermine's hotel in London that 'the agreement needed more time to be seen to work and that we should not precipitate an election by being too tough in backroom negotiation'.[29] He told the local press over the summer that 'The Steel/Callaghan agreement points the way to stability and a united country', and that 'the immediate results seem to me good'.[30] He taunted the Conservatives that 'I have seldom seen such a limp and exhausted parliamentary crew as the Tory leadership'.[31]

However, other considerations played an increasingly significant role in Wainwright's judgements, and by December only Party loyalty was keeping Wainwright from breaking ranks. Firstly, the Conservatives in Colne Valley seized the opportunity to paint Wainwright as having betrayed tactical Tory voters in the constituency who had backed him in 1974, by propping up a failed Labour administration. They wrote publicly to Margaret Thatcher at the start of the Pact declaring:

> Spurious claims by the sitting Liberal member for Colne Valley to represent the anti-socialist voter have now been totally exposed as being worthless following his complicity in the cynically opportunist deal concluded by the Liberal rump with the Government. He has earned the contempt of those who were persuaded to vote Liberal to keep Labour out and he will pay for this betrayal at the next General Election. We shall now work with redoubled vigour to terminate the political career of the present member for Colne Valley.

Colne Valley Conservatives, sensing their chance, went on to tell Mrs Thatcher that the constituency was 'at the very least a Conservative marginal', and their Prospective Parliamentary Candidate Stephen Kaye heaped blame on Wainwright for the economic failings of the Labour Government, including liquidations, personal bankruptcies, inflation, a drop in sterling and tax rises.[32] If Wainwright did not immediately recognise the scale of the strategic problem this raised, he was reminded of it by the County Council elections of May 1977. Though there were no County Council elections in Kirklees and therefore in Colne Valley that year, neighbouring urban Liberals fighting dominant Labour parties suffered disproportionately badly: all twelve Liberal seats on Greater Manchester County Council were lost, all six in Derbyshire, and ten out of the sixteen in Merseyside. Liberal Party Secretary General Sir Hugh Jones remembers that 'the county council elections opened up wounds wherever we lost councillors, and that was in three-quarters of our held seats'.[33]

When local contests were held at a lower level in Colne Valley, and at County level in May 1978, Councillor Gordon Beever remembers that 'the Lib-Lab Pact went down like an absolute lead balloon here and we did very, very badly at local elections on the back of it. The Tories for the first time ever got seats in the Colne Valley.' He remembers another Councillor, Heather Swift, saying that she had never been at an election count 'where you could cut the atmosphere with a knife'.[34] The Liberals held their ground (as they did in a parliamentary by-election in neighbouring Penistone in July) with six council seats in the constituency, but the Conservatives went from two to six seats, whilst Labour went from six to two.[35] The Lib-Lab Pact had let the Colne Valley Tory genie out of its bottle for the first time in nearly twenty years.

Wainwright at this point declared publicly against the Pact, though he had held his tongue for six months. Stephen Kaye mined the same vein as Conservative candidate at the 1979 election, conflating 'Labour and Liberal priorities' as 'profligate public expenditure' and writing that in the Pact 'Mr Wainwright and the Liberal Party showed its [sic] true colours'. On the eve of poll Kaye again raised the spectre of 'the Lib-Lab Pact, when the Liberals showed their true allegiance to Labour'.[36]

This turn of events did not go unnoticed in the Colne Valley Liberal Party. Although generally inclined to let Wainwright make his own decisions about parliamentary affairs, members were struck by the unpopularity of the Pact and its likely effect upon their electoral fortunes. Though Wainwright made the case for the Pact from the principle of national stability, and ultimately his judgement was accepted, if not shared, by Liberals in his seat, one loyal Wainwright supporter in Saddleworth remembers that 'we took flak for it every day'[37] and Nigel Priestley, subsequently Association Chairman and parliamentary candidate, witnessed the discussion at a meeting in the home of Jessie Kirby, one of Wainwright's longest-standing supporters:

> There was a very tense meeting about the Lib-Lab Pact, because some of the members were very upset about it. Richard was a man who still wanted to get results; whatever the reservations he might have had about the Pact, he certainly wasn't letting on. He had a way of giving a very good account for himself and yet retaining loyalty.[38]

Wainwright did not betray his doubts in his public statements, which kept to the commitment Wainwright had made to his colleagues. He even declared ahead of the autumn Liberal Council meeting that proportional representation was not a deal-breaking issue: 'I do not believe it is an issue on which the British people would want the Government to be brought down in an election.'[39] Even as the Pact was dying, Wainwright defended its achievements loyally to his activists. He told the Colne Valley Women Liberals in June 1978 that 'Liberal MPs were keeping the Labour Government to the centre of British politics' and even that Steel was 'prepared to have talks after the election to either side'. The minutes note that 'Mr Wainwright was then bombarded by questions and viewpoints.'[40]

Whilst the pressure to end the Pact was growing in his constituency, Wainwright found the benefits from it at Westminster were diminishing. He felt at a disadvantage in dealing with ministers, as he told his research assistant: 'I remember he said you'd go into the meeting, and there'd be the minister and about half-a-dozen very weighty bureaucrats, and he'd go in with his one advisor, and it was very difficult then to persuade the minister of anything.'[41] His good relations with Labour ministers notwithstanding, Wainwright grew doubtful of the Government's good faith and of the distance they were prepared to go to maintain the agreement. In September, he wrote to David Steel complaining about the 'rather unhappy contrast' between the understanding shown in negotiations over the Post Office Bill 'on matters where our votes have been needed, and, per contra, not shown on non-parliamentary aspects of the very same subject'. He was frustrated that Kaufman 'has parried my representations with civil service-type correspondence, raking together hypothetical difficulties'.[42] Later that month, Wainwright let his Leader know he was 'furious' that the Liberals had been given no credit for the appointment of Harold Lever to head an investigation into the problems of small businesses.[43] Fellow Liberal MP Geraint Howells later revealed that he and Wainwright had been to see Junior Minister Bob Cryer about this during the first few days of the Pact, but that 'we were not pleased with the result of our meeting'. Only by urging David Steel to press James Callaghan over this was anything achieved.[44] 'This was a cause as close as any to Liberal hearts' said Hoggart and Michie's account of the Pact the following year, 'and the Liberal MPs had been pressing for special treatment for small businessmen for months.'[45]

This deterioration in trust came to a climax in December, when the division in the Commons over the use of proportional representation for the forthcoming first direct elections to the European Assembly was lost. The Government had made this a free vote, but in July Liberal MPs had made their continued support for the Pact dependent upon the Cabinet using their 'best endeavours' to ensure the passage of the measure, and the Liberal Assembly in September had voted for the Pact on condition that 'a substantial majority' of Labour MPs voted for it. In the event, the defeat was caused partly by Tory Whips organising their MPs to block the measure, but fewer than half the Labour MPs voted for it, and eleven ministers, four from the Cabinet, voted against.

Liberal reaction ranged from dismay to righteous indignation, and Wainwright was closer to the latter. The one great long-term prize which might have been secured by Liberals through the Pact was lost and, worse still, was seen to have been lost. At a meeting of Liberal MPs, Wainwright voted with Cyril Smith, David Penhaligon and Emlyn Hooson to end the Pact; six of their colleagues voted to continue it, but only after it had become obvious that this was a resignation issue for Steel and after he had pretended to them that Callaghan would call an election if the Pact ended, inducing nausea amongst some. Wainwright had lost the vote but won the argument: the Pact would continue for the moment, but because of some MPs' loyalty to Steel rather than because of its inherent merits, and Steel himself had publicly to acknowledge that it would probably only last a matter of months more. Steel was also required to call a special Assembly in January to renew approval of the Pact.

A week after the Liberal MPs' vote, Steel found Wainwright and John Pardoe (who had abstained) had 'simmered down and are willing to accept that the agreement can go on till July with me giving notice in June of its ending'. It was Wainwright who went off to the Party's Standing Committee meeting with what Steel regarded as a 'satisfactory' Assembly resolution, giving Steel discretion over the termination of the agreement. Such was the strength of feeling against the Pact on the Committee that only by strengthening Steel's resolution to set a terminal date for the Pact in summer could Wainwright, together with Alan Beith and Steel's advisor Archy Kirkwood, secure an 8–6 vote in its favour. This was subsequently renegotiated by Steel, but Wainwright's role had been vital and clear: once again, he was the bridge-builder, the caution to leadership, the champion of purists who nonetheless could conciliate and wait, and who had the reputation and trust to hold the Party together.[46]

The January 1978 Assembly at Blackpool voted to continue the Pact rather than end it immediately by a margin of more than three to one, but the agreement's days were numbered. Wainwright opened the debate by introducing the main portion of the resolution which was accepted by both sides, asserting that the Pact had 'changed the direction of what had been a doctrinaire socialist government', but condemning Labour MPs who 'have undermined this constructive approach' and stating that the Pact's immediate aims of national interest would be fulfilled with the 1978 Budget. Wainwright himself argued that Britain's economic recovery had been possible only because of the Pact.[47] Yet, although now personally backing the motion giving Steel discretion, in a speech of sensitivity, passion and humour, he reached out as far as possible to radicals in this general appeal, particularly in his reaction to the failure of the proposed use of proportional representation for European elections:

> What nerveless, feeble and supine Liberals we would have been if we had not erupted immediately at this perverse sectarian Labour vote in favour of gerrymandering, carried out in cynical alliance with Mrs Thatcher's secretly whipped troops. In a general way, there is no doubt that their failure on PR, assuming they remain unrepentant, puts out of court any renewal of the present agreement.[48]

Despite an almost biblical rebuke to the Government, then, Wainwright left open the possibility that the agreement need not end immediately. However, the distance between Wainwright's position and Steel's was evident from Steel's closing speech in which he insisted 'I have to place in record that the Prime Minister delivered exactly what he undertook to deliver on PR', to delegates' cries of 'rubbish!'[49] This, though characteristically bold, was not designed to win over those fearful for Liberal identity; it was Wainwright's imprimatur, recognising their anger and anxiety, which was the most telling case for temporary, if indeterminate, continuation, and helped to secure such a convincing victory for Steel. As *The Times* noted, 'neither the wording of the motion nor the mood in the conference hall suggested that the delegates were voting to continue it indefinitely.'[50]

Through the first six months of 1978 there were occasional symbolic concessions to Liberal aims, and further disputes after Labour peers voted against PR for the proposed Scottish Parliament in April and Chancellor Healey proposed a large rise in National Insurance contributions in June, which Wainwright and Pardoe were able to restrain. Like Wainwright, however, most of the Party had lost faith in the Pact, and awaited its end. In March Steel explicitly acknowledged that the Pact would not extend into the next parliamentary session; on 24 July, the Liberal MPs voted down a Government measure on the dock labour scheme and it was lost. The Pact formally ended the following month.

Wainwright's heart was never in the Pact for the long term. He had initially been able to distinguish between the administrative promise and the strategic threats offered by the agreement, and took a typically pragmatic view that 'I don't really want it, but it's going to happen, so how do I best affect the outcome?', as his new research assistant Joanna Copsey (later Hannam) characterised it.[51] However, his secretary Caroline Cawston felt he was 'never that "easy" with it' and like many Liberals, Chris Greenfield understood, 'he felt that David [Steel] wasn't strong enough to drive a hard bargain with Callaghan.'[52] As time wore on, the tension between short-term benefits and long-term dangers became evident, and the latter loomed larger in Wainwright's mind. His instinct for fair dealing was offended by the failure of the Labour leadership to deliver on PR at European elections, too. Wainwright enjoyed aspects of the Pact, and it demonstrated the potential he had; but the advantages were always more superficial and short term than the dangers, and it took little time for Wainwright to recognise this. In subsequent Parliaments he took to interrupting sardonically at any mention of the Pact to shout 'the golden age',[53] and indignantly denied that 'during the Lib-Lab Pact any Liberal Member had access to any Government files or had the vestige of an opportunity to know what was taking place in the tax area.'[54] However, the other characteristic of Wainwright's demonstrated by the Pact – loyalty – meant this anger was not immediately evident. 'Despite his reservations', remembered David Steel, 'he was totally loyal in public to the Pact process.'[55]

It was fully expected by most of the political community that an October election would follow, and detailed arrangements were put in place at constituency and national levels for the Liberal campaign, with expenditure committed and activists booking annual holidays. Wainwright had announced detailed Liberal plans to tackle rising unemployment in August, and the September Assembly was assumed to be only weeks from an election, preparing the campaign under the slogan 'Break with the Past'.[56] Against that expectation,

Callaghan determined to hang on until 1979, only to see the Labour Party's electoral position undermined by the 'Winter of Discontent'.

Liberated from his self-denying ordinance, Wainwright went on the offensive against Labour, and particularly against the trade unions' leaders. At the beginning of the year he knew would see an election in which Colne Valley would judge him for his part in the Pact, Wainwright launched an uncompromising attack on Moss Evans, the leader of the Transport and General Workers' Union, with whom Steel had worked during the Pact,[57] and what he called 'Labour's "Old Boy" network.' Wainwright claimed Evans had openly admitted that he would not act in the national interest, and warned prophetically that pay deals not put to Parliament and trade unions' members would not stick. 'Militant leaders have, most unwisely, been given a big boost to their credibility by the spectacle of Government trying to use the trade unions' bosses as their agents', Wainwright told the Colne Valley Liberal Executive. 'The proper source of authority for incomes policy is Parliament.'[58] Of course, the Government had no authority in Parliament, and when Callaghan lost a vote of confidence in March 1979, Wainwright was raring to go, telling the BBC: 'Our thirteen Liberal MPs have been calling consistently for an election since last September. I'm delighted that at last the parties have got together and provided an election. It's more than high time.'[59] The Pact was long over, and normal business had resumed for Wainwright.

Notes

1 Labour lost seats at two by-elections in November 1976, and two Labour MPs left to form the breakaway Scottish Labour Party.
2 Steel, D., *A House Divided: the Lib-Lab Pact and the Future of British Politics* (London: Weidenfeld & Nicolson 1980), pp. 152–3.
3 Whitehead, P., *The Writing on the Wall: Britain in the Seventies* (London: Michael Joseph 1985), p. 260.
4 Douglas, R., *Liberals: The History*, p. 282.
5 See, for example, *Liberal News*, 5 July 1977, on the front page of which Smith explains his opposition to the Pact, then less than two months old.
6 Cited in Cook, C., *A Short History of the Liberal Party 1900–84* (London: Macmillan 1984), p. 164.
7 Whitehead, *The Writing on the Wall*, p. 260.
8 In contemporary cartoons, for example, Steel was depicted as a ball boy bringing Liberal votes to Callaghan and Healey on a tennis court (*Daily Telegraph*, 29 June 1978), and threatening to shoot Callaghan with a gun pointed at his own head (*The Sun*, 17 June 1977); Callaghan, on the other hand, was ridiculed as asking Steel when he could brush his teeth and go to bed (*Daily Mail*, 25 March 1977), and mocked with the image of the Liberal petrol pump refusing to supply his car with higher petrol taxes (*The Sun*, 1 April 1977).
9 Derbyshire, J.D. and Derbyshire, I., *Politics in Britain from Callaghan to Thatcher*

(London: Chambers 1988), p. 67.

10 Grimond, J., *Memoirs* (London: Heinemann 1979), p. 254; Beith, A., *A View from the North* (Newcastle: Northumbria University Press 2008), p. 89.

11 Whitehead, *The Writing on the Wall*, p. 259.

12 Caroline Cawston, interview, 3 June 2008; Martin and Hilary Wainwright, interview, 22 February 2008.

13 First and second meetings of Shadow Administration, April 1977. David Steel papers A/3/1.

14 Healey, D., *The Time of My Life* (London: Michael Joseph 1989), p. 403, and quoted in Whitehead, *The Writing on the Wall*, p. 260.

15 Cited in Steel, D., *Against Goliath: David Steel's Story* (London: Weidenfeld & Nicolson 1989), p. 139.

16 Cited in Michie, A. and Hoggart, S., *The Pact: The Inside Story of the Lib-Lab Government 1977–78* (London: Quartet Books 1978), pp. 167–8.

17 Healey, *The Time of My Life*, p. 403.

18 This remark was reported in interview, by Lord Trevor Smith, 22 June 2009, to whom Varley had made it over dinner in the Lords, but a similar conversation took place between Varley and Lord Shutt, and these confirm testimony Varley gave in writing to Lord Tordoff for use at Wainwright's memorial service in February 2003; interviews, Lord Shutt and Lord Tordoff, 3 June 2008 and 27 July 2009.

19 Sir Gerald Kaufman, correspondence with the present author, July 2009, and in *How to Be a Minister* (London: Faber & Faber 1997), p. 51. The original edition was published in 1980.

20 *Liberal News*, 28 June 1977.

21 Joel Barnett, Hansard 19 June 1968.

22 Hansard, 6 July 1983.

23 Caroline Cawston, interview, 2 June 2008.

24 Lord Barnett, interviews, 16 and 17 June 2009 .

25 *Huddersfield Daily Examiner*, 14 March 1977.

26 Ibid., 24 March 1977.

27 Ibid., 7 February 1978.

28 *Oldham Evening Chronicle*, 2 May 1979.

29 Cited in Steel, *A House Divided,* p. 161. The meeting took place on 26 and 27 June 1977.

30 *Oldham Evening Chronicle*, 20 July 1977; RSW, 'Positive Pact is Boosting Britain', *Oldham Evening Chronicle* August 1977 (exact date unknown).

31 Ibid., 2 July 1977.

32 *Huddersfield Daily Examiner* 26 March 1977. Kaye also wrote to the *Huddersfield Daily Examiner* on 2 May and 22 August attacking Wainwright's support for the Pact.

33 Jones, Sir H., *Campaigning Face to Face* (Brighton: Book Guild 2007), p. 117.

34 Gordon Beever, interview, 31 October 2008.

35 At the Penistone by-election of 13 July 1978, the Liberal candidate won 21.6 per cent of the vote, compared to 21.8 per cent at the previous General Election. The Conservatives rose from under a quarter to almost a third of the vote, and Labour dropped ten points to 45 per cent.

36 *Oldham Chronicle*, 30 April and 2 May 1979.

37 David Wheeler, interview, 26 July 2009 .

38 Nigel Priestley, interview, 30 October 2008.

39 *Huddersfield Daily Examiner*, 25 November 1977.

40 Colne Valley Divisional Women's Liberal Council AGM, 30 June 1978.

41 Chris Greenfield, interview, 1 December 2007.

42 RSW to Steel, 7 September 1977, David Steel papers 3/1. The present author is grateful to Dr Ruth Fox of the Hansard Society for pointing out this reference.

43 Steel, *A House Divided*, p. 181, 22 September 1977.

44 Geraint Howells, Hansard, 31 January 1990.

45 Michie and Hoggart, *The Pact*, p. 166.

46 Steel, *A House Divided*, p. 117, and *Against Goliath*, p. 139.

47 *Sunday Times*, 22 January 1978, p. 3.

48 *The Times*, 23 January 1978.

49 Ibid.

50 'The Liberals Set their course', ibid. p. 13.

51 Joanna Hannam, interview, 19 January 2009.

52 Caroline Cawston, interview, 2 June 2008; Chris Greenfield, interview, 1 December 2007.

53 See, for example, Hansard, 13 April 1981 and 19 May 1987.

54 Hansard, 14 July 1981.

55 David Steel, correspondence with the present author, 22 June 2008.

56 Jones, *Campaigning Face to Face*, p. 138.

57 See Steel, *A House Divided*, p. 123, where Steel describes Evans as 'a cheerful Welshman' on meeting him; on p. 177, however, Steel copies a note of a meeting between Liberal Employment spokesman Baroness Seear and the Secretary of State on 7 October 1977, where it is made clear that Evans and the TGWU 'were not party to the pact with the Liberals and did not recognise it as a constraint'.

58 Address to Colne Valley Liberal Association Executive, reported in *Liberal News*, 23 January 1979.

59 BBC Radio Manchester, 22 March 1979. The present author is grateful to David Wheeler for supplying this recording.

13 The SDP/Liberal Alliance

For the remainder of Wainwright's parliamentary career, the main continuing issue for the Liberal Party concerned its relationship with the Social Democratic Party (SDP), formed following the breakaway from Labour of twelve MPs, later joined by a further seventeen after the new Party had become established. The SDP was at first founded and led by former Labour Cabinet minister Roy Jenkins, who had spent the previous five years as President of the European Commission. In November 1979, Jenkins gave the Dimbleby lecture, in which he called for a realignment of British political parties around the 'radical centre', with a new group formed as the catalyst for existing forces in other parties.[1] This emerged first as the 'Council for Social Democracy' within Labour ranks, but attracted interest from outside current Party membership. In March 1981 the Social Democratic Party was launched amid great publicity and controversy as Britain's first new national party for eighty years.

The SDP's arrival presented Liberals with a dilemma. The policies which distinguished it from the Labour Party which its leaders had departed – constitutional reform, European integration, incomes policy in a free-market economy – were largely the ones which Liberals had been promoting for years in the teeth of opposition from the SDP's new leaders. There was now a choice between working with the new Party in an electoral and policy alliance, thereby potentially sacrificing the Liberal Party's hard-won independence and opportunities for representation to untrusted former foes; or trying to defeat a well-resourced opponent with credible national leaders which was offering co-operation and increased success. Both approaches had their difficulties, and both had their adherents in the Liberal Party.

The approach of Liberal Leader David Steel was very clear: he had been aware of Jenkins's plans since before the Dimbleby lecture, and had approved the formation of a new Party alongside the Liberals. The relationship brought him back in touch with some former Labour ministers with whom Liberals had worked in the Lib-Lab Pact, including David Owen, Shirley Williams and Bill Rodgers, and Steel regarded it as the pursuit of the long-term goal of realignment set by Jo Grimond in the late 1950s when Steel first joined the Party. Most leading Liberals concurred with, or at least acquiesced in, this policy, though some thought Steel too flexible and too keen in dealing with what would inevitably become a relationship with tensions built into it. Again as in the debate over the Pact, Cyril Smith was the most sceptical of the MPs, famously telling a member of the public on the BBC television programme *Question Time* that any new centre party should be 'strangled at birth'.[2]

The Alliance was formed with the support of an overwhelming vote at the Liberal Assembly in Llandudno in September. Cyril Smith gave his approval in the belief that since he had failed to strangle the SDP, the next best thing he could do was marry it. The partnership enjoyed immediate popular approval, securing the election of a Liberal MP at a by-election in Croydon in October, and the return to Parliament of the two leading Social Democrats not currently at Westminster, Shirley Williams and Jenkins, in November 1981 and March 1982. Gallup polls showed the Alliance matching or beating the other two parties from October to April, and in December it achieved over 50 per cent support.[3] The relationship it entailed, however, was a complex and cumbersome one, in which the right to contest parliamentary and council seats had to be shared out between the two parties, and joint policies had to be agreed at those elections. Both of these aims proved elusive during the seven years of the Alliance's existence, and the two parties' fortunes suffered accordingly.

As with the Lib-Lab Pact, Wainwright was loyal to the Leadership's pro-Alliance line in public from the outset, and he saw genuine promise in some of its effects; but he also shared the feelings of other Liberals ranging from indifference to anxiety. For practical purposes, the Alliance made little difference to Wainwright's work. The Liberal presence in the Colne Valley was so strong, and the SDP so insignificant – its membership in Colne Valley was rumoured to be in single figures – that it posed no organisational or strategic threat to normal political life in his constituency. 'There wasn't a big issue about the Alliance and the formation of the SDP' says Gordon Beever; 'people nodded and said "Oh yes?" It was a non-event to us in Colne Valley.' The view amongst activists was 'what these people do in Westminster is very much their own thing.'[4]

There were those in Colne Valley who thought that the arrival of the SDP brought badly needed modernity and professionalism to the third party's profile (the SDP, for example, was the first British party to accept subscriptions by credit card) as well as providing that credible national leadership. Wainwright's successor as candidate in Colne Valley, Nigel Priestley, attended the Bradford session of the SDP's conference in 1981, and returned enthused:

> For those of us who had been involved in the Liberals, and everything being 'muck and nettles', never any money, having to work hard, to see this glamour thing appear on your doorstep was amazing. It was at St George's Hall in Bradford, and I remember bringing back an SDP mug, and thinking what an amazing thing it was.[5]

Wainwright too saw some benefits which might come to the Liberals by asso-ciation with experienced ministers in terms of media coverage. The *Hudders-field Daily Examiner* encouraged the Alliance and counselled conciliation when the parties came into dispute, as over defence in 1986.[6] Wainwright gave the impression of valuing this increased profile to David Wheeler, whose mother won a prize at a local Party fund-raiser of a bottle of wine signed by Owen, Williams and Rodgers, with whom Wainwright had been on good enough terms to secure. Rodgers remembers being photographed with Wainwright at the Llandudno Assembly in a group which also included other Social Demo-crats with Jo Grimond and David Steel. Wainwright was 'looking cheerful and apparently about to address me' Rodgers recalls: 'Richard seemed pleased that the Liberals and SDP were getting together.'[7]

There were, however, other aspects of the Alliance which troubled or frus-trated Wainwright. Firstly, there were some in his constituency who saw the SDP as offering a repeat of their experiences in the Lib-Lab Pact. Bill Oldham, the Chairman of Kirklees Council the previous year, told Wainwright of his doubts:

> I don't think he was very sure what to make of it. I should say the Liberal Party round here at that time was split 50–50: quite a few were against it, and quite a lot were for it. It wasn't the best of times. I wasn't terribly keen on them [the SDP] to be honest, because I'm an old-fashioned Liberal.[8]

Another Councillor, Barry Fearnley, said that 'at the time I was so proud of us being Liberal, we'd worked hard to build the Liberal Party up, that we weren't too keen on the Democratic side, the Socialist side.' As with the Lib-Lab Pact, Wainwright had to persuade Oldham and Fearnley: 'He'd let you make up your own mind' said Fearnley: 'If you wanted to support Richard, you'd believe what he said, and you went along with that line. If he was wrong, he was wrong. We didn't know enough about the background at that time, the whole of it, as Richard Wainwright did.'[9] A report in *The Times* by a writer close to Wain-wright the month before the SDP was launched claimed that Liberals in West Yorkshire were 'not much interested in pacts or alliances with social demo-crats', and that on Wainwright's Friday night tour of the Liberal Clubs 'the talk was of local issues rather than national politics.'[10]

Wainwright bore these general hostilities in mind, and he himself had two specific reservations about the SDP: its leaders and its candidates. Amongst the leaders, Wainwright like most Liberals found some easier to come to terms with than others: his family learned that 'he didn't have a problem with the SDP, but he did with some Social Democrats'; his son Martin had not been impressed with the last ministerial defector from Labour, Christopher Mayhew, whose campaign as Liberal candidate at Bath in 1974 he had reported on, and Wain-wright may have feared more of the same.[11] The more immediately acceptable were Roy Jenkins and Shirley Williams, but even these did not escape critical comment: Wainwright later asked 'was it just for fun we worked hard through night after night opposing Roy Jenkins' deflationary and unenterprising Budgets, and Shirley Williams' dotty Bill for subsidising food?'[12] When Jenkins and Williams both stood for unpromising northern seats Wainwright was supportive, encouraging Liberals to go and help. However, the barbed tone of his appeal to York University students to travel to Warrington to help Jenkins in July 1981 indicated he was still sceptical:

> Roy Jenkins has rightly accepted that the electors of Warrington are an entirely proper jury to assess the worth of the Social Democratic Party. He will be wise to use his status as a former Chancellor and President of the EEC Commission to explain in detail how the British and European systems of government can be radically reformed so that he and his British SDP colleagues will be able to do very much better next time around.[13]

Wainwright's assistant at the time, Joanna Copsey (later Hannam), remembers him 'talking about Roy Jenkins in a suspicious way' and felt 'absolutely clear that he was deeply uncomfortable and had huge reservations' about the Alliance. After Copsey attended an early SDP public meeting in Putney at which Jenkins spoke, she says, 'I remember a distinct sense of a little frisson that made me feel slightly disloyal for going.' Wainwright did, however, 'get there' with Jenkins and Williams, as Copsey puts it.[14] He even chose to sit next to Jenkins when their portrait on the benches of the Commons was painted. He made no such journey with the SDP Leader from 1983 onwards, former Foreign Secretary Dr David Owen: for many Liberals, Owen was a *bête noir*, an avowed hawk on nuclear defence, and in the opinion of his critics dangerously Thatcherite on economic and social policy.

Wainwright needed no policy explanation for his dislike of Owen: he distrusted his self-confident, ambitious character which threatened Napoleonic leadership. When Caroline Cawston complained to Wainwright that Owen 'never registered there was anybody behind it when he opened a door' and consequently crashed into her, Wainwright warned: 'well, Carol, that transmits through every fibre of the relationship.'[15] Joanna Copsey had the same impression of Wainwright's view of Owen: 'He thought the man was an opportunist and not a politician based on principle; and I don't think he thought he was a great thinker, either.'[16]

Wainwright was also concerned around this time about the effect of the Alliance upon relations within the Liberal Parliamentary Party, taking decision-making into a clique around the two parties' leaderships. When three Parliamentary colleagues wrote to David Steel to propose in the wake of the 1983 election result the removal of the Leader's control over the manifesto and Party Political Broadcasts, the introduction of a deputy leader, and the establishment of a Strategy Commission, Wainwright expressed approval:

Privately, let me say that I have believed for quite a long time that the Parliamentary Party urgently needs at least one colleague wholly accountable to the PLP, and I believe that the cause has suffered from the lack of this. I also believe that key functions such as our relations with the media ought to be under the control of the PLP, presumably by way of an elected colleague. I am deeply disturbed at what now seems to be happening in the leadership.[17]

Most of the time Wainwright kept his criticisms to himself and his close colleagues, and Owen himself was unaware of the contempt in which he was held by Wainwright, remembering him as 'a very nice man' with whom he had little contact beyond giving a press conference together in 1983.[18] However, when Owen was pressing David Steel to introduce a policy of European-based nuclear deterrent in 1986, Wainwright spoke out in public to say that he was 'making a fuss' over an issue which could be resolved later. 'In my opinion', he continued, 'which seems to be shared with most Liberals with whom I have talked – it would be foolish and unnecessary to come out now, as Dr Owen seems to want, with a decision which will be taken by the Government of the day.' Wainwright suffered a rebuke from the Vice Chairman of the Kirklees SDP, and even Nigel Priestley, by this stage the prospective Liberal candidate for Colne Valley, expressed surprise and sadness.[19]

Other Social Democrats found Wainwright cordial even when he disagreed with them, and Wainwright showed here his usual realism about what could be achieved. SDP MP John Horam was Wainwright's co-Chairman of the Alliance Joint Policy Resolution Group prior to the 1983 election and was less enthusiastic about incomes policy than Wainwright, but found him to be an effective and positive negotiator: 'he is not the sort of person you forget. The Yorkshire accent, the personal authority, and the well-organized views all made an impression. He was a good man to work with; we never had any serious difficulties personally.'[20] It is a sign of the amused detachment with which Wainwright viewed the national pretentions of the Alliance Leaders that when he was taunted as to whether he or Horam would be Chancellor-designate at the 1983 election he replied, 'who knows whether it will be the policy of an Alliance government to have a Chancellor of the Exchequer?'[21]

Where negotiations became more tense was at regional level over seat allocation. Representatives were appointed by each of the parties to discuss and agree which Party would contest which seat at General Elections. A parallel if less uniformly formalised process took place for local elections, too. Liberals were anxious, and sometimes angry, at the prospect of withdrawing from electoral contests which they had been fighting for years, often with increasing success, and against some of the personnel of the untried new Party for which they were now expected to make way. Wainwright shared this scepticism about the campaigning strength of the SDP, and sympathised with displaced Liberals. He complained that 'the SDP began with a prevailing view that parliamentary elections are decided from the broadcasting studio and that work in the streets is mostly ritual.'[22]

West Yorkshire was one of 'the area units housing the hard cases' according to the Liberal Party's General Secretary at the time, and Wainwright took a keen interest in the allocation of seats there.[23] Even those in Colne Valley noted that there was, Gordon Beever remembers, 'a lot of aggro about that'[24] and David Whitwam called it 'the main point of contention'[25] in the Alliance. Alan Beith, who represented the Liberals in the Yorkshire negotiations, discussed them at length with Wainwright, whom he found to be 'very shrewd and sensible':

> He could see who in the SDP were sensible people capable of moving things forward, and who either didn't want to stand and were constructive, or who if there were misgivings or they wanted to stand out for something, it was soundly based on better prospects of winning the seat; and others who had less good reason to take a stand.[26]

This brutal focus upon proven electoral strength protected the achievements of Liberal activists, but gave little recognition to the potential of the new Party for growth, or the need for a broadly balanced outcome from the negotiations, and might have seemed inflexible from the SDP side of the table. Wainwright took satisfaction from the fact that the Yorkshire Pennine Liberal Federation which he had set up had helped keep seats out of the SDP's hands in the negotiations.[27]

Wainwright kept up his close analysis of the SDP's strength after the election, expecting to see little growth. He asked the Yorkshire Liberal Agent Jane Merritt for a briefing on the SDP for an upcoming discussion amongst Liberal MPs which he was to chair, saying which were active and to what extent they were 'obediently toeing the official SDP line of maintaining a quite separate existence from ourselves', which he described as being 'in rivalry with local Liberals'; what forms of co-operation were being adopted in other constituencies; and where Yorkshire SDP groups were 'lapsing into inactivity'.[28] Wainwright's view appears to have been that the SDP by this stage was either a nuisance or an irrelevance. On a tour of Humberside in October 1985 Wainwright refused to include a proposed visit to Bridlington because 'Bridlington is still SDP, who did not handle the constituency well at the last election.'[29]

Aware of Wainwright's doubts about the SDP, Chris Greenfield, who had worked for him and stood as a candidate in Leeds before going to teach in the Middle East, wrote him a letter about developments just after the Llandudno Assembly which both teased and sympathised with Wainwright:

> I understand that Leeds North ward now has an SDP (with Lib support) Councillor – does that mean that *you* now have one of the SDP's twenty councillors representing you in Leeds Council Chamber? Have there been any defections in Leeds, Colne Valley, Huddersfield or anywhere else interesting?

'There does seem to be a distinct likelihood', warned Greenfield, 'that the SDP will regard itself as the senior partner in the pact – with the danger that the Libs will lose out in the allocation of seats.'[30] Even in local elections, Wainwright told his Association Chairman David Ridgway that he was surprised at the concessions his fellow Liberals had been prepared to make in seat allocations in Kirklees, and said he would have held out for a better deal.[31]

Wainwright did not dismiss or disown the Alliance in public; indeed he expressed gratitude for the support in making economic policy of the SDP spokesman Ian Wrigglesworth,[32] and immediately after the 1983 General Election invested £2,000 in the founding of a joint Alliance magazine, *The New Democrat*, for which both he and his son Martin wrote.[33] However, Wainwright's correspondence and the testimony of his staff suggest that from an early stage he foresaw the end of the SDP, and the subsuming of much of its membership into a single, liberal, Party. As with local pacts with the Tories up to the early 1960s, and the Lib-Lab Pact in the 1970s, he had accepted a situation he found disagreeable, trying to get as much out of it as possible, until circumstances presented an opportunity to move on. Those circumstances were about to arrive.

Notes.

1 The lecture, 'Home Thoughts from Abroad', was broadcast on BBC television, 22 November 1979.
2 Cited in Joseph, J., *Inside the Alliance: An Inside Account of the Development and Prospects of the SDP–Liberal Alliance* (London: John Martin 1983), pp. 30–1.
3 King, A., (ed.), *British Political Opinion 1937–2000* (London: Politico's 2001), p. 15.
4 Gordon Beever, interview, 31 October 2008.
5 Nigel Priestley, interview, 30 October 2008.
6 'One Plus One Equals Three', Editorial, *Huddersfield Daily Examiner*, 16 June 1986.
7 Lord Rodgers, correspondence with the present author, 26 May 2009.
8 Bill Oldham, interview, 29 October 2008.
9 Barry Fearnley, interview, 31 October 2008.
10 Bradley, I., 'Liberals are Cool towards Pact', *The Times*, 9 February 1981, p. 4. Bradley acknowledges Wainwright's support in his *The Strange Rebirth of Liberal Britain* (London: Chatto & Windus 1985), p. 5.
11 Martin Wainwright, interview, 22 February 2008.
12 RSW, 'Green Paper: Our Different Vision', typed draft, 29 March 1989, p. 2, Wainwright papers file 11/5.
13 Address to University of York Politics Society, *Liberal News*, 16 July 1981.
14 Joanna Hannam, interview, 19 January 2009.
15 Caroline Cawston, interview, 2 June 2008.
16 Joanna Hannam, interview, 19 January 2009.
17 RSW to Cyril Smith, 2 September 1983, Wainwright papers file 8/23. The other two Liberal MPs proposing changes to Steel were David Alton and Simon Hughes.

18 Lord Owen, correspondence with the present author, 2 June 2008, and *Time to Declare* (London: Penguin 1992), p. 527.

19 'Owen Making a Fuss, says Wainwright', *Huddersfield Daily Examiner*, 9 June 1986.

20 John Horam, correspondence with the present author, 5 April 2009. Horam later went on to be Conservative MP for Orpington.

21 Hansard, 14 April 1983. The taunt had come from John Home Robertson.

22 RSW, 'An Open Letter to SDP Workers', *The Radical Quarterly* No. 5, Autumn 1987, p. 10.

23 Jones, Sir H., *Campaigning Face to Face* (Brighton: Book Guild 2007), pp. 202 and 204.

24 Gorden Beever, interview, 31 October 2008.

25 David Whitwam, interview, 15 April 2009.

26 Alan Beith, interview, 13 October 2008.

27 RSW to Gordon Beever, 5 August 1983, Wainwright papers file 5/B/23.

28 RSW to Jane Merritt, 4 January 1984, Yorkshire Liberal Federation papers, University of Bristol Special Collections.

29 Ibid., 20 June 1985, Yorkshire Liberal Federation papers, University of Bristol Special Collections.

30 Chris Greenfield to RSW, 9 October 1981.

31 David Ridgway, interview, 31 October 2008.

32 RSW to Michael Meadowcroft, 17 February 1988, Wainwright papers file 11/5.

33 Chris Layton to RSW, 18 July 1983. RSW, 'A Doorstep Incomes Strategy', *New Democrat*, Vol. III, No. 4 (1985), p. 21, around which time Martin wrote a regular 'Alliance Eye' column on events in the two parties.

PART FOUR: AFTER PARLIAMENT

14 The merger and the Liberal Democrats

The fundamental fault lines in the Alliance were not policy issues but organisational and strategic questions. Moreover, they did not usually cut cleanly between the Liberals and the SDP, but ran across them, dividing both. The subjects of recurrent argument had included which of the other two parties Alliance leaders would be most likely to go into government with in the event of no party having an overall Commons majority: ex-Labour Social Democrats were more hostile to their former tribe, and David Owen in particular had seemed to warm to elements of Thatcherism, whereas Liberals, though like Wainwright committed to the free market, generally regarded themselves as a Party of the Left. However, the same Liberals were often fighting Labour on the ground, and were intensely attached to the Party's independence, and so apprehensive about any co-operation.

There was also controversy over whether the Alliance should have a single leader: this had arisen during the 1983 campaign when Roy Jenkins had been titled 'Prime Minister-designate' to much anxiety amongst Liberals still fearful of an SDP takeover; by 1985, the fear was greatest amongst the Social Democrats, now evidently the smaller of the two parties and with a less obviously senior candidate for joint Leader, and the mockery of the 'two Davids' by *Spitting Image* worked too well to be without resonance amongst the public. There was the running sore of seat allocation which had exercised Wainwright; last was the question of merger, which combined all of these in a single civil war.

The idea that the Liberals and the SDP would eventually form a single Party had been the spectre at the feast of third Party politics since before even the birth of the SDP, and both parties had always had clearly identifiable pro- and anti-merger factions gearing up for this cathartic struggle.[1] When David Steel first discussed with Roy Jenkins the possibilities for the renewal of Liberal politics in 1980, Steel approved a new party as the vehicle on the assumption that the parties would eventually merge. David Owen's campaign for the leadership of the SDP in 1982, conversely, was based precisely on the anxiety of those Social Democrats who feared the disappearance of the new party's appeal in an old party which the SDP's membership had, by definition, rejected as a vehicle for their values. The idea of a merger had been floated after the anti-climax of 1983, but had been quickly ruled out by Owen as incoming Leader of the SDP.[2]

After the knock-back of 1987, the pro-merger factions in both parties were ready to take their opportunity, and their colleagues would have to take sides or withdraw. Wainwright, no longer in Parliament, could have avoided public exposure in this battle, but he followed the pattern of a lifetime and decided firstly what could be achieved and secondly how best to ensure that it occurred. He had decided some time earlier that the SDP should be temporary, and now merger was inevitable he was determined to ensure that the new party embodied as much as possible of the Liberal spirit. During its early stages Wainwright seems to have at times despaired of both the new party's potential to be the vehicle for Liberalism he wanted, and of his powers to influence the debate. He came to the conclusion that the work could be done; but he was increasingly aware that it would be others who would have to do it.

Joyce Wainwright reflected that merger was the issue on which her husband had changed his mind most dramatically during his political life.[3] It is probably fairest to set this change in the context of his earlier acclimatisation to the idea of the Alliance, but Joyce's comment nonetheless reflects the seriousness with which Liberals like Wainwright, who had seen their Party rescued from the brink of destruction, regarded the question of the formal dissolution of the Party. They faced the painful dilemma of a zoologist contemplating the point at which a great species, to the preservation and nurturing of which they had devoted their lives, must cross-breed in order to survive and prosper. It is no surprise that Wainwright, like other Liberals, hesitated.

This is also a distinctive episode in Wainwright's Liberalism because, for the first time in forty years, he could approach an issue without giving consideration to Party or electoral opinion. Where the need to keep faith with colleagues and supporters had affected the timing, if not the substance, of his pronouncements on the Alliance, the Lib-Lab Pact, Thorpe's leadership and the pacts with the Conservatives in the 1950s, this was Wainwright pure and unadulterated. It is testimony to his consistency that it so closely followed the pattern of other decisions he made.

The first event in the post-Alliance period for Wainwright was the loss of Colne Valley. Nigel Priestley failed to retain the seat Wainwright had won at five of the previous six contests. In the centenary year of the Colne Valley Association this was a bitter blow to Wainwright, especially as the victors were, for the first time ever in the seat, the Tories. Where Wainwright's first win had been the only loss for the Labour Party in the landslide of 1966, Colne Valley was the solitary Conservative gain of 1987. Publicly Wainwright blamed the national leadership, arguing 'the Steel/Owen campaign on TV seriously let down the effective local fighters'[4] and that 'no-one leading the Alliance's national campaign knew anything like enough of life in Britain's great conurbations';[5] to Party Headquarters he blamed the boundary redistribution of 1981;[6] but within the local Party he questioned the organisation of the campaign and the commitment of some members. The factor Wainwright was too modest to raise was the loss of his considerable personal vote. All of the key figures involved in the 1987 contest in Colne Valley – including the winner – have expressed the opinion that had Wainwright stood again, he would have won.[7]

The Alliance's national campaign certainly faltered, with the leadership evidently divided, but the total vote share of 22 per cent was well ahead of what it had been on previous occasions when Wainwright had won. The boundary changes are made implausible as an explanation by the fact that Wainwright secured his largest majority ever in 1983 on the new boundaries. The organisation of the local campaign did have weaknesses, some of which could be traced to the boundary changes, which introduced weaker local branches than the one in Saddleworth which had been lost: Chris Davies, the candidate for Oldham East and Saddleworth in 1987, found that eight out of ten of his members were in Saddleworth, and the other local branches were effectively derelict; at the other end of the new Colne Valley constituency, Wainwright had warned after the 1983 campaign that 'I don't think the Colne Valley Liberals were impressed by what they found in the Lindley and Crosland Moor wards when they were moved into the Colne Valley.'[8]

After the 1987 defeat Wainwright wrote to one of the Association officers saying 'zeal for the Liberal cause, especially when it has suffered defeat, makes me very forthright – with everyone'. He objected that no information about the campaign had been made available at the first meeting after the defeat, and that there was 'uncertainty as to the state of the Division's organisation' and 'hints that some other ward is skiving financially *and getting away with it*'.[9]

More importantly than this, however, a number of key figures in previous campaigns were gone: Harry Senior and Edward Dunford had died, and Joanna Hannam had been away on maternity leave during the candidate selection which had caused so much bad blood. Notes he made at the first Association meeting after the defeat indicate Wainwright thought that the staff brought into the constituency for the election had proved 'not equal to the Division's new task'.[10]

The main factor in the defeat, however, was outside the Liberal Association's control: the tactical scenario – always the starting point of any campaign in Colne Valley – had altered after 1983, because the Conservatives were now in second place, and therefore less susceptible to the appeals Wainwright had made for years to vote Liberal as the only means of defeating Labour. Even the local Labour Party's Chairman recognised the previous year's local election 'was not a good election for us in Colne Valley or for the district'. The Colne Valley Labour Party Executive reckoned that three council wards would have to be won next time 'to give the electorate confidence that Labour can win

Colne Valley in the General Election.[11] In 1987 Labour won one ward, to the Conservatives' seven and the Liberals' ten. Colne Valley was still a two-horse race; but one of the horses had changed.

The Liberal campaign was left with the equally unpromising alternatives of appealing for tactical votes to Labour voters whose Party the Liberals had fought tooth and nail for a century; or seeking to retain Conservatives who could now see Labour was a lost cause and their candidate had a real chance. It made matters worse that the Tory candidate was a determined young Yorkshireman not steeped in the defeatism of Colne Valley Conservatives, and with Wainwright's knack for gaining local press coverage. The demographic balance of the constituency was also shifting in the Tories' direction, with gentrification and new housing bringing new, prosperous young bourgeois voters – 'nesters' as Joyce liked to call them – in from outside. Graham Riddick, the Conservative candidate, had a sense of his forthcoming victory from some of these:

> My wife and I went out for dinner at The Weaver's Shed in Golcar, before we went to the count. We got chatting to two couples who were sitting on the table next to us – both of them were from Holmfirth. They told us that they had voted for me, and this was the first time they had ever voted Conservative; they'd always voted Liberal in the past.[12]

Riddick had discovered that Wainwright's personal appeal, and his political message to the Conservatives, had gone. Liberal candidate Nigel Priestley made some belated efforts to win over Labour voters, but he was up against a century of tribalism and a strong, familiar Labour candidate in Council Leader John Harman.

The effects of this defeat upon the Colne Valley Liberal Association were devastating as far as future parliamentary elections were concerned. An attempt to remove Priestley as the candidate after 1987 failed, having been resisted by Wainwright; in 1992, he slipped into third place and was forced to face a reselection contest against Gordon Beever, the Councillor who had been excluded from the shortlist back in 1985. This battle for the Liberal Democrat nomination involved fewer members than the one between Priestley and William Wallace – Wainwright noted the total votes cast as 164 – but was even closer: both aspirant candidates received eighty-one votes. Priestley eventually fought the 1997 election at which Labour outvoted the Conservatives and he as Liberal Democrat candidate came third again. Gordon Beever followed suit in 2001. Within less than ten years, Colne Valley had gone from being a proud historic Liberal stronghold to being a divided and apparently lost cause.[13] The Party at national level had gone through some radical changes, too.

The formation of the Liberal Democrats

The public argument as to whether the Liberals should merge with the SDP began immediately the 1987 election was over, and immediately it began Wainwright made known his view that the merger should go ahead:

> Liberal and SDP volunteers sharing election chores and composing election Focuses together found themselves indistinguishable from each other in aim and purpose. The election speeches of Roy Jenkins, Shirley Williams and Ian Wrigglesworth gave acceptable ammunition to Liberals and Social Democrats alike. If we do not pour our common elements into the new mould of one political party, we shall have neither the right nor the opportunity to press upon the voters our plans for re-uniting the country.[14]

His praise for isolated Social Democrat leaders, and his tone of damning with faint praise, reflected Wainwright's impatience with the SDP's continued existence. This must have been exacerbated by the observable fact that whilst the vote of the average Liberal candidate had fallen by a lone percentage point, amongst SDP candidates the decline had been nearly 12 per cent, and they had won none of their target seats.[15] Wainwright had anticipated the SDP's end for some time, and now focused upon the campaign to ensure that the price paid for merger was as low to Liberal interests as possible. 'Just remember', he said to Sir Cyril Smith over lunch in Huddersfield where they discussed their misgivings about merger: 'it's them joining us, not the other way around.'[16] Over the next three years Wainwright threw himself passionately, if not continuously, into that struggle, and at times he seems to have doubted whether it would be a price worth paying. It was to be the last time that Wainwright used his political weight to gain concessions for those who shared his opinions but not his reputation or his talents, as he had done in different contexts in every decade since leaving school.

Until the merger had been formally completed in March 1988, the focus of Wainwright's anger about the process was the Liberal Leader David Steel. As in the Lib-Lab Pact and the Alliance, Wainwright suspected that Steel was acting without consultation with Liberal colleagues, and with a rudderless approach to policy. Uninhibited by such obligations to other MPs or to the leadership which Wainwright might have felt before, and fearful for the Party itself rather than its relationship with others, he launched – partly in private but later in public – a series of bitter attacks on Steel's leadership.

The exchanges between Wainwright and Steel began in the week following the election, when Wainwright wrote to the Party Leader 'pleading for our two parties to get away from reflecting merely rural and maritime Britain, and starting to reflect town life which is overwhelmingly and increasingly modern Britain', and stressing that he would raise this in the media.[17] In autumn, with the two parties feverish with speculation about merger, Wainwright published an article warning of the weaknesses of the SDP's constitution, which he described variously as 'centralised', 'perverse' and 'seriously frustrating' to Liberals.[18]

Dissatisfied with Steel's 'bland' responses,[19] Wainwright launched his first direct public attack on Steel and his partnership with Owen, declaring that 'if I were a candidate now I wouldn't dream of going into an election with either of those two. They pretended to be buddies all through the election campaign and they were nothing of the sort.'[20] The following month, two days before the Harrogate Liberal Assembly voted on the principle of merger, he called upon Steel to resign, saying he 'has been a man of the failed Alliance and I believe he must be replaced. He bravely preached a partnership that did not really exist. And he failed to give our movement a compelling theme.'[21] After merger negotiations were initiated by the Assembly and SDP conference, Wainwright contacted Ian Wrigglesworth, former SDP MP for Stockton and now one of the SDP's representatives in the talks, about 'the question of Leaders by-passing the negotiating team'; Wrigglesworth wrote back agreeing that 'one of my greatest anxieties on this, as on other occasions has been David Steel's habit of trying to "bounce" his own party and others into things without proper democratic consultation and consent.'[22]

The discussions between the two seventeen-strong negotiating teams were tense and tortuous, causing walk-outs by members on both sides. During these months Wainwright seems to have been content to turn his attention to his work in other areas, and even argued with his daughter Hilary about the seriousness of the split in the Liberals. Over Christmas Wainwright read a draft of an article Hilary had written for the *New Statesman* condemning the growing distance between activists and leaders in all parties: he told her that he thought there was no significant policy difference between pro- and anti-merger Liberals, and indeed that policy output from the latter was unimpressive.[23]

In the New Year, however, the merger process descended into farce and Wainwright was drawn back into the controversy. Steel and the new SDP Leader Robert Maclennan decided to issue joint declaration of aims, *Voices and Choices for All*, parts of which were unexpected and incendiary in impact. These included the extension of VAT to children's clothes, fuel and newspapers, the ending of universal child benefit and a pledge of support for the introduction of Trident nuclear missiles in the UK. According to Roy Douglas, 'the Liberal MPs exploded in fury', and, being quickly disowned, the statement was nicknamed the 'Dead Parrot document' after the unfortunate animal in the *Monty Python's Flying Circus* sketch. It was quickly replaced by another statement drawn up by three leading policy-makers from each of the parties, in time to secure overwhelming approval for merger at a Special Assembly in Blackpool on 23 January. However, Steel and Maclennan had in Douglas's words 'angered nearly everybody'.[24]

Wainwright was certainly one of those incensed, and he must have been doubly furious to learn that after the Blackpool Assembly Jo Grimond and other leading Liberals had urged Steel to consider standing for the leadership of the merged Party,[25] and to read later in *The Guardian* that 'Mr Steel will have the leadership of the new party if he wants it.'[26] In a speech at Leeds in the first week of February, he attacked Steel and Maclennan as unfit to lead, particularly because of the 'farce and shame' of the 'parrot' document. 'It was', Wainwright intoned, 'not the first time that David Steel intended to publish under his name sixth-form essays which ought to have been sent back marked "only 1 out of 10".'[27] The speech was not only reported in the Yorkshire press and broadcast on regional television – along with an interview with Wainwright – but also in the *Financial Times* and *The Scotsman*, from where Steel complained that his Conservative opponents in his constituency could gather ammunition.[28]

There followed three weeks of angry correspondence between Wainwright and Steel. Wainwright was indignant and outspoken in his tone; Steel infuriatingly unflappable and decorous whilst dismissing Wainwright's arguments. Refusing to announce his retirement as Leader, Steel implored Wainwright 'do please come and see me rather than as Jo used to say "confide in the nearest journalist"!';[29] he later accused Wainwright of giving Graham Riddick, the Conservative MP for Colne Valley, material to use against his Liberal Democrat opponent Nigel Priestley;[30] and ended the exchanges saying 'your letters are beginning to fall into the category of those underlined spasmodically in green ink and copied to the Queen. I cannot follow the by-ways of your argument.'[31]

Steel could scarcely have designed a better approach for infuriating Wainwright. His references to Jo Grimond and the Colne Valley – like Steel's claim earlier in the merger process that David Penhaligon, who had died tragically in a car accident, would have been well placed to lead a merged Party – touched on the most sensitive of associations for Wainwright. He countered Steel that 'one bonus from my speech is that for the first time since June you have asked me to see you', though he was 'the only person to whom the Yorkshire media can turn for a comprehensive view' in the absence of any Alliance MP from the region; he rebuked Steel as 'a real Mrs Malaprop in using Jo's words to me', and regarded the claim that he was undermining any Liberal candidate as hypocritical:

> Did you make this a priority when you (self-indulgently and foolishly as I have thought) spent your Eastbourne speech deriding and denouncing some of your Commons colleagues, all of whom intended to fight the next election? And your finger-wagging came from the floodlit Leader, not from a retired man holding no office whatever in the Liberal Party as such.

'Only a megalomaniac', Wainwright continued, 'would expect to transform your style of leadership by discussion, when even a series of disasters arising

201

from your irresponsibility about policy failed to prevent you creating the "parrot" which will drive every Liberal on the defensive so long as you are Leader. If our paths cross soon, I shall be glad of a talk', he conceded; 'but not at the Yorkshire Assembly. I am surprised you even contemplate appearing there.'[32] Wainwright repeated his demand that Steel step down, and called for a leadership campaign longer than the three months envisaged by Steel. When in April Steel finally decided not to run for the leadership of the new Party, it followed his recognition that 'I could no longer rely on a coalition of support from the MPs and the mass membership' and that 'the "parrot" episode had dangerously eroded my "political capital" amongst the party activists.'[33] Wainwright's reproaches were a particularly clear indication of this to Steel.

For good measure, in the midst of this correspondence Wainwright published an article in *The Guardian* dilating upon Steel's 'downgrading of policy' and predicting that 'if David Steel were to lead the new Party into the next session of Parliament, serious parliamentary candidates are more likely to request him to stay away than to visit them.'[34] At the same time he wrote to other leading Liberals, including Malcolm Bruce MP, parliamentary candidate Viv Bingham, who expressed approval of the *Guardian* piece,[35] and Councillor John Marshall in Harrogate, to reiterate his concerns. 'I felt obliged to warn you', he told Marshall, 'that the irresponsible declaration last month was not an isolated incident of Steel policy-making and cannot be expected to be the last of its kind whilst he is leader.'[36]

A certain amount of Wainwright's unusually panicky tone can be attributed to a feeling that his great sense of responsibility was no longer matched by his erstwhile ability to influence events at Westminster: like all retired MPs, he was coming to terms with being out of the loop. For the most part, however, his reaction was a reflection of genuine anxiety that the merger process was going to end in the destruction of any sort of meaningfully liberal party. The proof of his continued strategic caution is to be seen in his resistance of the siren call of those Liberals who refused to join the merged Party, best-known amongst whom was Wainwright's protégé Michael Meadowcroft, whom Wainwright had once described as 'a consummate politician'.[37] At the same time as he campaigned against Steel, Wainwright was in correspondence with Meadowcroft about a pamphlet the latter had written, *Merger or Renewal?* in which he began to set out the case for a continuing independent Liberal organisation after the merger. Wainwright was supportive but non-committal, hoping at this stage to maintain links between all types of Liberal, whatever the outcome of the negotiations.[38]

In March the launch of the Social and Liberal Democrats took place. Its early manifestations cannot have been encouraging to Wainwright: his preferred leader, Alan Beith, was defeated in July by Paddy Ashdown, using a 'one member, one vote' system which Wainwright disliked because it failed to recognise the difference between committed activists and armchair subscribers in the way the old Liberal electoral college had done. In September the Party adopted the shortened name 'Democrats' for media purposes, against Wainwright's insistence to Ashdown that the word 'Liberal' be retained.[39]

Wainwright joined the SLD, but continued to keep a foot in both Liberal camps as Meadowcroft founded the Liberal Movement, intended initially as a meeting-point for former Liberal Party members who had refused to transfer to the new Party as well as those who had joined it. Just before Ashdown was declared Leader of the SLD, Wainwright was ceremonially awarded the 'Liberal Roll of Honour' at the Liberal Movement's conference in Wolverhampton, where he made a speech highly critical of the Alliance.[40] Ambivalent as this might have looked at the time, it was Wainwright's attempt to do as he always had, and keep faith with all parts of the Liberal family. That task was becoming more demanding than ever.

In February 1989, Meadowcroft published a more substantial defence of his refusal to join the SLD, in which he attacked the conduct of the Party from the time of the Lib-Lab Pact because 'the Liberal leadership thereafter never again promoted Liberalism as a distinctive and essential philosophy', and condemned the SLD as suffering from 'a lack of principle and confidence'.[41] Wainwright nonetheless wrote to him to encourage him to take up an approach he had received from the SLD branch in his old seat of Leeds West.[42] Wainwright also wrote a highly critical review of the chief policy statement issued by the SLD, *Our Different Vision* by Professor David Marquand.[43] By this stage, however, though Wainwright's heart was partly with the Liberal Movement, his head recognised that the SLD was the only show in town. In February he spent a week with Joyce in a rented cottage in North Yorkshire helping the SLD candidate in the Richmond by-election, contributed to the campaign's funds and advised Campaigns Director Chris Rennard, one of the Liverpudlian helpers in Colne Valley in the 1970s.

The experience must have been a salutary one for Wainwright. First of all Wainwright's preferred candidate was not chosen; and second, the SLD candidate was faced with competition from a representative of the continuing Social Democratic Party and an 'Official Liberal' anti-merger candidate. The result was that whilst the candidates of the former Alliance gained 54 per cent of the vote between them, the seat was retained by the Conservative candidate, William Hague. Humiliatingly, David Owen's 'Continuing' SDP were runners-up and the SLD third. The need to rally behind the organisation was painfully clear, and became more so when the Greens gained more than twice the vote of the SLD at the European elections in June.

The time had come to make a decision about which vehicle of Liberalism to support, although Wainwright was neither swift nor joyous to make it. After a meeting in the first week of October, Michael Meadowcroft made another bid to get Wainwright fully involved in the Liberal Movement and out of the SLD.[44] When Wainwright replied nearly a fortnight later, he declined the invitation in the most downbeat and apologetic terms:

> My energies, such as they are, will be spent on Electoral Reform (STV), Charter 88 and (marginally) the Liberal Movement. I shall not for the moment actually resign formal membership of SLD, in order not to risk handicapping stout colleagues who are still working to redeem SLD.[45]

A number of developments had helped drive Wainwright to this conclusion: Steel was gone from the leadership, as was David Owen from the Party and almost from the political scene; Wainwright mentioned Owen and the fact that the SLD had finally decided upon the title 'Liberal Democrats' after a ballot of members the result of which was announced between Meadowcroft's letter and Wainwright's reply.[46] Wainwright agreed with Meadowcroft that there was a 'gaping hole in the party's essential equipment' around policy-making, a larger version of one the Liberals had had previously. 'In my view', he went on, 'any group supporting a distinctive political faith would do well to be a "Movement" rather than a "Party"'. He offered the *tu quoque* defence for the Liberal Democrats that he had during his career asked himself about the effectiveness of the Liberal Party, 'and on several occasions concluded that, at the time, it was doing more harm than good to Liberalism', but acknowledged that 'I realise that vast numbers of Liberals remain outside.'[47] The problem was that some of those outside were preparing to challenge the fledgling Liberal Democrats at the polls without offering any real prospect of doing better – in 1990 the anti-merger Liberal Party fought five by-election campaigns against SLD candidates, never winning more than 3 per cent of the vote. Wainwright the realist backed the Liberal Democrats with a somewhat heavy heart. Meadowcroft could only say that 'I sense that you've had quite a struggle with your response but I know that it will disappoint many friends.'[48]

At the end of the year Wainwright wrote to Paddy Ashdown complimenting him on his New Year's address to the Party with its focus on policy, and offering him advice on the need for investment in unproductive emerging Eastern European economies, and for the careful presentation of such measures.[49] Ashdown knew Wainwright as 'a wise old head' from the controversies in the Parliament of 1983, when he acted as a bridge and represented 'the sensible viewpoint'. As Liberal Democrat Leader, Ashdown could not count the number of times he sought Wainwright's advice, knowing that his attitude to the Liberal Democrats was that 'he would not have wanted it that way, but he understood why it had to be that way'. Ashdown found Wainwright was 'a talisman – if it was all right with Richard, it was all right with...'[50] Wainwright was back in his old role, in a new Party.

Wainwright as a Liberal Democrat

From January 1990 onwards, Wainwright resumed his position as a critical but generous friend to his Party leadership, and was especially active in Yorkshire. He had already agreed to be President of the Yorkshire Liberal Democrats, and set aside a week in September to attend the Party conference, which he also did in 1992 and 1993. In May 1990 he represented the Liberal Democrats on Yorkshire TV and Radio Leeds and the following February he told the Yorkshire Liberal Democrats' conference at Harrogate that they had 'ripe territory' to work.[51] By August 1991 the Wainwrights were hosting Strawberry Teas for the Liberal Democrats of Leeds North West at their new home.[52] Joyce joined the Yorkshire Women's Liberal Democrats, and over the next ten years Wainwright attended candidates' selections in Colne Valley, Leeds, Pudsey, Skipton and Shipley. He gave testimonials supporting the nomination of candidates for Bradford in 1992 and Easington in 1997.

Wainwright took a particular interest in the Saddleworth by-election of 1995,[53] donating funds to the local Party, speaking at candidate Chris Davies's adoption meeting, and spending several days campaigning in his old constituency, including a successful press call at Uppermill market. Davies remembers the continued value of Wainwright's endorsement with seasoned voters and activists who were 'a hundred per cent "Richard Wainwright Liberals".'[54] Wainwright had campaigned at Saddleworth in 1987 and 1992, and had already helped in the successful Ribble Valley by-election campaign of 1991, but according to Joyce he was especially gratified to see Davies's victory at Saddleworth, for he had first encouraged him as another young canvasser in Colne Valley visiting from Liverpool in the 1970s.[55] Perhaps it gave the Liberal Democrats authenticity for Wainwright that under their banner one of his apprentices had won back part of his old seat – and against a Labour campaign personally directed by Peter (now Lord) Mandelson. In 1995 and 1996 Wainwright monitored the involvement of his successor as MP for the Colne Valley, Graham Riddick, in the 'Cash for Questions' scandal, and wrote to the local press reproaching him.[56]

Wainwright's active involvement in the Party dwindled after 1997, when he retired as President of the Yorkshire Liberal Democrats. With forty-six seats at that year's General Election, the Party had secured the best representation it had enjoyed in the Commons since Wainwright was ten years old. In his eightieth year he could begin to let others take up the unfinished business of Liberal politics, but as late as November 2000, his diary entries include a meeting with new Party Leader Charles Kennedy.

As well as his time, Wainwright gave the Liberal Democrats money, as generously and anonymously as he had done for the Liberals. Wainwright offered £3,000 to pay for a poll of the Colne Valley in the run-up to the 1992 election with the aim of demonstrating that the Liberal Democrats were best placed to oust the Conservatives, and at the same election he donated £150,000 to the national Liberal Democrat campaign with the stipulation that it was to be devoted to developing and publicising Party policy and providing detailed ammunition for candidates in the form of briefings.[57] 'I wouldn't give a penny towards a national press advertisement' he insisted, 'which I think is tantamount to saying to the public: "We don't have enough active supporters to bring our case to your doorstep so we are using the medium employed by the salesmen of toffees, hair cream and pulp fiction". At election times I enjoy mocking at parties who have to rely on posters and adverts.'[58]

Lastly Wainwright continued to lobby the Liberal Democrat leadership on policy and strategy. He wrote a string of letters throughout the 1990s to Liberal Democrat MPs including Ed Davey, Nick Harvey, Archy Kirkwood, Bob Maclennan and Paddy Ashdown, resisting what he perceived as the threat of diluting distinctive Liberal Democrat positions on the economy, Europe, electoral reform, devolution and regional government. In 1993, for example, Wainwright gave Ashdown a detailed analysis of the draft 'New Agenda' Paper still under preparation by the leadership.[59] The overarching theme of these warnings was, as it had been in the Lib-Lab Pact and the Alliance, the need to guard against the weakening of Liberal Democrat independence as the Party drew closer and closer to New Labour in the run-up to the 1997 election. Wainwright feared that Ashdown was being drawn into agreeing statements that were 'almost meaningless, and perhaps intended to be' and that he was 'repudiating Keynesian solutions and almost endorsing Thatcherite economics'.[60] He told Ashdown that some of the Leader's writing in national newspapers worried him.[61]

Most of this correspondence was cordial, but Wainwright never disguised concerns. When Labour took office in 1997, and Liberal Democrats joined a Cabinet Committee, Wainwright again fired off a warning shot that 'our relationship with Labour must be one of tension', as Ashdown quickly agreed.[62] When Robert Maclennan acquiesced in serious limitations of the Freedom of Information Bill under Jack Straw's Home Secretaryship, Wainwright wrote to *The Guardian* to support Hugo Young's accusation that 'Lib Dem MPs who sit on the Lab/Lib Cabinet Committee failed to resist a deeply flawed draft Freedom of Information Bill' and that 'Lib Dem activists, who have to answer for their Party on the doorstep and in the media, need to hear more from Mr Maclennan.'[63] After sixty-three years in the Party, Wainwright remained one of those Liberals who were its conscience and its watchman, rarely acknowledged, always loyal, but pivotal in its fate.

Wainwright was undoubtedly a Liberal Democrat: he had made a difficult journey shared by many other Liberals, in which he had accepted many aspects of the new Party with which he was not comfortable – it lacked the religious dimension of the old Liberal Party; it was larger than the old Party; it was a more national affair with a different approach to policy-making – but many of these problems had presented him with dilemmas before 1988. For Wainwright, the question was not whether the Party was perfect, but whether it was viable as a vehicle for Liberalism. More than one of Wainwright's former colleagues and supporters has pointed to the record of Vince Cable as an exemplar of what Wainwright would have wanted to see Liberal Democrats doing. Cable went to Cambridge, and fought his native York as a Social Democrat when Wainwright was fighting his last campaign in Yorkshire; more importantly, he is a believer in government action but also economic orthodoxy; and he is a witty and intelligent debater who does not crave national leadership, or in Roy Hattersley's less generous compliment, 'realises that apparent contempt for image building is the best image of all'.[64] Wainwright's unfinished business is being carried on.

Notes

1 The present author's own experience of this preparedness of both sides in the merger debate was of working for five months of 1987 in the General Election Unit of the SDP in Cowley Street, writing for the Party's newspaper, *The Social Democrat*. He was appointed upon assurances to the paper's Editor from colleagues in the Party's youth movement – exaggerated, as it happens – that he was 'sound' (i.e. Owenite, anti-merger), and was able to witness from his position the departure almost immediately after the election of senior officials of the Social Democrats to run the pro-merger 'Yes to Unity' campaign.

2 Owen, D., 'No Fear of Merger', *The Social Democrat*, 8 July 1983, p. 8.

3 Joyce Wainwright, interview, 22 February 2008.

4 RSW, 'Where Our National Campaign Let Us Down', *Liberal News*, 19 June 1987.

5 RSW' 'Split Britain Faces Trouble', *Yorkshire Post*, 13 June 1987.

6 RSW to Nick Harvey, Liberal Democrat Joint States Candidates' Committee, 2 January 1993, Wainwright papers file 12/1.

7 Graham Riddick, interview, 16 March 2009.

8 RSW to Gordon Beever, 5 August 1983, Wainwright papers file 5/B/23.

9 RSW to David Ridgway, 16 July 1987, Wainwright papers file 5/B/16.

10 Colne Valley Divisional Liberal Association Executive minutes, 2 July 1987.

11 Colne Valley Labour Party minutes, 16 and 20 May 1986, Huddersfield University Archives file HLP 23.

12 Graham Riddick, interview, 16 March 2009.

13 It should be noted that the success of the Liberal Democrat candidate Nicola Turner in retrieving second place in another tight three-way contest in Colne Valley at the 2010 election shows the enduring Liberal support there on which Wainwright drew and which he nurtured.

14 RSW, 'Where Our National Campaign Let Us Down', *Liberal News*, 19 June 1987.

15 Outwin, D., *The SDP Story* (Maidenhead: Hartswood 1987), p. 75.

16 Sir Cyril Smith, interview, 29 May 2008.

17 RSW referred back to this correspondence in a letter to Steel of 10 February 1988, Wainwright papers file 11/4.

18 RSW, 'An Open Letter to SDP Workers', *Radical Quarterly*, No, 5, Autumn 1987, pp. 8–10.

19 RSW to David Steel, 10 February 1988, Wainwright papers file 11/4.

20 'Liberal Savages Steel', *Yorkshire Post*, 14 August 1987.

21 Ibid., 16 September 1987. The call for Steel's resignation was also reported in the *Yorkshire Evening Press* of the previous day.

22 Ian Wrigglesworth to RSW, 30 October 1987. RSW had written to him on 26 October, Wainwright papers file 11/4.

23 RSW to Michael Meadowcroft, 10 February 1988, Wainwright papers file 11/5. The article appeared as Wainwright, H., 'Who's Afraid of Political Activists?', *New Statesman*, 8 January 1988, pp. 11–13.

24 Douglas, R., *Liberals: The History of the Liberal and Liberal Democrat Parties* (London: Hambledon & London 2005), p. 297.

25 D'Arcy, M., '12 Days that Shook the Merger', *The Social Democrat*, 28 January 1988, p. 5.

26 RSW to David Steel, 12 February 1988.

27 *Huddersfield Daily Examiner, Yorkshire Post* and *The Scotsman*, 4 February 1988 .

28 David Steel to RSW, 11 February 1988, Wainwright papers file 11/4.

29 Ibid., 5 February 1988, Wainwright papers file 11/4.

30 Ibid. 11 February 1988, Wainwright papers file 11/4.

31 Ibid., 15 February 1988, Wainwright papers file 11/4. On 18 February, Wainwright sent a lengthy and more conciliatory reply including the cryptic remark 'sorry about the red ink in my letter to you of 12 Feb. I was brought up to use it in my former firm, but I realise that it is now out of fashion.'

32 RSW to David Steel, 12 February 1988, Wainwright papers file 11/4.

33 Steel, D., *Against Goliath: David Steel's Story* (London: Weidenfeld & Nicolson 1989), p. 294.

34 RSW, 'The Time Has Come for David Steel To Go', *The Guardian*, 15 February 1988, p. 34.

35 Viv Bingham to RSW, 16 February 1988, Wainwright papers file 11/4.

36 RSW to John Marshall, 25 February 1988, Wainwright papers file 11/4.

37 Cited in Jones, Sir H., *Campaigning Face to Face* (Brighton: Book Guild 2007), p. 76.

38 RSW to Michael Meadowcroft, 10 and 17 February 1988, Wainwright papers file 11/5.

39 Lord Ashdown, interview, 12 September 2008.

40 *Liberal Movement News*, No. 3, p. 1. Wainwright addressed the conference on 17 July 1988.

41 Meadowcroft, M., *Liberalism Today and Tomorrow* (Coventry: The Liberal Association 1989), pp. 4 and 25.

42 RSW to Michael Meadowcroft, 22 March 1989.

43 The review, a typewritten draft, is dated 29 March 1989, Wainwright papers file 11/5.

44 Michael Meadowcroft to RSW, 8 October 1989, Wainwright papers file 11/5.

45 RSW to Michael Meadowcroft, 20 October 1989, Wainwright papers file 11/5.

46 The ballot result – showing 70 per cent in favour of 'Liberal Democrats' as the Party

title – was announced on 16 October 1989.

47 RSW to Michael Meadowcroft, 20 October 1989, Wainwright papers file 11/5.

48 Michael Meadowcroft to RSW, 24 November 1989, Wainwright papers file 11/5.

49 RSW to Paddy Ashdown, 31 December 1989, Wainwright papers file 12/1.

50 Lord Ashdown, interview, 12 September 2008.

51 'Party's Ripe Pickings', *Yorkshire Post*, 25 February 1991, p. 13.

52 Barbara Pearce to RSW and JW, giving notice of members' meeting, 7 August 1991, and thanking Joyce and RSW for organising the Strawberry Tea, Wainwright papers file 12/1.

53 RSW to Chris Rennard, 5 June 1995, Wainwright papers file 12/2.

54 Chris Davies, interview, 24 July 2009.

55 Joyce Wainwright, interview, 22 February 2008.

56 Wainwright papers file 5/B/35. Riddick was one of those named in a 1994 *Sunday Times* report as having received payment in exchange for asking parliamentary questions. Riddick resigned as a Parliamentary Private Secretary and was briefly suspended from the Commons.

57 RSW to Jim Wallace MP, Chief Whip, 16 April 199, Wainwright papers file 12/1.

58 Ibid., 9 January 1992, Wainwright papers file 12/1.

59 RSW to Paddy Ashdown, 26 May 1993, Wainwright papers file 12/1.

60 RSW to Archy Kirkwood, 26 April 1993, Wainwright papers file 12/1.

61 RSW to Paddy Ashdown, 5 May 1993, Wainwright papers file 12/1.

62 RSW to Paddy Ashdown, 23 July 1997; Ashdown to RSW, 30 July 1997, Wainwright papers file 12/1.

63 RSW to *The Guardian*, 24 June 1999, Wainwright papers file 12/2.

64 Hattersley, R., '*Free Radical* by Vince Cable', Book Reviews, *The Guardian*, 14 November 2009.

Conclusion

Wainwright's retirement was not all party politics: in fact, he refused the opportunity to continue his parliamentary career in the House of Lords. As the most experienced retiring Liberal MP, he was the obvious choice to receive the lone Peerage which was offered to the Liberal Party by Margaret Thatcher in 1987.[1] However, he had throughout his career maintained a fiery opposition to the then still largely hereditary composition of the Lords. When asked if he would contemplate joining the Lords, Wainwright had a stock set of replies, one of the less graphically insulting of which was 'you only visit a graveyard; you don't live in one.'

Even Liberal Peers did not escape Wainwright's wrath. Frank Byers, by then Leader of the Liberals in the Lords, objected to a letter Wainwright had written to *The Times*, saying 'your description of the work of the Lords is a total travesty and based on your complete inexperience of how the place works';[2] a year earlier, Byers reported his colleagues 'absolutely shocked' by a speech made by Wainwright at Oldham whilst Chairman of the Liberal Party, at which he called for an end to the Honours system. 'The Lords', Wainwright declared, 'is the most exquisite instrument of humbug for neutralising radical movements because it wields the deadliest of all British weapons – power to bore the public.' Every debate in the Upper House, he taunted, should begin with a somnolent rendering of:

> Drool Britannia,
> Britannia Shields the Knaves,
> Britons always, always, always
> Shall be slaves.[3]

In response to Byers's horror Wainwright could say only that he approved of 'the way in which first-class Liberals with manifest grass-roots connections with the Party have been made Life Peers', but warned: 'I am concerned lest further offers from the PM of a rash of Honours shall be seen to push us much too far towards the hopeless structure of the other two parties.'[4] It was true that the Liberal Lords had throughout the post-war era outnumbered the Party's

MPs, and had maintained a quite distinctive existence from them. Wainwright declined to add to this number not only by his own refusal to join them, but even during his retirement to support nominations for close friends and supporters whose names were being put forward for Peerages.[5]

Some of Wainwright's time was invested in organisations around but not part of the Liberal Democrats, including Charter 88, the Electoral Reform Society, the Wider Share Ownership Council, the Liberal Democrat History Group and the Centre for Reform (now Centre Forum), a think-tank which he funded generously.[6] Wainwright remained involved in the Joseph Rowntree Reform Trust, and was made a Fellow of Huddersfield Polytechnic in 1988. He and Joyce travelled to Cyprus, Italy, France and Cornwall, and visited the theatre at Leeds. He saw more of his family, especially his grandchildren in whose education he took a keen interest, and his garden remained a source of relaxation and pride. In May 1989, Wainwright moved from The Heath to a bungalow built in its grounds. A matching house was built for his gardener at the same time; but he kept a substantial part of The Heath's gardens, and continued to open them to the public.

Retirement from public life was not without its difficulties for Wainwright: his health, mental and physical, deteriorated, and both he and Joyce spent periods in hospital, Wainwright staying at The Retreat, a Quaker-run psycho-logical centre in York. Friends visiting Wainwright at Leeds noticed that latterly, despite his determination to carry out unaided the duties of the host, he was weakening, and sometimes lacked the purposeful demeanour he had exhibited as an MP. The decline in his ability – politically and physically – to put into practice the convictions which had driven Wainwright so power-fully throughout his life, and which still burned within him, was frustrating. In the circumstances, he used his talent for planning to relatively good effect in keeping himself occupied. He remained engaged in enquiry and discussion about politics until his death on 16 January 2003. A Service of Thanksgiving at a packed Leeds Parish Church on 21 February brought together many of the personalities whom Wainwright had worked with and motivated in tribute to his remarkable impact.

Wainwright's success

Almost any successful Liberal parliamentary candidature in the 1960s is a matter of legitimate curiosity; but the fact that Wainwright was able to win Colne Valley from third position, to retrieve the seat after defeat, and from that platform and others to exercise the influence he did over the Party's fate, is a matter of significant historical interest. Wainwright's success rested upon a combination of four factors: his personality, his background, his constituency and his Party.

Wainwright's personal attributes which account for his success are acknowledged by both his critics and his supporters: he was a man of enormous charm, wit and articulacy, whose analysis was worthy of a hearing and likely to win friends; he was impressively organised, and persevered not only with his quest to win and win back Colne Valley but with his ambitions for the Liberal Party; most striking of all is his commitment to his core beliefs and his willingness to lose friends for them. In an age in which catch-all parties and superficial leaderships were becoming commonplace, Wainwright stands out as a politician who on a series of issues made himself unpopular, or lost benefits to himself, by being unfashionable. His decision to join the Liberal Party and stay in it through its lowest points is only the most extended example: his refusal to fight in the Second World War; his opposition to capital punishment and support for immigration; his readiness to put his head above the parapet in the Thorpe affair; and his refusal to take a seat in the House of Lords; he even opposed Scottish devolution because he thought it would damage the North, and the Liberal animal rights group because they objected to beagling. All of these illustrate a preparedness to risk unpopularity rather than connive in what he believed to be wrong, often motivated by his faith.

This was never a martyrdom accompanied by self-pity or righteousness, however, even when angry or sad: in fact it emerged only at times of greatest necessity, and for most of his political life Wainwright's other characteristic was loyalty, even to leaderships and arrangements about which he had the greatest private doubts. One of Wainwright's great skills was the ability to judge the point at which he could by individual action move others towards what he thought the right path, even if at cost to himself. This combination emerged in great national controversies, but also in the reaction of so many of his constituents who regarded Wainwright as a man who would give a straight answer.

Some of Wainwright's personality traits were enhanced by his social background. He was doted upon as the only son of a prosperous professional who prepared his son for public life from childhood. At home, school and university Wainwright's life was littered with contacts – present and future leading figures from the academic, political, artistic and business worlds – and experiences which would give him confidence and support in his political career. Moreover, Wainwright's family background gave him the financial security with which to be ambitious and independent. Wainwright probably made a net loss on being an MP. He paid the wages of his Agent and an organiser, as well as hiring two staff and purchasing equipment with which to undertake printing. Much of this was done through the Yorkshire Pennine Liberal Federation which Wainwright established in 1967 to assist neighbouring seats, and into which he was investing £2,400 per year in addition to these other costs by the early 1980s.[7] Through Yorkshire business contacts he was also able to add to this: at one Party dinner in Saddleworth, the first prize in the raffle was a Mini motor car supplied by an associate of Wainwright's in Leeds.[8]

At national level Wainwright set up the Local Government Department at Liberal Headquarters, hired economic advisors and assistants (some of whom he continued to pay when they were drawn into the pool of MPs' staff), gave substantial sums to appeals run by Cyril Smith in the 1970s, and supported the Liberal Democrats' first General Election campaign with a six-figure sum. He also made possible the funding of many Liberal candidates through his place on the Board of the Joseph Rowntree Trust, one of whose grants is credited by Paddy Ashdown with rescuing his political career a year before entering Parliament when he was down to his last £150.[9]

All of this was done without publicity, but it had two key effects: Wainwright's campaigning was a more consistent and substantial operation than most Liberals could hope to run – Colne Valley, for example, was one of only eighteen constituencies with a full-time Liberal Agent in 1970[10] – and thus he was not outspent by the two main parties; and secondly, these gifts were anonymous to outsiders but their origin was known to the recipients, and they took due note of the preferences of the benefactor. Wainwright, of course, could not help this, but it made him a difficult man to ignore, and he used that to give voice to Liberals who might not otherwise have been heard.

The other effect of his background which benefited Wainwright was his marriage. Joyce's magnificent contribution to Wainwright's success is set out above, but their children were called upon to campaign, and largely did so very effectively: when, two years before his death, Wainwright and Joyce visited Luise Nandy, the daughter of Frank Byers, with his own children Martin and Hilary, they reminisced and teased Wainwright about the work to which they were put. 'We had the same kind of experience' said Nandy; 'we got dragged around from a very early age.' Like Wainwright's children, she had canvassed, been photographed, and travelled in the tannoy car. 'You had to mind your P's and Q's' she remembered: 'we had to learn how to shake hands.'[11] Hilary wrote to her grandfather from school that 'last week Miss Blake said that we could go home a day earlier because it would be so near Easter if we did not, but when I told Mummy, she immediately "suggested" (commanded) that I should go canvassing with her, but at least that's better than school!'[12]

It is far less likely that Wainwright would have arrived in Parliament, and certainly that he would have stayed so long, but for his decision to contest the Colne Valley in particular. He may have been, as he was described in Joyce's account of the 1964 election, 'one of the finest candidates in any party in the country',[13] but in few other constituencies was there the existing Liberal organisation and culture, and the distinctive social and economic mix, of Colne Valley; and there were few constituencies – certainly very few outside Yorkshire – where Wainwright's credentials as a local representative would have been so readily recognised. High-quality Liberal candidates failed across the country in the 1960s, but they did not have a network of Liberal Clubs, local press support and a constituency party with three Liberal MPs in living memory to build upon. Doubtless many would have failed to capitalise upon these assets as effectively as Wainwright – this was no safe seat – and assuredly there are other seats which at the right time would have responded to Wainwright's appeal; but the special chemistry between Wainwright and the Colne Valley brought repeated success.

The fourth factor in Wainwright's success is the one to which he least often gave credit: the standing of the Liberal Party nationally. The electoral politics of Colne Valley were often at odds with those of the rest of the country for Liberal candidates, because a rising Labour vote usually drained Liberal support, whereas in Colne Valley it drove supporters of a weakened Tory Party to Wainwright. This tactical explanation for his success was assumed by leading psephologists, and was a key element in Wainwright's own campaigning. Wainwright also liked to mock and criticise the strategies and campaign materials of Liberal Party Headquarters, an attitude for which there was sometimes cause, but which was something of 'a routine event in the case of the Liberal Party' in the words of one of those criticised, David Owen.[14] This disdain overlooked the important, if underperformed, role played by public perceptions of the Party as a national force. Local tactical considerations, the examination above argues, were only one part of Wainwright's success, and did not account for his election despite a high Conservative vote in February 1974, 1979 and 1983. It is also difficult to deny the link between national and local Liberal fortunes visible as Wainwright secured second place in Colne Valley at the tail end of the Orpington boom; when Wainwright lost his seat in 1970 on the only occasion the Liberal Party gained less than 10 per cent of the vote nationally after 1959; and when he secured his largest ever margin of victory (despite very unfavourable boundary changes) in 1983 at the only time the third Party gained over a quarter of the vote nationally. However much Wainwright disliked it, national politics affected local performance, and he benefited and suffered by it.

This brings us to one of Wainwright's weaknesses. It is a liability of almost every mature politician that they lose pace with change, and Wainwright was no exception. His approach to campaigns placed a faith in doorstep campaigning and policy research which, even in as stable and cohesive a community as Colne Valley, became regrettably but unarguably less relevant towards the end of his career. His insistence that Colne Valley could be recovered after 1987 by a tour of the Liberal Clubs such as he had made in 1970, and his assertion to the Liberal Democrats' Chief Whip four years later that 'what gave the party credibility in various electorally lean years was its publicly accepted ability to produce pioneer policies of real quality',[15] suggest that he was reluctant to see that if voters had ever been persuaded by detailed policy-making, it made less impression by the 1990s. 'He was so keen to support policy research'